Praise for
The Magical Universe o
by Matthew Levi Stevens:

MW01285264

Nina Antonia

(Rock journalist extraordinaire, author of the acclaimed biography *Johnny Thunders – In Cold Blood*, also the recent collection of poetry & prose, *13 Knots*)

"A magical act is always a triumph or failure of the will." – William S. Burroughs.

In writing *The Magical Universe of William S. Burroughs*, author Matthew Levi Stevens has triumphed. If Burroughs was a multi-dimensional tight-rope walker, Stevens has unravelled the threads to create a superlative supernatural treatise of *Il Hombre Invisible*'s life and work. Whether an initiate to the world of Burroughs or a seasoned scholar, this book opens new and fascinating vistas. Vitally unorthodox and yet true to the core, this is an essential text for anyone looking to go beyond the page into an alternative reality, where magic lives.

Michael Butterworth

(Publisher, editor, author. With David Britton, co-founder of Savoy Books and co-author of the notorious *Lord Horror* and its various sequels)

Very impressed . . . You have told me something I didn't know about Burroughs, and that was the importance of magic in his life . . . Shines a light into the creative processes of William Burroughs.

Paul A. Green

(Writer, poet, broadcaster and bluesman, his many works include *Beneath the Pleasure Zones* and *The Gestaltbunker: Selected Poems 1965-2010*)

This is a unique and significant study of Burroughs, taking us into a zone other critics have often avoided – the occult beliefs and practices that permeated WSB's life and work. Deftly weaving together insightful readings of the texts with vivid biographical detail and original research – sparked by a memorable encounter with Burroughs in the 1980s – Matthew Levi Stevens creates a fascinating and revealing portrayal of Burroughs-as-magus, channeller of the zeitgeist.

Oliver Harris

(Professor of American Literature at Keele University, and author of *William Burroughs and the Secret of Fascination*)

I was very impressed by the sheer amount of material you put together, which itself makes your point . . . There's definitely a readership, and it will do Burroughs good to have this kind of approach (rather than the cultural and political ones that dominate in academic studies.)

Graham Masterton

(Author, and correspondent, editor and friend to William S. Burroughs during the *Mayfair Academy* years)

Fascinating book, very well written and a very fresh look at William's thinking.

Malcolm Mc Neill

(Artist, collaborator with William S. Burroughs on *Ah Pook Is Here*, as documented in his memoir *Observed While Falling* and album *The Lost Art of Ah Pook*)

I finished The Magic Universe of WSB and really enjoyed it. You've joined a lot of dots my friend. It's a wealth of information and you've finally connected the huge number of artists, writers and musicians who are indebted to the man. Thank you for including me in the list. You write really well of course, so it was also a pleasure to read.

Marc Olmsted

(Poet, musician, and short film-maker, including *Burroughs on the Bowery*. His memoir, *Don't Hesitate: 23 Years of Knowing Allen Ginsberg*, has just been published)

An excellently researched (and very readable) account of Burroughs' interest in the occult sciences surprised me with info I'd wondered about for a long time. A perfect companion to David S. Wills' recent *Scientologist! William S. Burroughs and the 'Weird Cult'*: accessible scholarly breakthrough into the grey room of the Old Man himself. For both the academic and the fan, a must!

Jim Pennington

(Publisher, printer, bookist. In 1970 founded Aloes Books, publisher of *White Subway*, an invaluable collection of Burroughs' small press pieces)

very compulsive reading

John Power

(Author of *Pagans and Witches of Essex* and *Madaece: Beat Zen, Psychedelia and Beyond in the Counterculture*)

It is amazing that in all the books that have been devoted to the work of William Burroughs that his biographers have only managed to remark on his all-pervasive interest in magick as a quaint footnote or even as just an aberration. Such authors have generally tried to just focus on Burroughs links to the Beat Generation writers and his remarkable literary innovations. At last Matthew has been able to combine a deep knowledge of occultism, as well as that of literature, in a feat of bisociation that puts the central preoccupation of Burroughs' magical outlook in its proper place to explain his life and literary achievements. This a very important addition to the corpus of Burroughs studies, and it is bound to annoy and even confound the old guard of Beat commentators. This ground breaking volume is destined to become a classic, opening up new insights into Burroughs' world view and methods.

Michael Stevens
(Author of *The Road to Interzone: Reading William Burroughs' Reading* and *A Distant Book Lifted*)

I believe your study is surprisingly informative, highly readable and a necessary addition to Burroughs studies.

I am surprised that such a huge part of Burroughs' interests has gone mostly unexplored until your work. Anyone with just a passing interest in WSB would know of his interest in magic and it appears in most all of the biographies in at least minor detail, but never so involved and detailed as your account.

I love your study.

Paul Weston
(Lecturer, Blog Talk radio presenter, and author, *Aleister Crowley and the Aeon of Horus*, "the successor to Robert Anton Wilson's *Cosmic Trigger* for the 21st Century")

Just read your Burroughs work in one sitting so that should indicate to you that I liked it.

I'd say I liked it a hell of a lot in fact. The subject matter and cast of characters is very appealing.

I have never read any of the critical Burroughs works and bios but I can say I really enjoyed yours and it has stimulated my feeling of magical creativity.

I'm sure it will be well received.

David S. Wills

(Founder and editor, *Beatdom* magazine, author of *Scientologist! William S. Burroughs and the "Weird Cult"* and the novel *The Dog Farm*)

What Stevens has done is compose a very readable, very informative book that goes well beyond the usual story. For the Burroughs scholar – like your humble reviewer – there is plenty of new information. He has thoroughly explored the origins of Burroughs' magical inspiration and traced the genesis of his beliefs and the trajectories of his influence far beyond previous consideration.

Of particular interest are the interviews Stevens has conducted with people like C.J. Bradbury Robinson, and his research into the life of Cabell McClean, both of which yield a wealth of previously untapped information. Additionally, Stevens has documented the relationship between Burroughs and musicians like Genesis P-Orridge, detailing how they took him as inspiration not just because of his literary achievements, but rather his magical explorations.

I give all this background information because I do not think one can assess a writer's motives without knowing something of his early development. His subject-matter will be determined by the age he lives in – at least this is true in tumultuous, revolutionary ages like our own – but before he ever begins to write he will have acquired an emotional attitude from which he will never completely escape.

Writing a book is a horrible, exhausting struggle, like a long bout of some painful illness. One would never undertake such a thing if one were not driven on by some demon whom one can neither resist nor understand.

George Orwell, Why I Write.

The
Magical Universe
of
William S. Burroughs

By

Matthew Levi Stevens

For All the Wild Boys, and Girls, Psychick Youth of All ages, and Cosmonauts of Inner Space,

For the various members of the Johnson Family I have been lucky enough to meet along the way,

And for the Lost Boys in the Land of the Dead :

Cabell, Ian, Mikey . . .

. . . and William.

May they All find their place in The Western Lands.

Published by
Mandrake of Oxford
PO Box 250
OXFORD

Contents

Art & Photo Credits

FRONT COVER: Original artwork by Emma Doeve. Incorporates detail of a portrait of WSB, image treatment by Peter 'Sleazy' Christopherson, reproduced with the kind permission of Anthony Blokdijk, Maldoror Stichting/Den Haag.

Page 12
1. Graham Masterton and William S. Burroughs, with tour guide, at Scientology HQ, Saint Hill, East Grinstead. Photo by Antony Balch, Autumn 1967, reproduced with the kind permission of Graham Masterton.

Pages 71-77
2. *"everything is permitted"* – original artwork by Billy Chainsaw, reproduced with his kind permission.

3. WSB at NL Centrum, Amsterdam. Photo by Brecht van Teeseling, reproduced with the kind permission of Anthony Blokdijk, Maldoror Stichting/Den Haag.

4. *Nothing Here Now But The Recordings* (Industrial Records, 1981.) WSB spoken word/tape cut-up LP. Cover design and photography by Peter 'Sleazy' Christopherson.

5. *Piccadilly Burroughs*, original artwork by Philip Willey, reproduced with his kind permission.

6. *Statements of a Kind* – program for *The Final Academy*. Cover art by Neville Brody.

7. *"Wild Boys Very Close Now"* – original artwork by Emma Doeve, reproduced with her kind permission.

8. *The Wild Boys Are Coming* – original artwork by Emma Doeve, reproduced with her kind permission.

9. William S. Burroughs, Duke Street, St. James, 1971. Original photo by Baron Wolman, reproduced with his kind permission.

Pages 135-142
10. William S. Burroughs with Genesis P-Orridge, at the time of their first meeting, Duke Street, St. James, 1973. Photo taken by WSB's "Dilly Boy" companion, Johnny Brady.

11. *Black Sun Bill*, recreation of collage for Wild Fruits fanzine, 1988. Incorporates portrait of WSB, original photo by Ruby Ray, San Francisco 1980, reproduced with her kind permission.

12. *Wild Boys: Zimbu Xolotl Time* – original artwork by Emma Doeve, reproduced with her kind permission.

13. WSB at NL Centrum, Amsterdam. Photo by Brecht van Teeseling, reproduced with the kind permission of Anthony Blokdijk, Maldoror Stichting/Den Haag.

14. Geff Rushton (aka 'John Balance') & Peter 'Sleazy' Christopherson of Coil with WSB. Taken in Lawrence, Kansas, 1992, at the time of the filming of the video for Ministry's *Just One Fix*, which featured WSB and was directed by Sleazy.

15. *The Electronic Revolution* (Dutch language edition, 1988.) Cover design and image treatment by Peter 'Sleazy' Christopherson. Reproduced with the kind permission of Anthony Blokdijk, Maldoror Stichting/Den Haag.

16. Original artwork by Billy Chainsaw, reproduced with his kind permission.

17. Original artwork by Billy Chainsaw, reproduced with his kind permission.

18. The author, outside Dalmeny Court, 8 Duke Street, St. James. Photo by C. J. Bradbury Robinson, August 2013, reproduced with his kind permission.

1. Graham Masterton and William S. Burroughs, with tour guide, at Scientology HQ, Saint Hill, East Grinstead. Photo by Antony Balch, Autumn 1967, reproduced with the kind permission of Graham Masterton.

Foreword

Sometime in the nineteen-seventies, following a reprint of my book, *Magic: An Occult Primer*, a letter was forwarded to me by my then publisher. Poorly typed and in an envelope which, unless my memory deceives me, bore no postage stamp, it came from William S. Burroughs. I still have it somewhere. In it the writer made plain his interest in magic. In real magic that is, not the smoke and mirrors kind.

Given that Burroughs' tireless ambition was to encounter a reality beyond that accessible to our five senses, with magic perceived as an effective means to that end, it is remarkable that the subject has hitherto received but scant attention. This work, by Matthew Levi Stevens, who must have encountered Burroughs at around the time he wrote to me, sets out to make up for that deficit. In it he chronicles the man's interest and examines the part magic and occultism generally played both in his life and in his work. Stevens sets about the task with gusto, indicative of his respect and, indeed, affection for "Uncle Bill", as well as his familiarity with the topic itself. He draws on Burroughs' own writings, and on those of the growing number of people, supporters and critics alike, who have commented on him and his literary output.

It is a job well done. And one that is all the more welcome because long overdue.

David Conway, 2014.

Author's Note

> The standardised explanation was published.
> I shall oppose it with heresy.
> *Charles Fort,* Lo!

It is assumed that the interested reader will have at least some basic idea regarding the life and work of my subject, William S. Burroughs. It is not my intention here to try and write yet another full-length biography, or attempt a work of in-depth literary criticism – many others have already done so, and probably far more successfully than I could ever manage. Indeed, I will be drawing on a number of such texts throughout this book to illustrate and support my examination, and all such sources will be duly noted.

I have also drawn extensively from my own correspondence, encounters, and interviews with a number of individuals mentioned in the text – these, too, are duly noted.

Likewise, I am not in this instance especially interested in the various famous or perhaps infamous aspects of WSB's life – such as his connection to the Beats, drug addiction, homosexuality, or the shooting of his common-law wife – and will only really address these inasmuch as I see them as being directly relevant to the central premise.

It has been decided to follow a broadly chronological line for the sake of narrative, but allowing for occasional digressions when it will permit a more thorough consideration of the subject at hand.

Introduction

> I am a man of the world. Going to and fro and walking up and
> down in it.[1]

Love or hate him, venerate or revile him, the life and work of William Seward
Burroughs continues to inspire and intrigue. In addition to the work, since
his death in 1997 we have seen further biographies, celebrations, collections
of letters, and critical studies, as well as restored and even previously
unpublished texts. The first serious attempt at a "life" was the mammoth
Literary Outlaw by Sanche De Gramont (writing as 'Ted Morgan'), written
over a number of years with extensive co-operation from both the subject
himself and his intimates. Published in 1991 while Burroughs was still alive,
it is a giant of a book that all other examinations of his life & times must
surely stand either on the shoulders – or else in the shadow – of. Also
written within the writer's lifetime, and by another long-term associate and
close friend, was *El Hombre Invisible* by Barry Miles (first published 1992, and
slightly revised 2010.) Immediately following Burroughs' death in 1997 was
Graham Caveney's *The Priest They Called Him* – a book that boasted of its
wish to explore the icon and the myth, rather than the man or his work.
Despite being visually lavish to the point of inducing eyestrain or a migraine,
it couldn't seem to help but wear its preconceptions and prejudices on its
sleeve.

It was, of course, inevitable as we reached the centenary of his birth, that
the life and work of William Burroughs should be celebrated, considered,
and examined like never before. The beginning had been *William Burroughs:
The Algebra of Need* by Eric Mottram – critic, editor, poet – but, and perhaps
more importantly, also lecturer and reader in American Literature at King's
College, London: that had been written as long ago as 1971, with a revised
edition in 1977, while Burroughs was still very much alive and still writing.

The most recent has been *William Burroughs and the Secret of Fascination* in 2003, by Oliver Harris, Professor of American Studies at Keele University – who "Aside from James Grauerholz, Executor of the Burroughs Estate . . . may well be the most eminent living scholar of William Burroughs and his works."[2]

There has been reassessment and re-examination of various aspects of both life and work, starting with Burroughs and Homosexuality in Jamie Russell's *Queer Burroughs*, then *Retaking the Universe: William S. Burroughs in the Age of Globalization*, edited by Davis Schneiderman and Philip Walsh; there was Burroughs and Literature in Michael Stevens' *The Road to Interzone* – an encyclopaedic study of "reading Burroughs' reading" that is equally essential and fascinating to fan *and* scholar alike – and, more recently, Graphic Novel Burroughs in Malcolm Mc Neill's candid memoir, *Observed While Falling*, written to accompany an outstanding volume, *The Lost Art of Ah Pook*, which showcases the original illustrations Mc Neill created during the seven year collaboration with Burroughs. We have also had Mayfair Burroughs in the *Introduction* to his old friend Graham Masterton's experiment in "intersection writing" *Rules of Duel*.

As well as a fairly steady trickle of Literary Theory, also there has been Phil Baker's worthy *William S. Burroughs* (in the *Critical Lives* series), and, more recently, the commendable *Scientologist! William S Burroughs and the "Weird Cult" by David S Wills*. My own contribution, *A Way With Words*, published just in time for the centenary and written in collaboration with C. J. Bradbury Robinson – a friend to Burroughs during his time at Duke Street, London, during the late 1960s-to-early-1970s – was an attempt to shed some light on an otherwise little-known episode of his life that had, thus far, been overlooked by *all* the 'official' biographies. It remains to be seen what consideration, if any, it will receive – either from Burroughs scholars or from the fans.

You could be forgiven for thinking that no *turn* had been left *unstoned*, so to speak. That almost everybody who had ever *known* or even *met* William Burroughs had been interviewed, or else had written about it. That there wasn't that much left to say about Uncle Bill that we didn't know already.

Well, *think again . . .*

The fact that these and other works have continued to find not only new things to say about him, but also *new voices* that we have not heard before – and, that at the time of this writing, a new "definitive and official" biography, *Call Me Burroughs: A Life* by Barry Miles, is due to be published to mark the "Burroughs Centenary" – begins to make the Rime of this particular Postmodern Mariner seem more like a *Rashomon* than ever before . . .

Which brings me neatly to the theme of my ongoing research, of which this book is hopefully both distillation and expression, which I suppose had its first beginnings over 35 years ago, when I first encountered the literary work of Burroughs as a 13 year old schoolboy, and was doubtless then confirmed when I first met the author in the flesh less than 3 years later, barely a month shy of my 16th birthday, and found myself suddenly in the middle of a conversation about the occult:

The Magical Universe of William S. Burroughs.

The Magical Universe Of William S. Burroughs

> In the magical universe there are no coincidences and there are no accidents. Nothing happens unless someone wills it to happen. The dogma of science is that the will cannot possibly affect external forces, and I think that's just ridiculous. It's as bad as the church. My viewpoint is the exact contrary of the scientific viewpoint. I believe that if you run into somebody in the street it's for a reason. Among primitive people they say that if someone was bitten by a snake he was murdered. I believe that.[3]

In talking about *The Magical Universe of William S. Burroughs*, I am thinking, really, of two things:

> Firstly, and probably most obviously, is the material that appears in the output of Burroughs the Writer that can be seen as describing or referring to some magical, mystical or occult idea – invocations of Elder Gods of Abominations, descriptions of sex-magick rituals, references to amulets, charms, ghosts, omens and spells – the kind of thematic set-dressing that we all know and love, from Hammer Horror Movies to *Weird Tales*, from H. P. Lovecraft to Dennis Wheatley and *The X-Files* . . .

Secondly, and perhaps less obviously, there is the *personal* interest and involvement of Burroughs the Man with belief systems and practices that come from those strange "other" territories that lay outside the bounds of either conventional mainstream religion or scientific materialism – and in this I would include his explorations of L. Ron Hubbard's Scientology, Konstanin Raudive's Electronic Voice Phenomena, Wilhelm Reich's Orgone Accumulator, and various other areas that can perhaps be considered fringe science (perhaps even 'pseudoscience'), as well as contested knowledge of a more traditional kind: partaking of the Vine-of-the-Soul, Ayahuasca, with

Amazonian shamans, attending the Rites of Pan with the Master Musicians of Joujouka in the Rif Mountains outside Morocco, participating in a sweat-lodge with a Native American Indian medicine man – and even, latterly, an engagement with that most postmodern of occultisms, Chaos Magic.

This is not perhaps as surprising as it might first seem when you take into consideration a number of statements made in Ted Morgan's excellent biography of Burroughs, *Literary Outlaw*, where he declares unequivocally:

> As the single most important thing about Graham Greene was his viewpoint as a lapsed Catholic, the single most important thing about Burroughs was his belief in the magical universe. The same impulse that lead him to put out curses was, as he saw it, the source of his writing . . .

> To Burroughs behind everyday reality there was the reality of the spirit world, of psychic visitations, of curses, of possession and phantom beings . . .[4]

As Burroughs put it himself:

> Among so-called primitive peoples, if a man is killed in a fall from a cliff, the friends and relatives of the victim start looking for a killer . . .

> Primitive thinking? Perhaps . . .[5]

Even among critical response to Burroughs, controversial and almost inevitably divided as it is, from the very beginning there has been recognition of this more mythical, or even *magical*, aspect to his work. The author of *I Am A Camera* and *Mr Norris Changes Trains*, Christopher Isherwood, who met Burroughs in Los Angeles and New York, described him in a review of his 1981 novel, *Cities of the Red Night*, as an "awe-inspiring poetic magician," and a reviewer for the *New York Times* once wrote:

> In Mr Burroughs's hands, writing reverts to acts of magic, as though he were making some enormous infernal encyclopaedia

of all the black impulses and acts that, once made, would shut the fiends away forever.[6]

A Clockwork Orange author, Anthony Burgess, would caricature Burroughs in his novel, *Enderby Outside*, after befriending him in Tangier. Burroughs would visit for afternoon tea, and sit and read Jane Austen's *Persuasion* to his wife, Lynne Burgess, when she was ill in bed. Later, the two writers would meet again in London, and become drinking companions.[7] When Burroughs asked Burgess whether he met with any other writers socially, he received the scathing reply "No, they're all a lot of swine" – but he was happy to express his admiration for the author of *Naked Lunch* thus:

> Mr Burroughs joins a small body of writers who are willing to look at hell and report what they see.[8]

Author of such New Wave sci-fi as *The Atrocity Exhibition* and *Crash*, J. G. Ballard – with whom Burroughs shared something of a mutual appreciation in the 1960s, when they were both still concerned with pushing back the boundaries of experimental literature and attempting to "create a new mythology for the Space Age" – considered him "the most important writer in the English language to have appeared since the Second World War", once characterising him as a "hitman for the apocalypse." Although Ballard felt from their meetings that there was a limit to how far he could relate to Burroughs *personally*, being neither a drug user nor a homosexual, he still went on record as saying:

> . . . William Burroughs has fashioned from our dreams and nightmares the authentic mythology of the age of Cape Canaveral, Hiroshima, and Belsen. His novels are the terminal documents of the mid-twentieth century, scabrous and scarifying, a progress report from an inmate in the cosmic madhouse.[9]

Poet and actor, Heathcote Williams, who was associate editor of the literary journal *Transatlantic Review* when he met Burroughs in 1963, has written of the latter's interest in the Mayan Codices and Sacred Calendar, adding:

> Bill had an unusual belief in the significance of numbers and
> also in coincidences, which he had a kind of nose for.[10]

In a recent reminiscence for the "Burroughs Centenary", Williams continues:

> I was in a cab with him once going down the Brompton Road
> when he announced that the number 23 was "the death
> number." I expressed surprise, if not disbelief, but my reaction
> was shortly to be transformed into astonishment when he
> pointed out a shop front that we were just passing and then said
> emphatically. "See that? Kenyon's the Undertakers … now tell
> me the street number." Sure enough it was 239 Brompton Road.
> There was a distinct 2 and a 3 in the funeral parlour's street sign.
>
> Then Bill leant forward and asked me to tell him what my
> phone number was. I was living in the *Transatlantic Review* office
> at the time and it was KNI (Knightsbridge) 2389. 2 and 3 again.
> This was all said in the most deadpan, matter-of-fact way –
> nothing of the drumrolling of some stagey mind reader. Lastly
> he asked, "How old are you Heathcote?" I took a moment to
> answer "23."
>
> He concluded by saying, "Watch out for 23." It was
> bewildering.[11]

Co-author of the cult classic *Illuminatus!* trilogy, Robert Anton Wilson, was
also made aware of Burroughs' fixation with the number 23:

> I first heard of the 23 enigma from William S Burroughs, author
> of *Naked Lunch*, *Nova Express*, etc. According to Burroughs, he
> had known a certain Captain Clark, around 1960 in Tangier,
> who once bragged that he had been sailing 23 years without an
> accident. That very day, Clark's ship had an accident that killed
> him and everybody else aboard. Furthermore, while Burroughs
> was thinking about this crude example of the irony of the gods
> that evening, a bulletin on the radio announced the crash of an
> airliner in Florida, USA. The pilot was another captain Clark and
> the flight was Flight 23 . . .[12]

Pioneering "Industrial music" group Throbbing Gristle would further mythologize the meeting of Burroughs and "Captain Clark" – as well as the significance of the number 23, of course – in their song *The Old Man Smiled*, with lyrics including:

> Can the world be as sad as it seems? At this the Old Man smiled, Sitting there in Tangier . . . 23 days and 23 hours of the day . . . Sitting in a café in Tangier, And down to his table came Captain Clark, He'd worked on the ferry for 23 years and a day . . . So I walked round the corner, To a room in the Bowery . . . And Captain Clark welcomes you aboard, Flight 23 . . . [13]

Even the first-ever attempt at a critical study of Burroughs, *The Algebra of Need*, by Eric Mottram, makes a telling choice of language early on in describing what it sees as being, at least in part, the purpose of his work:

> . . . Burroughs realizes that the black magic of mass communications must be counterattacked by white magic of analysis and resistance.[14]

Lest one think that this is a "boys only" club, the chorus of appreciation and critical evaluation of Burroughs also includes a number of contributions from women:

The radical 'No Wave' Post-Punk writer Kathy Acker, infamous for her commitment to the use of creative plagiarism and other *avant garde* literary techniques with which to create a heady mix of pulp and porn, once described how she made use of sections from *The Third Mind* by William S. Burroughs and Brion Gysin "as experiments to teach myself how to write." Acker found in Burroughs a prose writer who "was dealing with how politics and language came together" – inspiring her to hijack everything and everybody from Rimbaud, Pasolini and Genet, even Burroughs' own *The Wild Boys*, to create her own sex-positive, post-feminist vision in works such as *Blood and Guts in High School* and *Empire of the Senseless*. On being informed of Burroughs' death in 1997, Acker affirmed:

For me, William was the American writer who wrote by thinking about how language is used. Who dissected the relations between language and power . . . He saw evil as possession, a virus . . . William spent a life-time investigating anti-viral medicines, from EST to Tibetan Buddhism to Shamanism . . . And then he says, "Writers don't write, they read and transcribe." This is the mystic's stance. A writer reads and so is read . . . William wrote by reading the future that is now ours.[15]

The novelist and critic Angela Carter, author of such works as the collection of "Adult Fairy Tales" *The Bloody Chamber*, the magical realist novel *The Infernal Desire Machines of Doctor Hoffman*, and the extended Feminist essay *The Sadeian Woman and the Ideology of Pornography* – who wrote during his lifetime that Burroughs was "the only living American writer of whom one can say with confidence he will be read with the same shock of terror and pleasure in a hundred years' time" – has left for us to consider one of the most thought-provoking evaluations of the true nature and intent of his work of all:

> . . . Burroughs' project is to make time stand still for a while,
> one which is more frequently that of religion than of literature
> and there are ways in which Burroughs' work indeed resembles
> that of another William, the Blake of the self-crafted mythology
> of the Prophetic Books, although it must be said that
> Burroughs is much funnier.[16]

The woman who was probably closest to Burroughs in 1970s New York – as a fellow artist, writer, and also friend of longstanding – was the High Priestess of Punk, poet and performer Patti Smith, who summed up her feelings:

> . . . William seemed to have a connection with anything and
> everything – you know, you'd see a movie like *Blade Runner*, and
> then you'd find the phrase "blade runner" came from him – the
> term heavy metal is attributed to him, soft machine – there's so
> many phrases, names of groups, come from William's work . . .
> He's like – another kind of Bible.

He's up there with the Pope, you can't revere him enough![17]

Perhaps the last word, for now, before we begin at the beginning, belongs to Burroughs himself:

> It is to be remembered that all art is magical in origin – music sculpture writing painting – and by magical I mean intended to produce very definite results . . .[18]

In The Beginning
Was The Word . . .

. . . I will examine the connections between so-called occult phenomena and the creative process. Are not all writers, consciously or not, operating in these areas?[19]

When the American writer William S. Burroughs passed away at the ripe old age of 83 back in August 1997, the media coverage was definitely more in keeping with his status as a counter-cultural icon than it was for his literary fame – or infamy – alone. All the usual well-rehearsed lines were trotted out, about how he was the Harvard-educated product of the WASP elite and scion of the family that founded the Burroughs Corporation, who had turned his back on it all to become a junkie queer, trawling the steaming jungles of South America, sleazy "Interzone" of Tangiers, and shady back-streets of Paris and London for drugs and boys. That somewhere along the line he became an unlikely mentor to Jack Kerouac, Allen Ginsberg and the Beats, who had opened the way for the Cultural Revolution of the Sixties. William Burroughs had originally exploded onto the literary scene back in 1959 with his breakthrough novel, *Naked Lunch*, causing hip critics everywhere to claim they had seen the future – even if nobody was really sure that they understood it. With his three-piece suit, glasses, hat and raincoat, Burroughs seemed like the ultimate undercover hipster, and *that voice* certainly didn't hurt: pitched somewhere between T. S. Eliot and W. C. Fields, mixing camp twang and knowing drawl with the educated tones of an old-fashioned Southern gentleman. From the moment he received that ultimate Sixties imprimatur of cool, being included by The Beatles on the cover of *Sergeant Pepper's Lonely Hearts Club Band* (he's in there between Marilyn Monroe and Fred Astaire), William Burroughs was the rock rebel's choice of Literary Outlaw: from David Bowie and Jimmy Page to Patti Smith, Tom Waits, and Sonic

Youth, experimental bands like Throbbing Gristle, Psychic TV, and Coil, to Bill Laswell's Material, The Black Dog, Bomb The Bass, and the Disposable Heroes of HipHoprisy – even Nirvana's Kurt Cobain and REM would record collaborations with him – generations of alternative rock stars, experimental dance musicians, and sonic alchemists have collaborated and paid homage.

As if that was not enough, in the words of his biographer, Barry Miles, Burroughs "had made more records than most rock groups and appeared in dozens of films and documentaries" – as well as all manner of collaborations with the various musical artists already mentioned, there had been releases of numerous Spoken Word albums: sometimes straightforward recordings from his many public appearances, and others with his distinctive, gravelly drawl set against a musical accompaniment. In later life, Burroughs would also contribute lyrics to other artist's projects, such as when he performed on the song *Sharkey's Night* for his friend, New York performance artist and musician, Laurie Anderson – and, perhaps more significantly, when he wrote the libretto for conceptual artist Robert Wilson's opera, *The Black Rider: The Casting of the Magic Bullets.*

Burroughs had engaged with film early on, collaborating with his friend, film-maker Antony Balch, to create a trilogy of cut-up inspired films. The list of experimental and underground films that have drawn inspiration or even contributions from Burroughs is considerable, but there is also his influence and even appearance in more "mainstream" fare: Ridley Scott's sci-fi classic, *Blade Runner*, although adapted from the seminal novel *Do Androids Dream of Electric Sheep?* by Philip K. Dick, acknowledges in its credits a debt to Burroughs for the title – and "el hombre invisible" wasn't quite so "invisible" when he appeared as the old junky priest, Father Tom Murphy, alongside Matt Dillon and Kelly Lynch in Gus van Sant's *Drugstore Cowboy*, or even after his cameo as Julie Hegarty's butler in his young friend Howard Brookner's Gangsters-and-Prohibition-Era romantic comedy, *Bloodhounds Over Broadway*, alongside Randy Quaid, a young, up-and-coming Madonna, Rutger

Hauer, and, once again, Matt Dillon.

Lastly, there was what he referred to as his "second career," Painting. William S. Burroughs had always been intensely interested in visual imagery – after all, one of the longest-running collaborations and friendships of his life has been with the artist Brion Gysin – his articles, essays and novels demonstrate a keen interest in the hieroglyphics of the Ancient Egyptians and the Central American Maya; and his fascination with the Mayan glyphs, Sacred Calendar, and Lost Books inspired the genre-defying, proto-graphic novel project, *Ah Pook Is Here*, which he worked at with English graphic artist, Malcolm Mc Neill, on-and-off for over seven years in the early 1970s. In addition to his earlier scrapbook experiments, and collaborations with Gysin for *The Third Mind*, as the 1980s progressed, Burroughs collaborated on drawings and prints with artists Robert Rauschenberg, Jean Michel Basquiat, and Philip Taaffe – eventually deciding to focus on painting full-time as a visual artist in his own right. Throughout the last decade of his life, Burroughs would tour the world with his paintings, with shows in London, Los Angeles, New York, Paris, Rome, Tokyo and Venice. It was perhaps ironic, that Burroughs' career as a painter brought him more money than he had ever earned as a writer – bringing him at last, in old age, some degree of comfort and security. Although his work, which was usually of a broadly "abstract expressionist" kind – made with collage, dripping, stencils, spray-paint, and, infamously, shotgun blasts, that some dismissed as just "an old man's hobby" – Burroughs was willing-and-able to cash-in on his own cult-status to sell to Hollywood movie stars and counter-culture celebrities like Timothy Leary for up to $10,000.

The Ambivalence
Of Possession

> Audrey was a thin pale boy his face scarred by festering spiritual
> wounds. "He looks like a sheep-killing dog," said a St Louis
> aristocrat. There was something rotten and unclean about
> Audrey, an odor of the walking dead. Doormen stopped him
> when he visited his rich friends. Shopkeepers pushed his change
> back without a thank you. He spent sleepless nights weeping
> into his pillow from impotent rage . . .[20]

Norman Mailer once famously said that William S. Burroughs was "The
only American novelist living and working today who may conceivably be
possessed of genius," and as often as this was repeated down the years
Burroughs himself was at pains to point out that it was not saying that he
had genius or *was* a genius, but that he may at times have been lucky enough
to be *possessed* by genius. Interviewed at The October Gallery in London in
1988, he had this to say on the subject:

> To me 'genius' is the *nagual:* the uncontrollable – unknown and
> so unpredictable – spontaneous and alive. You could say the
> magical.[21]

The fact that his answer uses a term, *nagual,* derived from the world of the
Yaqui Indian sorcerer, as described by Carlos Castañeda in *The Teachings of
Don Juan* and subsequent books, is telling indeed . . .

> In the Carlos Castañeda books, Don Juan makes a distinction
> between the tonal universe and the nagual. The tonal universe is
> the everyday cause-and-effect universe, which is predictable
> because it is pre-recorded. The nagual is the unknown, the
> unpredictable, the uncontrollable. For the nagual to gain access,
> the door of chance must be open. There must be a random
> factor.[22]

. . . But there is also another kind of 'possession' that was very much a concern for William Burroughs, Man and Writer. From an early age, as much as he felt a definite sense of being "other" and not really belonging or fitting in anywhere, as much as he knew he was homosexual, he also believed in the idea of *The Magical Universe*. He was aware that an integral part of that universe was that there were inimical – even hostile – forces that threaten us, that may need to be bargained with and from time-to-time appeased, and that one of the dangers posed is that of possession:

> My concept of possession is closer to the medieval model than to modern psychological explanations, with their dogmatic insistence that such manifestations must come from within and never, never, never from without (As if there were some clear-cut difference between inner and outer.) I mean a definite possessing entity.[23]

As a young man he had already had direct experience of a sense that there was *something* inside him that did not have his best interests at heart, which was not under his control, and was even at odds with his conscious desire or will:

> In 1939, I became interested in Egyptian hieroglyphics and went out to see someone in the Department of Egyptology at the University of Chicago. And something was screaming in my ear: 'YOU DON'T BELONG HERE!' Yes, the hieroglyphics provided one key to the mechanism of possession. Like a virus, the possessing entity must find a port of entry . . .[24]

Later on, in the *Foreword* for the autobiographical *Queer* (written in the 1950s but unpublished until 1985), Burroughs talks about the appalling circumstances of the shooting accident that caused the death of his common-law wife, Joan Vollmer, when their so-called 'William Tell act' went disastrously wrong, after she dared him to shoot a glass off her head:

> I live with the constant threat of possession, and a constant need to escape from possession, from Control. So the death of

> Joan brought me in contact with the invader, the Ugly Spirit,
> and manoeuvred me into a lifelong struggle, in which I have had
> no choice except to write my way out.[25]

The simple truth is, however, that William Burroughs had always been a scribbler: in numerous articles and interviews he describes at length his literary efforts from childhood on, and the somewhat precocious sense that the bookish, physically awkward, shy young Billy had of himself as an aspirant writer – an image that was as hopelessly Romantic as it was coloured by a flouting of moral convention:

> As a young child I wanted to be a writer because writers were
> rich and famous. They lounged around Singapore and Rangoon
> smoking opium in a yellow pongee silk suit. They sniffed
> cocaine in Mayfair and they penetrated forbidden swamps with
> a faithful native boy and lived in the native quarter of Tangier
> smoking hashish and languidly caressing a pet gazelle.[26]

Childhood's End

> I was born in 1914 in a solid, three-story, brick house in a large
> Midwest city. My parents were comfortable . . . All the props of
> a safe, comfortable way of life that is now gone forever.[27]

William Seward Burroughs was born 5th February 1914 in the American
Mid Western city of St. Louis, Missouri. The family home was a red brick
three storey house with a slate roof at 4664 Berlin Avenue, with a lawn in
front and a large back yard where his father and the gardener would tend
roses, peonies, iris and a fish pond.

Despite his famed descent from the inventor of the Burroughs Adding
Machine – after whom he was in fact named – and although the family of
William Seward Burroughs were fairly comfortably off, due to a loss of
stocks and shares in the company that bore their name they were never by
any means *rich*, and young Billy was always painfully aware of his family's
status as "poor relations" compared to the members of St. Louis Society
that comprised most of their neighbours, friends, and his classmates, many
of whom were genuinely wealthy. As an outsider, it was inevitable that he
would come to reject the values of a 'polite society' that he saw as essentially
dishonest and hypocritical, and wanted no part in anyway. But it could of
course also be argued that this is a classic passive-aggressive tactic of a
wounded child: reject *them* before they reject *you*.

On the surface, it sounds like a comfortable enough childhood. Even though
they were by no means rich, the Burroughs' family were certainly well off,
and lived in a big house in a fashionable upper middle-class neighbourhood.
They were able to send their sons to good schools, and retain a level of
domestic help that would be unthinkable today except to the *very* wealthy.
They had a nanny for the boys, a maid, a gardener, and a cook, all of whom
would contribute to the shaping of the young boy's attitudes and outlook in

surprisingly significant ways. For almost from the beginning there were dark shadows gathering around young Billy Burroughs:

> Actually my earliest memories are colored by a fear of nightmares. I was afraid to be alone, and afraid of the dark, and afraid to go to sleep because of dreams where a supernatural horror seemed to be always on the point of taking shape. I was afraid some day the dream would still be there when I woke up. I recall hearing a maid talk about opium and how smoking opium brings sweet dreams, and I said: 'I will smoke opium when I grow up.'[28]

As a child, Burroughs was already a loner: he felt cut off from his emotionally absent father, and shut out from the male-bonding between his older brother, Mort, and dad. His mother was also remote – Burroughs actually described her as "ethereal" – and with a horror of the body typical of her genteel Bible Belt upbringing. At the same time she could also dote on Billy to the point of embarrassment, almost smothering him. Perhaps more importantly, she claimed to be psychic: Burroughs would later write of the mother of his fictional alter-ego, Audrey, that "she adored crystal balls, séances, wallowing in ectoplasm"[29] – and from the description, his own mother, Laura Lee Burroughs, was clearly the model:

> My mother's character was enigmatic and complex. Sometimes old and knowing, mostly with a tremulous look of doom and sadness, she suffered from head and back aches, was extremely psychic, and was interested in magic.[30]

In the same novel, *The Place of Dead Roads*, Burroughs takes obvious delight in describing his protagonist, Kim, in a way which clearly wears the more antinomian aspects of engagement with the occult on its sleeve:

> Kim is a slimy, morbid youth of unwholesome proclivities with an insatiable appetite for the extreme and the sensational. His mother had been into table-tapping and Kim adores ectoplasms, crystal balls, spirit guides and auras. He wallows in abominations,

unspeakable rites, diseased demon lovers, loathsome secrets imparted in a thick slimy whisper, ancient ruined cities under a purple sky, the smell of unknown excrements . . .

In short, Kim is everything a normal American boy is taught to detest.[31]

For all its defiant posturing, this portrait of his alter-ego probably gives us an authentic enough snapshot of how much of an *outsider* Burroughs felt as a boy – but it also affirms how much his later occult interests are specifically related to memories of his mother. Laura claimed strong intuitions, bordering on the mediumistic: she once advised her husband against a prospective business partner, saying that she just *knew* that the man was a crook, and turned out to be right. Another time, she woke from a dream in which she had seen her older son, Mort, covered in blood, who told her "Mother, we've had an accident" – it later transpired that he had, in fact, been in an accident, "at that very moment."

From the various biographies and interviews – also a close reading of his work, which betrays a considerable amount of autobiographical detail – a picture emerges of Billy as an isolated loner, bookish and dreamy, who as far back as he can remember had a sense that there were forces and powers, and ways of knowing things, that were beyond what could be seen in the world or explained easily. He appears to have been almost unnaturally sensitive:

When I was four years old I saw a vision in Forest Park, St. Louis. My brother was ahead of me with an air rifle. I was lagging behind and I saw a little green reindeer about the size of a cat. Clear and precise in the late afternoon sunlight as if through a telescope.

Later, when I studied anthropology at Harvard, I learned that this was a totem animal vision and knew that I could never kill a deer.[32]

But this "magic of childhood" also had a darker side: the young Burroughs was afraid of the dark, afraid of storms, and troubled by nightmares to the extent that he was often afraid to go to sleep:

> I was subject to hallucinations as a child. Once I woke up in the early morning light and saw little men playing in a block house I had made. I felt no fear, only a feeling of stillness and wonder. Another recurrent hallucination or nightmare concerned 'animals in the wall,' and started with the delirium of a strange, undiagnosed fever that I had at the age of four or five.[33]

Equally portentous for the young Burroughs was the introduction to folklore and superstition of a particularly dark shade from two of the household staff, the cook and the nanny – a sinister double-act, who sound like something straight out of *The Turn of the Screw* by Henry James. Described by Burroughs years later as a "buxom old crone," the Irish cook initiated the young boy into the quaint art of *Calling the Toads* – a process involving a kind of low humming and no doubt a lot of patience, whereby you would call a toad to come to you, presumably for the purpose of making it into some kind of Witch's Familiar. The only toad native to Ireland is the Natterjack, found in County Kerry and County Wexford, which as well as having a loud, rattling, croak of a mating call, curiously enough had a couple of traditional associations with Witchcraft. The Natterjack (or *Bufo calamita*) – also known as "the walking toad" – can secrete a thick white poison known as "toad's milk" through its skin, a source of the powerful psychoactive alkaloid, bufotenine, highly toxic but sometimes hallucinogenic, which was said to have been an ingredient in some traditional "flying ointments" used by Witches. The Natterjack was also a source for the infamous Toad's Bone Amulet, first mentioned in Pliny's *Natural History*, of which it was said:

> When they have taken out the bone the Devell would give them the power of Witch craft, and they could use that power over both Man and Animales.[34]

The Irish cook would also tell little Billy about strange and potent spells, such as the *Curse of the Blinding Worm*, in which the idea was to take a piece of mouldy bread, run a sewing needle through it, and then bury it under the fencepost of a pigsty while intoning "Needle in thread, needle in bread, eye in needle, needle in eye, bury the bread deep in the sty." Apparently the "blinding worm" would somehow be conjured forth from the bread and go into the eye of your intended victim, blinding them. If you wanted to protect yourself from possible rebound, you also intoned "Cut the bread and cut the thread, and send the needle back on red." Such details would stay with Burroughs, shaping his belief in and experience of "The Magical Universe," as well as informing his later work as a writer – many years later, when he had first moved to the Empress Hotel in London, he encountered an old Irish woman who must have reminded him of the cook, and woke up screaming from a nightmare in which a white worm was crawling out of his eye . . .

The English graphic artist, Malcolm Mc Neill, later wrote of a strange and somewhat sinister incident, which recalled the Curse of the Blinding Worm. Mc Neill first met Burroughs in London in 1970, when he embarked on what would turn into a lengthy collaboration with him, ultimately intended to be a pioneering new form of book, combining artwork and text, *Ah Pook Is Here* – which has never appeared in its intended form, sadly, despite seven years of on-and-off collaboration, and several hundred pages combining Mc Neill's original images with Burroughs' text. As Mc Neill has written, regarding critical response to the work they did together:

> . . . if there was one instance in Burroughs' career that did produce something magical it was *Ah Pook Is Here*. In time that will become more apparent. Right now it's still essentially ghettoized in the 'graphic novel' section. As *[Burroughs scholar]* Jed Birmingham suggests it was in fact Burroughs' ". . . attempt to articulate a definitive statement of his personal and creative worldview" – a word and image collaboration that might actually

constitute ". . . his total work of art." True art by definition being a magical process.[35]

By the mid-1970s, Mc Neill had followed Burroughs from London to New York, in the hope of completing the *Ah Pook* project, and when Burroughs vacated his Franklin Street apartment in 1976 to move to the now infamous "Bunker" on the Bowery, he offered the lease to Mc Neill, leaving behind a rocking chair and an old freestanding wardrobe. Before long, Mc Neill could sense something in the flat, prompting him to ask Burroughs if he had ever "seen anything unusual" while he had been living there:

> "Like what?" he asked.
>
> "Smudges," I said. "Sometimes I see black smudges out of the corner of my eye."
>
> "Whereabouts exactly?"
>
> "By the door. Near the wardrobe."
>
> "Hmmm . . . that would make sense," he said.

Returning home, Mc Neill immediately examined the wardrobe in question from all sides, eventually standing on a chair to look on top:

> There I discovered a small note in Bill's handwriting.
>
> Two dried up lemon slices were alongside and it was sprinkled with salt. It was a curse, the 'Curse of the Blinding Worm' to be exact, one of the many he'd recited to me back in London. They'd been taught to him . . . when he was a child, he'd said. Beneath the note was a newspaper clipping – an unflattering review of *Exterminator!* by Anatole Broyard.[36]

This was not so much a case of "life imitating art," perhaps, as art with a magical intention attempting to initiate events in everyday life. Mc Neill later observed:

> The fact that the loft nearly burned down soon after the

discovery of the note, was an added factor that confirmed Burroughs' other remark in the Morgan bio, that sometimes a curse can "bounce back and bounce back double." Though he didn't say so – cursing amounts to dialogue.[37]

Things would take an even more sinister turn for Burroughs as a child with the children's nanny – "Nursey" as she was called – a Welsh woman called Mary Evans. At first little Billy *adored* Mary, would follow her everywhere, and have tantrums when it was her day off – leading his first biographer, Ted Morgan, to suggest that she was using "the old nursemaid trick of sexually stimulating the boy to pacify him"[38] (a suggestion that has been repeated ever since.) Mary was also full of folklore and superstition from her native land, and young Burroughs lapped it up – in particular, a curse that she taught to him which was said to induce its target to fall down stairs, "Slip and stumble, trip and fall – down the stairs and hit the wall."

Many years later, Burroughs the Writer would make use of the rhyme, incorporating it into a sequence in *The Place of Dead Roads* in which his youthful protagonist, Kim Carsons – clearly a partly idealised self-portrait – seeks to avenge himself on one of the many tormentors of his unhappy adolescence:

> Once he made sex magic against Judge Farris, who said Kim was rotten clear through and smelled like a polecat. He nailed a full-length picture of the Judge to the wall, taken from the society page, and masturbated in front of it while he intoned a jingle he had learned from a Welsh nanny:
>
> Slip and stumble (lips peel back from his teeth)
>
> Trip and fall (his eyes light up inside)
>
> Down the stairs
>
> And hit the wallllllllllllllll!
>
> His hair stands up on end. He whines and whimpers and howls

the word out and shoots all over the Judge's leg. And Judge
Farris did fall downstairs a few days later, and fractured his
shoulder bone. The Judge swore to anyone who would listen
that a scrawny, stinking red dog . . . suddenly jumped out at him
on the stairs . . .

. . . Kim knew that he had succeeded in projecting a thought
form.[39]

Mary Evans would also be the focus and source of another sinister secret
from childhood that would remain with Burroughs throughout the rest of
his life. When he was still only four years old, Mary Evans took the young
Burroughs on an outing on her day off, accompanied by her veterinarian
boyfriend, apparently. Almost immediately after, little Billy's beloved "Nursey"
was dismissed suddenly, under a cloud, leaving the lingering suggestion of
something inappropriate – abuse, even. Years later, after an intensive period
of analysis had still not been able to get to the bottom of it, Burroughs
would write:

The memory he could never reoccupy, even under deep narco-
analysis. Whenever he got close to it, excitation tore through
him, suppressed below the level of emotional coloring, a neutral
energy like electricity. The memory itself never actually seen or
re-experienced, only delineated by refusals, disgusts, negation.[40]

What is not at all clear is *what*, if anything, actually happened, but trying to
make sense of the different versions on record of what Burroughs *felt* he
had remembered, what is immediately striking is both their inconsistency
and also a sense of escalation – and the suggestion that comes across loud
and clear is one of some kind of sexual abuse: he thought he saw Nursey
having sex with a girlfriend – he thought he saw Nursey having sex with her
boyfriend – he thought the boyfriend, a vet, had made him watch as he put
down animals – he thought Nursey had tried to force him to perform fellatio
on the boyfriend, and that "in defense" he had bitten the boyfriend's penis
– and, finally, he thought he had been made to watch while the boyfriend

performed some kind of backstreet abortion on Nursey, and then burnt the foetus in an incinerator.

Whatever the "truth" of this incident, the important thing is, clearly, that Burroughs, on some level, *believed* that he had been the victim of such abuse. The author and former Kleinian psychoanalyst, C. J. Bradbury Robinson – who has an especial interest in child psychology and early sexual development, and was also a close friend to Burroughs during his years in London – has put it to me:

> . . . one might ask why he *wanted* to believe this about himself?[41]

But to my mind, the most helpful attitude is that put forward by C. G. Jung in the *Prefatory Note* to his *Answer to Job*:

> "Physical" is not the only criterion of truth: there are also psychic truths which can neither be explained nor proved nor contested in any physical way . . . Beliefs of this kind are psychic facts which cannot be contested and need no proof.[42]

If we accept that the notion of his childhood abuse was indeed just such a "psychic fact" to Burroughs, then this single event is key in understanding much about his later writing, sexual orientation, personality – and even occult beliefs.

It would instil in him a lifelong fear of possession, of being at the mercy of another's Control.

It would confirm in him the apprehension that the universe was governed by inimical, even hostile, forces.

It would be the beginning of his lifelong struggle with what he would come to think of as The Ugly Spirit.

Cut-Shift-Tangle

> As soon as you walk down the street like this – or look out the window, turn a page, turn on the TV – your awareness is being Cut: the sign in that shop window, that car passing by, the sound of the radio . . . *Life IS a Cut-up.*[43]

As well as the monstrous masterpiece that is *Naked Lunch*, William Burroughs is also best remembered, perhaps, for championing the experimental technique of the Cut-ups – what appears to be at first glance the almost ludicrously simple idea of introducing collage techniques into writing. The cut-up in all its various forms may very well be the pre-eminent creative breakthrough of the 20th Century. From the earliest beginnings with Picasso and Braque, collaging simple materials from everyday life onto their canvases; then the Dadaist poet Tristan Tzara, creating a poem by pulling words out of a hat – as much as it was probably a publicity stunt – pointing the way forward for more serious writers, such as T. S. Eliot with *The Waste Land*, who wanted to be able to convey the voices in our heads, the constant verbalisation of the world around us, both within and without; and eventually the appropriation of such techniques by more experimental rock musicians – invariably informed by borrowings from theories of Art and Literature – and Hip Hop DJs like Grandmaster Flash, and later DJ Spooky, who subtitles himself "That Subliminal Kid" after a character in Burroughs' *Nova Express*:

> 'The Subliminal Kid' moved in and took over bars cafes and juke boxes of the world cities and installed radio transmitters and microphones in each bar so that the music and talk of any bar could be heard in all his bars and he had tape recorders in each bar that played and recorded at arbitrary intervals and his agents moved back and forth with portable tape recorders and brought back street sound and talk and music and poured it into his recorder array so he set waves and eddies and tornadoes of sound down all your streets and by the river of all language . . .[44]

Arguably the use of sampling in contemporary music began with the electroacoustic manipulation of prepared recordings on magnetic tape in *musique concrète*. This gradually spread through the more *avant garde* forms of Rock music, to surface first in Industrial, and then – with the emergence of increasingly more affordable and convenient methods of digital sampling – in House Music, until eventually cut-and-paste has become a universal standard in a world where *everything* is just so much *information*, to be manipulated and processed. For better or worse, such techniques probably more accurately mirror the way the world is experienced by most people in an increasingly accelerated, fragmentary, and *seemingly random* datascape. Sampling, montage, collage: these methods really *do* come closer to representing or expressing what the facts of perception are for most of us in this Post-Technological, Post-Modernist, Information Overload.

In *The Third Mind*, a joint manifesto with friend and long-term collaborator Brion Gysin – both a product *of* and named *for* their creative "meeting of minds" – Burroughs acknowledges their predecessors:

> Of course, when you think of it, *The Waste Land* was the first great cut-up collage, and Tristan Tzara had done a bit along the same lines. Dos Passos used the same idea in *The Camera Eye* sequences in *U.S.A.*[45]

Reference is also made to literary collaborations by Joseph Conrad and Ford Madox Ford, W. H. Auden and Christopher Isherwood, and, later, to the stream-of-consciousness of Djuna Barnes' *Nightwood*, and *A Vision* by the poet (and initiate of the Hermetic Order of the Golden Dawn) W. B. Yeats – based largely on experiments in 'automatic writing' with his wife, George. There were also other precursors, such as André Breton and Philippe Soupault, who had written their collaboration, *The Magnetic Fields*, via automatic writing techniques, as well as their friend, Robert Desnos, who had written poems in trance during séances, as Brion Gysin would have been aware from his early encounter with Paris Surrealist circles.

Almost from the beginning, however, there was another aspect to the cut-ups which was acknowledged just as emphatically: that they had the potential to be *oracular*. To William Burroughs, who would undoubtedly become the greatest champion of the technique, they introduced an element of randomness, and also of Time: as he would later put it, whereas the basis of fiction was "once upon a time" – with the cut-ups it was "once in *future* time."[46] Years later, when he was teaching classes at Naropa College, Burroughs explained this apparently prophetic aspect thus:

> When you experiment with cut-ups over a period of time you find that some of the cut-ups in re-arranged texts seemed to refer to future events. I cut-up an article written by John-Paul Getty and got, "It's a bad thing to sue your own father." This was a re-arrangement and wasn't in the original text, and a year later, one of his sons did sue him.[47]

The much-mythologized "happy accident" by which the cut-ups were discovered – or rediscovered – was born out of an increasingly pressure-cooker intensity of "slippery times together . . . psychic symbiosis"[48] between Burroughs and his new friend, the painter Brion Gysin, with them living in-and-out of each other's rooms, minds, and lives as much as any married couple. The cross-referencing and mutuality would, inevitably, extend to their art and writing – each appearing in the other's work – and reasonably can be considered the most long-standing, intimate, and influential of collaborations for both of them. In a video tribute to Gysin recorded for the Dublin *Here To Go Show* in 1992, Burroughs stated unequivocally:

> Brion Gysin is the only man I have ever respected, the only person of either sex. He was completely enigmatic because he was completely himself.[49]

Gysin, who was no stranger to *avant garde* techniques and occult intrigue, after a poor start in Tangier with neither making a favourable impression on the other, had got to know Burroughs at last in no uncertain terms in the cramped, dingy rooms of the now legendary Beat Hotel in Paris: steering his new friend through the emotional rapids of heroin withdrawal, and allowing him to watch him at work on his art. Burroughs was wide open without the safety blanket of junk, and Gysin felt vulnerable and exposed working in front of his new friend. He rarely if ever let people see him paint, saying it was a more private act than masturbation. It must have been an incredibly raw bonding indeed. It was as if the first cut-up that they created together, this "project for disastrous success"[50] as they called it, was with their very souls: and it was out of this commingling, "The Third Mind" as it would come to be known, that all their subsequent collaborations would proceed. The very notion of The Third Mind was itself a kind of psychic cut-up, named for the idea in Napoleon Hill's 1937 'self-help' book, *Think and Grow Rich*, that :

> No two minds ever come together without, thereby, creating a third, invisible, intangible force which may be likened to a third mind.[51]

September 1959, and the making of myths was in the air: at the same time that the newly notorious William Seward Burroughs was being feted by Snell and Dean for their profile in *Life* magazine that would help mint the image of the Harvard-educated gentleman junkie behind the unspeakable *Naked Lunch*, legend has it that Brion Gysin was in his room at the Beat Hotel, using a Stanley knife to cut through paper to make mounts for some drawings he was working on. In recent years, Gysin's "apprentice to an apprentice" Terry Wilson, himself an accomplished practitioner of the "complete and systematic derangement of the senses"[52] of the cut-up and The Other Method, has brought the story into question, saying it is "almost *too* good to be true . . ."[53]

Burroughs would later write in *The Third Mind*:

> He was looking at something a long time ago... fade-out to #9 rue Git le Coeur, Paris, room #25; September, 1959... I had just

returned from a long lunch with the *Time* police, putting down a con, old and tired as their namesake: "Mr Burroughs, I have an intuition about you... I see you a few years from now on Madison Avenue... $20,000 per year... life in all its rich variety... Have an Old Gold." Returning to room #25, I found Brion Gysin holding a scissors, bits of newspaper, *Life*, *Time*, spread out on a table; he read me the cut-ups that later appeared in *Minutes to Go*.[54]

In the process of cutting paper for mounts, Gysin had sliced into copies of the *New York Herald Tribune* spread out as a cutting mat. Seeing the various strips of paper and reading the chance combinations his blade had produced, he laughed so uproariously the neighbours were concerned for his sanity. When Burroughs returned, Gysin showed him the results – almost as an afterthought, "an amusing Surrealist diversion" – but Burroughs was immediately struck by the technique and its potential:

> The cut up method brings to writers the collage which has been used by painters for fifty years. And used by the moving and still camera. In fact all street shots from movie or still cameras are by the unpredictable factors of passersby and juxtaposition cut ups. And photographers will tell you that often their best shots are accidents... writers will tell you the same. The best writing seems to be done almost by accident but writers until the cut up method was made explicit – all writing is in fact cut-ups; I will return to this point – had no way to produce the accident of spontaneity. You cannot will spontaneity. But you can introduce the unpredictable spontaneous factor with a pair of scissors.[55]

Among Burroughs' earliest cut-ups were phrases that meant nothing at the time, but which in hindsight took on an eerie prescience. The early newspaper cut-up piece *Afternoon Ticker Tape* included the line "Come on, Tom, it's your turn now" – and shortly thereafter a newspaper from home, the *St. Louis Post-Dispatch*, included the headline *TOM CREEK OVERFLOWS ITS BANKS*. They could also refer sometimes to quite mundane events:

In 1964 I made a cut-up and got what seemed at the time a

totally inexplicable phrase: "And here is a horrid air conditioner." In 1974 I moved into a loft with a broken air conditioner which was removed to put in a new unit. And there was three hundred pounds of broken air conditioner on my floor – a horrid disposal problem, heavy and solid, emerged from a cut-up ten years ago.[56]

This was similar to the seemingly arbitrary content of dreams, which Burroughs had been paying serious attention to for some time, as a result of both his experiences with analysis and interest in parapsychology:

I have experienced a number of precognitive dreams that are often quite trivial and irrelevant. For example I dreamed that a landlady showed me a room with five beds in it and I protested that I didn't want to sleep in a room with five people. Some weeks later I went to a reading in Amsterdam and the hotel keeper did show me a room with five beds in it.[57]

As his friend and collaborator, the artist Malcolm Mc Neill, would later confirm:

Given the fundamental uncertainty that defines the human condition this is only to be expected. The ability to access *future* time, above all, is at a premium. The long record of shamans, mystics, seers, prophets, psychics, and clairvoyants reveals a propensity that has conceivably existed since humans became conscious of time.

It's a phenomena we call prescience; the knack of knowing ahead. Writers and artists have also been known to access such information from time to time and Bill Burroughs was among them. He had the ability to '*write* ahead.'[58]

Right from the beginning, Burroughs immediately made the connection between their literary endeavours and more esoteric pursuits:

You will recall *An Experiment with Time* by Dunne. Dr Dunne found that when he wrote down his dreams the text contained many clear and precise references to so-called future events.

However, he found that when you dream of an air crash, a fire, a tornado, you are not dreaming of the event itself but of the so-called future time when you will read about it in the newspapers. You are seeing not the event itself, but a newspaper picture of the event, pre-recorded and pre-photographed.[59]

This caused him to speculate:

Perhaps events are pre-written and pre-recorded and when you cut word lines the future leaks out.[60]

As a more paranoid worldview began to evolve – in which he saw *Life* and *Time* magazines, the newspapers, and ultimately *all* media – as channels for the Control Machine, more about disseminating *disinformation* than really keeping the public informed, Burroughs felt that the cut-up was a way to break through the Word Lines of this insidious, all-pervading enemy and get to The Truth:

The word of course is one of the most powerful instruments of control as exercised by the newspaper and images as well, there are both words and images in newspapers... Now if you start cutting these up and rearranging them you are breaking down the control system.[61]

This was an attitude he would extend increasingly to *all* communications, and eventually all relationships: an early tape-recording from the Beat Hotel has Burroughs and his conspirators discussing a "creepy letter" which Gysin says he "can't bear to hear again" – but it is explained that Burroughs "is going to cut it up – then we'll hear what he's *really* saying!"[62]

This newfound shared enthusiasm would not last though, and in some respects ended in tears: of the original collaborators who launched the cut-ups on an unsuspecting world with *Minutes to Go* in 1959, poet Gregory Corso distanced himself from what he saw ultimately as an assault on the Muse, and the already unstable Sinclair Beiles would become so upset during the often heated discussions that he would have to leave the room to throw up. Gysin himself felt that, ultimately, he was unable to make the cut-ups work for him the way they worked for Burroughs: instead he focused more on the Concrete Poetry of the Permutations. He would take short, simple phrases and run them through every conceivable combination and juxtaposition, producing hypnotic, mantra-like formulae that it was hoped would expose something about the basic mechanisms of the Word Virus, which both he and Burroughs were increasingly sure must be the basic unit of Control. A short text by Gysin later included in *The Third Mind* offers both an explanation and one of the earliest examples:

Words thank you for your collaboration, but they can also create themselves on their own, thus:

Come to free the words

To free the words come

Free the words to come

The words come to free

Words come to free thee!

The possible permutations are $5x4x3x2x1 = 120$ lines.
Therefore a 120 line poem without an author. Where is the poet Brion Gysin?[63]

But even with such an apparently impersonal process as this, Brion the self-mythologizer was able to see occult forces at work, claiming:

The permutations discovered *me* – because permutations have been around for a long time; in the whole magic world permutations are part of the Cabalistic secret . . .[64]

Gysin has described how "William followed by running the cut-ups into the ground, literally" and was "always the toughest of the lot. Nothing ever fazed him."[65] Together they worked their way through the *New York Herald Tribune, Saturday Evening Post, Time, The Observer,* and (of course) *Life* magazine

– with Burroughs showing a particular enthusiasm for news features on cancer – and then began combining the strips of newsprint with Rimbaud, Shakespeare, and the *Song of Songs* from the King James Bible. Later they would include material from Huxley's *The Doors of Perception*, and *Anabasis* by St. John Perse (in the Eliot translation, a particular favourite of Burroughs that he was still sampling 23 years later for *The Place of Dead Roads:* "a great principle of violence dictated our fashions") – in fact pretty much *anything* they happened to be reading, or had to hand – including of course the "Word Hoard" that was left over from writing *Naked Lunch*.

Talking in the 1970s to Terry Wilson for the book of expanded interviews *Here to Go: Planet R101*, Brion Gysin described how Burroughs would work with the material – and I think his choice of words is instructive:

> On the wall hangs a nest of three wire-trays for correspondence which I gave him to sort out his cut-up pages. Later, this proliferated into a maze of filing cases filling a room with manuscripts cross-referenced in a way only Burroughs could work his way through, more by magic dowsing than by any logical system. How could there be any? This was a magic practice he was up to, surprising the very springs of creative imagination at their source.[66]

The cut-ups would get a more public airing – for the first time beyond the relatively underground bohemian circle around the Beat Hotel in Paris – when U.K. publisher John Calder arranged for Burroughs to appear at the Edinburgh Conference in August 1962. Despite the notoriety of *Naked Lunch*, he was still something of a newcomer and relative unknown when he was invited to speak as part of a panel on *The Future of the Novel*. There was a clear standoff between the old guard, who dismissed all the sex and drugs as immoral and irrelevant, and these new techniques as unintelligible – and the mapmakers of the new consciousness, "cosmonauts of inner space" in the immortal phrase of Burroughs' friend and ally, the Scottish-Italian Beat writer and fellow addict, Alex Trocchi.

Burroughs stole the show with his presentation of an attempted "new mythology for the Space Age" – and an explanation of the innovative techniques that had made it possible, the cut-ups, and their further extension in the newly-developed *fold-in* – but when he tried to stress the *magical* applications of these new techniques, claiming that he had actually caused a plane to crash, the Anglo-Indian writer Khushwant Singh protested "Are you *serious?*" Burroughs' deadpan reply of "Perfectly" prompted a curious comparison from the poet and critic Stephen Spender, who queried the analogy between science and writing:

> It sounds to me like a rather medieval form of magic rather than modern science.[67]

It is in fact informative to compare this with a statement Burroughs himself made, in which his comparison of cut-ups with mediumship is explicit:

> Cut ups often come through as code messages with special meaning for the cutter. Table tapping? Perhaps.[68]

The Beat Hotel

"The years in the Beat Hotel were full of experiments . . . it was
the right time, the right place, and the right people meeting
there together, there were lots of experimental things going on .
. ."

Brion Gysin, interviewed by Terry Wilson.[69]

It is to be remembered that the atmosphere around Burroughs and Gysin in
those early days at the Beat Hotel in Paris was steeped in the occult, with
daily experiments in mirror-gazing, scrying, trance and telepathy, all fuelled
by a wide variety of mind-altering drugs – and so it is not so surprising to
think that they may have considered these new developments in such terms.
There were also two new additions to this sorcerous circle: one was Mack
'Shell' Thomas, a saxophone player from Texas who dabbled in junk, and
taught Burroughs his technique for getting rid of unwanted visitors who
had outstayed their welcome (apparently you were to visualise them *outside*
the room, while looking at them and thinking alternately "I hate you – I love
you – I hate you – I love you"[70] until they would follow the psychic nudge
and leave.) The other was the larger-than-life figure of Jacques Stern: an
eccentric French intellectual, claiming relation to the Rothschilds, left crippled
by a childhood bout of polio, but who eased his sufferings with the best
junk his apparently abundant riches could buy.

As to the actual techniques mentioned, *scrying* is a very old and almost universal
practice whereby the "scryer" gazes into a crystal ball, mirror, or other
reflective surface, so as to access a form of spirit vision – usually (but not
exclusively) for the purpose of divination, or fortune telling. Gysin very
probably knew of the 10th Century Persian epic poem, the *Shahnameh* or
"Book of Kings", in which there are descriptions of the practitioners of
pre-Islamic sorcery, gazing into a sacred cup as a way of "observing all of

the seven layers of the universe." He would conduct scrying marathons, sitting cross-legged in front of the mirrored armoire in his tiny room at the Beat Hotel for up to 36 hours, tears streaming down his face from unblinking eyes, as friends passed the occasional cigarette, cup of coffee, or joint to help keep him going. He later described how:

> . . . you see great galleries of characters, running through . . . scientists . . . in their sort of 19th century labs . . . whole events or whole scenes sort of frozen . . . And faces which never existed, and great chieftains of unknown races, and so forth and so on, going back and back further and further in time and history . . . after certainly more than 24 hours of staring . . . where there seemed it was a limited area that one could see only a certain distance into, uh, where everything was covered with a gently palpitating cloud of smoke which would be about waist-high . . . that was the end, there was nothing beyond that . . .[71]

Burroughs would frequent an occult bookshop, *la Table d'Emeraude* (doubtless named for the "Emerald Tablet" of fabled mage Hermes Trismegistus, he of "as above, so below" fame), in which he bought a small and shiny stainless steel ball on a chain – probably meant for dowsing of some kind – but which he would use for scrying. When Burroughs hung the ball in his room, Gysin looked into it and said he could see scenes of Tangier, particularly his former restaurant. When Burroughs looked as well, he saw a vision of a Moslem funeral – the two scryers agreeing that they saw a body being carried downstairs – and when Jacques Stern reported that he had independently had a vision of "a coffin in the library"[72] it seemed like a confirmation – of *something* . . .

Brion also had an Arab necklace that he said was magical, with an amber bead strung on it. After Burroughs had been working on a section of what would become *Naked Lunch*, featuring a delightful new character named "Fats Terminal" – described in one place as a translucent, foetal monkey, with a round, lamprey disk-type mouth – Brion was able to show him that very face in the amber bead. A letter to Allen Ginsberg included in the first volume of *Collected Letters* gives a pretty clear picture of the increasingly occult world Burroughs was exploring:

> The para-normal occurrences thick and fast . . . I saw Stern lose about seven pounds in ten minutes when he took a shot after being off a week. (That flesh you gain back when you kick is soft and ectoplasmic at first, and it melts literally at touch of junk). On another occasion he felt my touch on his arm across six feet of space . . . After writing the "Fats Terminal" section, I saw Fats' face in an amber bead Brion Gysin showed me from magic, Arab necklace . . .[73]

Burroughs began to pursue his own mirror-gazing experiments, both as a form of meditation and to explore trance states, and they were beginning to produce some quite bizarre side effects:

> Once I looked in mirror and saw my hands completely inhuman, thick, black-pink, fibrous, long white tendrils growing from the curiously abbreviated finger-tips as if the finger had been cut off to make way for tendrils . . . And Jerry, who was sitting across the room, said: "My God, Bill! What's wrong with your hands?"
>
> "My hands?" I said innocently.
>
> "They are all thick and pink and something white growing out the fingers."
>
> Many people have commented on my growing invisibility . . . So the material is a catalogue of actual events.[74]

A further disturbing occurrence was reported, that went beyond either invisibility or strangely transformed fingers and hands:

> What is happening now is that I literally turn into someone else, not a human creature but man-like: He wears some sort of green uniform. The face is full of black boiling fuzz and what most people would call evil – silly word. I have been seeing him

for some time in the mirror. This is nothing, of course. But when other people start seeing him without being briefed or influenced in any way, then something is really there . . . he comes through so clear that people stare at me in restaurants.[75]

Unfortunately, Stern soon turned out to be something of a manipulator, fantasist and con-man, given to mean-tempered irascibility and paranoid outbursts, but for a while Burroughs bought into his act, later saying:*Jacques Stern had psychic powers . . . I was easily impressed in those days.*[76]

When things later cooled between them – and Shell was busted on his return to the States, having been foolish enough as to try and sneak heroin through Customs while dressed in "Beatnik" clothes and carrying his saxophone – Burroughs was genuinely disappointed. As he wrote to his old friend and confidante Ginsberg:

> Stern in complete seclusion. Answers no letters – at least none of mine. Says the presence of people is painful to him. I think Gysin is afraid of me as notorious carrier of Black Fuzz, bad luck and death. Of the three mystics I had hoped to form nucleus and get something definite and useable via cross-fertilization – Shell, Gysin, and Stern – and then there was none. I continue to see visions and experience strange currents of energy, but the Key – the one piece that could make it useable – Stern had part of it, and so did Shell (Gysin more a catalyst or medium in strict sense): "You can look anywhere, no good, *no bueno* – hustling myself."[77]

At the point that the second volume of his Collected Letters – *Rub Out The Word: The Letters of William S. Burroughs 1959-1974* – opens, William S. Burroughs had been living outside of the USA for the best part of a decade, was settled in the Beat Hotel in Paris, and his breakthrough novel, *Naked Lunch*, had just been published by the Olympia Press. He was about to be profiled in *Life* magazine – the subject of a pained exchange with his outraged mother, Laura Lee Burroughs, in which Burroughs compares himself with former "Wickedest Man in the World,"[78] Aleister Crowley – and his newfound friend and collaborator Brion Gysin has just had the "happy accident" that leads to the cut-ups, of which we will hear *much*.

The Beat Godfather, The Great Beast, & The Necronomicon

> There is also the question of the actual relations between formal ritual magic and writing. People who are into ritual magic like Aleister Crowley – he may have been a competent black magician but he is not a good writer, in fact he's not readable.[79]

With regard to Crowley, Burroughs certainly had an intermittent awareness of – and recurring interest in – the man who had styled himself "The Great Beast", even going so far as to title one of his abstract "spirit paintings" in 1988, *Portrait of Aleister Crowley*. Numerous occasional references crop up in interviews and throughout his fiction down the years, even if they are not always consistent – but to be fair, as self-styled Magus, occultist extraordinaire, and Prophet of a New Aeon, Crowley himself was a complex and not always consistent figure, and so any attempt at commentary is bound to be prone to similar complications . . .

As late as 1996, a phone interview with Robbie Conal and Tom Christie included the following exchange:

> Interviewers: You're interested in the occult, aren't you?

> Burroughs: Certainly. I'm interested in the golden dawn *[sic]*, Aleister Crowley, all the astrological aspects.[80]

Back in the mid-1970s, when Burroughs was introduced to Led Zeppelin guitarist Jimmy Page in New York, to record an "interview" for *Crawdaddy* magazine, to break the ice they discussed mutual friends and acquaintances back in London:

Burroughs thought he and Jimmy might know people in common since Burroughs had lived in London for most of the past ten years. It turned out to be an interesting list, including film director Donald Cammell, who worked on the great *Performance*; John Michell, an expert on occult matters, especially Stonehenge and UFOs; Mick Jagger and other British rock stars; and Kenneth Anger, auteur of *Lucifer Rising* . . .[81]

I was especially mindful of this when I interviewed Graham Masterton, and took some effort to put it to him as precisely as possible:

MS: What William described as "the Magical Universe" is a recurring theme throughout his life & work, despite the efforts of some to deny it (or at least relegate it to a sort of eccentric footnote.) The Sixties were clearly a time when people were open like never before to all sorts of new thinking and re-examination of older ideas, including magic, mysticism, and non-Western beliefs. Brion & William had been exposed to folk-magic in Morocco, and in London they knew the likes of Kenneth Anger – Donald Cammell – Anita Pallenberg – Jimmy Page – who all had more than a passing interest in Aleister Crowley, ritual magic(k), and witchcraft; also the recently published letters favourably describe visits to 'psychic healers' like Major Bruce MacManaway. What impression did you get (if any) of his interest or involvement in such things?

GM: We talked a great deal about the supernatural and particularly about near-death experiences and hallucinations and whether there was any kind of life after death. I always got the impression that he believed the human mind was capable of far more than we realize (which was one of the reasons he was so interested in Scientology and Wilhelm Reich's "orgone box" and such things) and that we all have what you might describe as a soul. But he saw it from a scientific rather than a religious perspective.[82]

In an interview recorded some years later – after William had died, in fact – James Grauerholz introduced a note of playful ambiguity:

. . . Burroughs considered Crowley a bit of a figure of fun, referring to him as "The Greeeaaaaat BEEEEAST!" in that behind-closed-doors, queeny comic delivery he used sometimes: his voice rising straight up in pitch, into an hysterical falsetto . . [83]

But also evinced a certain lack of correct information, surprisingly, when he went on to say:

William knew quite a bit about Crowley's life and work, and he certainly dug deep into the *Necronomicon* (anonymous but often attributed to Crowley) when it became available in a snazzy, black-morocco, tooled-leather hardback binding. He appreciated much about Aleister Crowley.[84]

The *Necronomicon*, in fact, is an entirely *fictitious* work – created by "Weird Tales" author, H. P. Lovecraft, as the ultimate "damned book" or grimoire of occult blasphemies – in effect, the bible of his existentialist science fiction horror stories, the Cthulhu Mythos. Although a number of tribute or even spoof "Necronomicons" have been created as a sort of homage to Lovecraft and his works – and it is certainly true that a number of contemporary occult practitioners have experimented with this material, in an exercise of extended Post-Modern play-acting, including one-time apprentice and secretary to Crowley, Kenneth Grant – there is no evidence that Crowley had even so much as *heard* of Lovecraft and his fictitious grimoire, yet alone had anything to do with it (the best efforts of conspiracy theorists, esoteric scholars, and occult pranksters notwithstanding!)

Burroughs also had a recurring tendency to equate the most (in)famous dictum of "The Great Beast" with the alleged "Last Words" of the Old Man of the Mountain:

Old Aleister Crowley, plagiarizing from Hassan I Sabbah, said: " 'Do what thou wilt' is the whole of the Law" . . . And then Hassan's last words were "nothing is true; everything is permitted." In other words, everything is permitted *because* nothing is true. If you see everything as an illusion, then everything is permitted . . .[85]

An amusing incident is related by Malcolm Mc Neill in his memoir of the time spent working with Burroughs, and the friendship that evolved between the two. This particular anecdote concerns the Middle Aged Writer proposing a very different and particular kind of "collaboration" to the Young Artist:

On the evening in question, after lighting up his umpteenth [*cigarette*], he suddenly switched to a conspiratorial tone.

"So Ma-a-a-alcolm . . . the Old Man of the Mountain says, 'Do as thou wilt shall be the whole of the law.'"

"*Yes*, Bill . . ."

"So why don't we, then? We've known each other a while now."

By then his left hand had made its way to my side of the table. Kind of like a crab, I thought. My knees came together. It occurred to me we were in a steakhouse, and suddenly a whole lot was at stake.

"Well, Bill," I said, "I guess I'll wilt."

"I was forgetting – you like gi-i-i-i-rls."

We finished the meal as if nothing had happened . . .[86]

The spirit of Aleister Crowley even gets a walk-on part, indirectly-speaking at least, in *The Place of Dead Roads*:

Tom introduces Kim to Chris Cullpepper, a wealthy, languid young man of exotic tastes. He is into magic and has studied with Aleister Crowley and the Golden Dawn. They decide on a preliminary evocation of Humwawa, Lord of Abominations, to assess the strength and disposition of enemy forces . . .[87]

The scenes of ritual magic which occur subsequently are clearly influenced more by Chaos Magic and Freestyle Shamanism, however, than the more formal Ceremonial Magic of Crowley or the Golden Dawn, for all the inclusion of "barbarous names of evocation"[88] and use of sex as a means of raising energies:

> Chris has set up a stone altar in the old gymnasium with candles and incense burners, a crystal skull, a phallic doll carved from a mandrake root, and a shrunken head from Ecuador.
>
> Kim leans forward and Marbles rubs the unguent up him with a slow circular twist as Chris begins the evocation . . .
>
> UTUL XUL
>
> "We are the children of the underworld, the bitter venom of the gods."
>
> . . . Tom is changing into Mountfaucon, a tail sprouting from his spine, sharp fox face and the musky reek.
>
> Kim feels something stir and stretch in his head as horns sprout . . . a blaze of silver light flares out from his eyes in a flash that blows out the candles on the altar. The crystal skull lights up with lambent blue fire, the shrunken head gasps out a putrid spicy breath, the mandrake screams
>
> IA KINGU IA LELAL IA AXAAAAAAAAA[89]

A somewhat bizarre illustration of the interconnectedness of all of Burroughs' creativity – writing, thinking, and, increasingly latterly, painting – also how his continuing belief in "The Magical Universe" is a central and unifying factor, is a startling admission concerning "Humwawa" in an interview ostensibly about his visual art:

> I've got a real muse thing going. Some of my paintings are directly influenced by them – and I don't mean the standard nine muses either. I like to invoke all sorts of muses, like *Humwawa*, Lord of Abominations! His head is a mass of reeking entrails. He arrives on a *whispering* south wind, with his brother

Pazuzu, Lord of Fevers and Plagues. They come in on a *whispering, fetid* south wind.[90]

This is another example illustrative of the kind of "creative confabulation" that can occur for a number of reasons where issues of art, creative imagination, and the occult intersect. The most common reason simply being *misunderstanding* or *misremembering* where arcane or esoteric material is concerned – a secondary reason being an *unintentional* and perhaps *unrealised* error of recall (especially when factors such as heavy and habitual use of alcohol and drugs are concerned) – and, thirdly, perhaps a more *intentional* conflation of ideas for artistic, creative, or even occult reasons, such as might occur in play with "conspiracy theory" style thinking for satirical effect.

Of the aforementioned "spoof *Necronomicons*" created by fans and fellow horror writers dabbling in occult themes alike, the most successful and well-known must surely be the so-called "Simon *Necronomicon*" (thus called because the only authorial attribution is to an alleged editor and translator, "Simon"), which first appeared in 1977. Described with some affection by Social Historian, Professor Owen Davies, as a "well-constructed hoax"[91] the book – which appears most likely to have originated in the occult circles around Herman Slater's *Magickal Childe* bookshop in New York – of course *claims* to be the authentic "dark grimoire of forbidden lore" referenced by Lovecraft and his literary followers, but it is in fact nothing of the sort. Rather, the material contained within the book draws mainly on Ancient Middle-and-Near Eastern Mythologies such as the Assyrian, Babylonian, Chaldaean, and Sumerian, with just enough allusions to the works of both H. P. Lovecraft *and* Aleister Crowley woven in to try and establish a plausible connection (at least, if you don't question some of the apparent reasoning *too* rigorously . . .) The book clearly caught something of the zeitgeist: after the initial, limited edition "Schlangekraft, Inc." imprint Sold Out, it was bought by a mainstream publisher, and has not been out of print since.

One of the more curious coincidences, at least as far as we are concerned (although I can almost hear the ghost of William S. Burroughs moaning "There are *no coincidences . . .*") is that when the first edition of the Simon *Necronomicon* came out, it bore the perhaps somewhat surprising endorsement:

> "Let the secrets of the ages be revealed. The publication of the *Necronomicon* may well be a landmark in the liberation of the human spirit." – William S. Burroughs

Varying versions of how this might have come about have been put forward: one suggested by occult author Peter Levenda – who many consider to be in fact the most likely candidate for "Simon" – being that Burroughs simply used the same publisher as whoever it was behind Schlangekraft, Inc., and that when he saw the *Necronomicon* being printed there remarked it was "a dangerous book . . . the theological equivalent to a loaded gun." The book's illustrator, Khem Caigan, who collaborated with "American Magus" Harry Smith in compiling a concordance of the so-called Language of the Angels, Enochian, as recorded by Elizabethan sorcerer-scholar John Dee (and later used by The Golden Dawn and "The Great Beast" Aleister Crowley) – has given an equally plausible and down-to-earth explanation:

> It was about that time that William Burroughs dropped by, having caught wind of a "Necronomicon" in the neighbourhood. After going through the pages and a few lines of powder, he offered the comment that it was "good shit." He might have meant the manuscript too . . .[92]

Whatever the truth of the matter, it is interesting to note that Burroughs incorporates references to "Humwawa" and "Pazuzu" into his Magical Universe – perhaps most famously in the *Invocation* at the start of *Cities of the Red Night*, which also includes a mention of "Kutulu, the Sleeping Serpent who cannot be summoned."[93] *Humwawa* and *Pazuzu*, brother-demons from Ancient Mesopotamian mythology, who are both monstrous, chimaeric entities associated with fevers, plagues, and storms, do not appear *anywhere* in the fiction of H. P. Lovecraft – but they *do* both feature *heavily* in the

Necronomicon put together by "Simon" for Schlangekraft, Inc. Likewise, the reference to "Kutulu" is probably derived from the same source, wherein the variant spelling of the originally Sumerian "Kutu" (meaning "underworld") has been made, doubtless to suggest some equivalency to the central embodiment of evil in Lovecraft's nightmarish mythos, Cthulhu.

Success Will Write *Apocalypse* Across The Sky . . .

Io Pan! Io Pan!

Devil or god, to me, to me,

My man! my man!

Come with trumpets sounding shrill

Over the hill!

Come with drums low muttering

From the spring!

Come with flute and come with pipe!

Aleister Crowley, *Hymn to Pan*.[94]

The earlier volume of Burroughs' collected correspondence, published as *The Letters of William S. Burroughs 1945 to 1959*, ended with a letter to Allen Ginsberg, and the later collection, *Rub Out The Words: The Letters of William S. Burroughs 1959-1974*, picks up quite literally where it left off, with another written to him the very next day (30th October 1959). We are in fairly familiar territory here – Burroughs giving thanks to Ginsberg for a supply of mescaline, catching up on gossip about mutual acquaintances Gregory Corso and Jacques Stern, and an amusing anecdote about Henri Michaux:

> It seems that M*[ichaux]*. was hurrying home after swallowing his mescaline tablet . . . closed the door and bolted it and drew the curtains and turned out the light and got into bed and closed his eyes and there was Mr. B[urroughs]. and Mr. M. said:
>
> "What are you doing here in my vision?"

And B. replied: "Oh I live here."[95]

So far so good, but things *Cut-Shift-Tangle* at an accelerating rate: the real story here is William S. Burroughs coming of age as a writer, differentiating himself from his former Beat peers, and finding his own voice (even if its name is Legion.)

Defending his work at the 1962 International Writer's Conference on *The Future of the Novel*, critic Mary McCarthy said that one of the things that set Burroughs apart was his "planetary perspective,"[96] and it has been argued that he belongs more with the writers and thinkers of the European *avant garde* tradition. Editor Bill Morgan describes in his *Introduction* how these letters give:

> . . . witness to an era in which Burroughs became the centre of a new coterie of creative people who were not related to the Beat Generation. With their assistance, Burroughs became an influential artistic and cultural leader whose reputation spread well beyond the literary world . . .[97]

As well as old friends Alan Ansen, Paul Bowles, Corso and Ginsberg, Burroughs' new horizons expand to include, amongst others, Antony Balch, Charles Henri Ford, Timothy Leary, Norman Mailer, Barry Miles, Jeff Nuttall, Michael Portman, Ian Sommerville, Terry Southern and Alex Trocchi; but the single most important figure is without doubt Brion Gysin, who soon replaces Ginsberg as Burroughs's most trusted collaborator and confidante – although unlike Ginsberg, *never* lover – as Gysin himself was at pains to later point out to Terry Wilson:

> Burroughs and I saw each other more than a lot. No, not 24 hours a day. No matter what people may say, we were never lovers. Allen Ginsberg writes that he has one set of ideas about making it sexually with friends, I have another. Not a matter of principle. Friends just don't turn me on, I guess.[98]

2nd December 1959, Burroughs writes to Ginsberg:

I have met my first master in Brion.[99]

They quickly overcame previous rather cool impressions from Tangier, and plunged into the slippery psychic symbiosis of "The Third Mind." From tales of famed medium Eileen Garret and Hassan-i Sabbâh, Old Man of the Mountain and Master of the Assassins, to the ecstatic trance music of Morocco, Brion was a spellbinding storyteller indeed. As psychedelic guru Timothy Leary would later write in his memoirs:

> . . . Brion dispenses blessings, visions, communications, poetic sermons, and wicked gossip – the world of the occult is his planet. Gysin is one of the great hedonic mystic teachers. He has played starring roles in the great spiritual movies of our times. He led the rescue party that found and saved John Cooke from the black magicians of Algeria and brought the great crippled wizard back to the living. He performed the rites and lefts in Eileen Garrett's temples and absorbed the message of that fantastic medium. It was Brion Gysin who could tell you anything you wanted to know and tell you in witty, polished epigrams . . .[100]

As well as the myth of the "Hash-Head Assassins"[101] Gysin was also full of tales of the magic and mystery of the Master Musicians of Joujouka, a collective of Berber Sufi trance musicians originating from the small village of that name, south of Tangier in the foothills to the west of the Rif Mountains. As Gysin would later write in respect of his first encounter with the stirring, primal, hypnotic music of reeds, pipes, and goat-skin drums:

> Magic calls itself The Other Method for controlling matter and knowing space. In Morocco, magic is practiced more assiduously than hygiene though, indeed, ecstatic dancing to music of the brotherhoods may be called a form of psychic hygiene. You know your music when you hear it one day. You fall into line and dance until you pay the piper.[102]

Something about it certainly caught Gysin's imagination, and, through him, Burroughs' also, and together they would build up a considerable personal mythology around the Master Musicians and the folklore of their mountain village. After managing to attend the Festival of Bou Jeloud up in Joujouka for the first time, Gysin claimed:

> . . . I recognized very quickly that what they were performing was the Roman Lupercal, and the Roman Lupercalia was a race run from one part of Rome, a cave under the Capitoline Hill . . . and in this cave goats were killed and skinned and a young man of a certain tribe sewn up in them . . . and the point was to go out to the gates of Rome and contact Pan, the God of the Forests, the little Goat God, who was Sexuality itself, and to run back through the streets with the news that Pan was still out there fucking . . .[103]

As far as Gysin was concerned, when the villagers of Joujouka celebrated their annual feast, in which a young boy was chosen to dance the part of Bou Jeloud, sewn into the skins of freshly killed goats:

> Their secret, guarded even from them, was that they were still performing the Rites of Pan under the ragged cloak of Islam.[104]

Burroughs wholeheartedly embraced Gysin's interpretation that Bou Jeloud was an avatar of the Greek god Pan that had survived from pagan times, as had been put forward by the pioneering socio-biologist, Edvard Westermarck, in his 1933 study, *Pagan Survivals in Mohammedan Civilization*. So, to Burroughs, the "magical music" of the Master Musicians was, quite literally, a manifestation of the Pipes of Pan, joining his literary armoury of occult references and psychic techniques, and becoming a recurring theme throughout his writings, both fiction and non-fiction alike:

> The boy . . . dances in front of our party for a few seconds. Pan the Goat God, Master of Skins, Master of Fear, ageless enigmatic impersonal, looks out through his eyes. He can look out through many eyes.
>
> Listen to this music, the primordial sounds of a 4,000-year-old rock 'n' roll band . . . listen with your whole body, let the music penetrate you and move you, and you will connect with the

oldest music on earth.[105]

Like a message-in-a-bottle thrown out into the sea of time for subsequent generations to pick up on, between them they would cast a spell on artists, writers, and above all musicians: Brian Jones of The Rolling Stones, Ornette Coleman, Bill Laswell, Lee Ranaldo of Sonic Youth, Talvin Singh, Jane's Addiction, and many others, would all follow in their footsteps in the hope of catching a little of the magic of the Master Musicians of Joujouka as they celebrated the Rites of Pan.

> Mariners sailing close to the shores of Tuscany heard a voice cry out from the hills, the trees and the sky: "The Great God Pan is dead!" Pan, God of Panic: the sudden awareness that everything is alive and significant. The date was December 25, 1 A.D. But Pan lives on in the realm of the imagination, in writing and painting and music. Look at Van Gogh's sunflowers, writhing with portentous life; listen to the Pipes of Pan in Joujouka . . .

> Every dedicated artist attempts the impossible. Success will write APOCALYPSE across the sky . . .Pan God of Panic, whips screaming crowds, as millions of faces look up at the torn sky . . .

> *LET IT COME DOWN*

> Caught in New York beneath the animals of the village, the Piper pulled down the sky.[106]

The Lost Boys

> The magical theory of history: the magical universe presupposes that nothing happens unless someone or some power, some living entity *wills it to happen*. There are no coincidences and no accidents.[107]

Meanwhile, back at The Beat Hotel . . . Curses, mirror-gazing, spells and trances, and the non-chemical expansion of awareness made possible through Cut-ups, Flicker, and Playback – all would be diligently explored with Bill's new acolytes and lovers: the Cambridge mathematician, Ian Sommerville ("the Technical Sergeant"), who would facilitate the Dreamachine and tape-recorder experiments, and spoilt rich-kid jailbait, Mikey Portman ("the Medium") – who, despite his bad habits, good looks, money and youth (or, perhaps, even *because* of them) would eventually drive Burroughs to distraction.

These two Lost Boys were each, in their way, vital to the collaborations being undertaken by Burroughs and Gysin in the 1960s, and how they sought to extend their "Third Mind" to others. Indeed, the *Acknowledgment* for Burroughs' 1962 novel, *The Ticket That Exploded,* gives notice of the importance of this new spirit of collaboration:

> The sections entitled *in a strange bed* and *the black fruit* were written in collaboration with Mr. Michael Portman of London. Mr. Ian Sommerville of London pointed out the use and significance of spliced tape and all the other tape recorder experiments suggested in this book. The film experiments I owe to Mr. Antony Balch of Balch Films, London. The closing message is by Brion Gysin.[108]

Born 3rd June 1940, Ian Sommerville was a brilliant young man from a working-class background in Darlington, in the North of England, whom a scholarship had enabled to go to Cambridge to study Mathematics. During the Summer Holidays, he had gone to Paris and found part-time work in the Mistral bookshop, where a chance recommendation from Harold Norse ("this kid *likes* older guys"[109]) had lead, inadvertently, to what would perhaps be the love of Burroughs' life. Gysin later said of Sommerville:

> Ian Sommerville was a mathematics scholar at Jesus, Cambridge, just over in Paris for the holidays. He was skinny and quick as an alleycat with bristly red hair that stuck up all over in pre-punk style. He was crisper than cornflakes and sharp as a tack. He crackled and snapped with static electricity and panicked at the idea of rain on his hair.[110]

The characters 'Technical Tilly' and 'The Subliminal Kid' in Burroughs' 1960s cut-up novels are based on Sommerville, and he gets a further credit in the *Foreword Note* to *Nova Express*:

> The section called "This Horrible Case" was written in collaboration with Mr. Ian Sommerville, a mathematician – Mr. Sommerville also contributed the technical notes in the section called "Chinese Laundry" . . .[111]

Many years later, Ian would be the basis for the character of the photographer, Tom Dark, in *The Place of Dead Roads*, and he would appear regularly in the various dreams recorded in the final works, *My Education* and *Last Words*. Ian Sommerville would also play a key role as the Third Mind's very own "systems advisor" after a startling visionary experience Gysin had in the back of a bus in December 1958. As he recorded in his diary:

> Had a transcendental storm of colour visions today in the bus going to Marseilles. We ran through a long avenue of trees and I closed my eyes against the setting sun. An overwhelming flood of intensely bright colors exploded behind my eyelids: a multidimensional kaleidoscope whirling out through space. I was swept out of time. I was out in a world of infinite number. The vision stopped abruptly as we left the trees. Was that a vision? What happened to me?[112]

When Burroughs later read *The Living Brain* by W. Grey Walter, he made the connection with his friend's strange visionary experience immediately. Walter, an American-born British neurophysiologist, had been researching the effect of controlled flicker on states of consciousness via the use of precisely calibrated stroboscopes, and with the help of early EEG equipment had put forward a model of varying brainwave frequencies corresponding to different states of consciousness. Apparently a flicker rate of 8-to-13 cycles a second induced what Walter dubbed "alpha rhythms" – which "predominantly originate . . . during wakeful relaxation with closed eyes" and, interestingly, also during REM sleep (i.e. during *dreaming*.) Obviously Brion had experienced a spontaneously-occurring flicker experience, no doubt caused by the exact rhythm of the sunlight flickering through the trees as the bus drove past, thought Burroughs. Walter himself had actually suggested the possible evolutionary impact of something similar in an uncharacteristically poetic flight of speculation in his book:

> Oddly enough it is not in the city, but in the jungle conditions, sunlight shining through the forest, that we run the greatest risk of flicker-fits. Perhaps in this way, with their slowly swelling brains and their enhanced liability to break-downs of this sort, our arboreal cousins, struck by the setting sun in the midst of a jungle caper, may have fallen from perch to plain, sadder but wiser apes.[113]

New Year, 1960, and Burroughs sent Gysin a postcard proclaiming "Blitzkrieg the citadel of enlightenment!"[114] The question was, though, *how* to reliably reproduce the flicker effect? The answer came from their young friend, Ian Sommerville, who had also read Walter's book, and, after returning to his studies at Cambridge, had written:

> I have made a simple flicker machine; a slotted cardboard cylinder which turns on a gramophone at 78 rpm with a light bulb inside. You look at it with your eyes shut and the flicker plays over the eyelids. Visions start with a kaleidoscope of colours on a plane in front of the eyes and gradually become

2. *"everything is permitted"* – original artwork by Billy Chainsaw, reproduced with his kind permission.

3. WSB at NL Centrum, Amsterdam. Photo by Brecht van Teeseling , reproduced with the kind permission of Anthony Blokdijk, Maldoror Stichting/Den Haag.

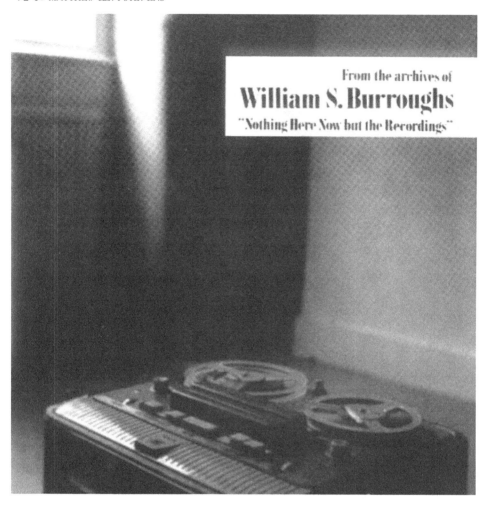

4. *Nothing Here Now But The Recordings* (Industrial Records, 1981.) WSB spoken word/ tape cut-up LP. Cover design and photography by Peter 'Sleazy' Christopherson.

5. *Piccadilly Burroughs*, original artwork by Philip Willey,
reproduced with his kind permission.

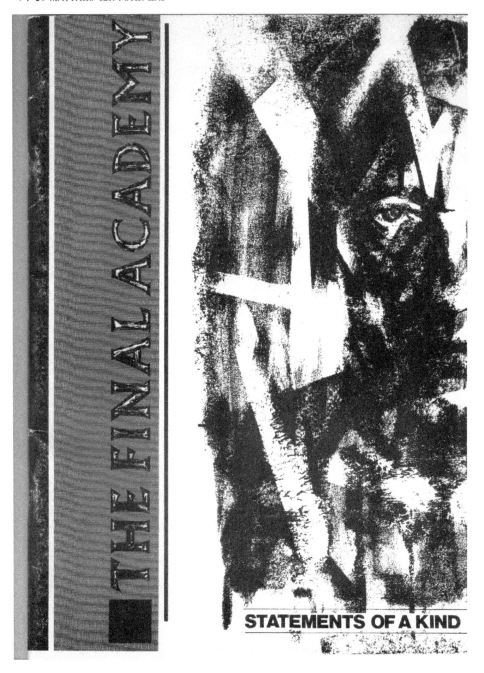

6. *Statements of a Kind* – program for *The Final Academy*. Cover art by Neville Brody.

7. *"Wild Boys Very Close Now"* – original artwork by Emma Doeve, reproduced with her kind permission.

8. *The Wild Boys Are Coming* – original artwork by Emma Doeve, reproduced with her kind permission.

9. William S. Burroughs, Duke Street, St. James, 1971. Original photo by Baron Wolman, reproduced with his kind permission.

more complex and beautiful, breaking like surf on a shore until whole patterns of colour are pounding to get in . . .[115]

As Gysin would later remark of Sommerville:

He was an extraordinary technician, had obviously ever since childhood been the sort of boy who can fix things, or make things, or mend things, or invent things . . .[116]

Gysin, inevitably, was quick to promote both the Dreamachine and his discovery of it – going so far as to register a patent, *Procedure and apparatus for the production of artistic visual sensations*, for his "invention"[117] (although many later felt that the credit really should have gone to Sommerville.) Ever the charismatic raconteur and self-mythologizer, Gysin would spin a web of wonder about "his" flicker device, writing that:

The Dreamachine may bring about a change of consciousness inasmuch as it throws back the limits of the visible world . . .

This, surely, approaches the vision of which the mystics have spoken.

He would also create a suitably esoteric and esteemed pedigree, telling interviewers:

. . . one knows of cases – in French history, Catherine de Medici for example, had Nostradamus sitting up on the top of a tower . . . and he used to sit up there and with the fingers of his hands spread like this would flicker his fingers over his closed eyes, and would interpret his visions in a way which were of influence to her in regard to her political powers . . . they were like instructions from a higher power . . . Peter the Great also had somebody who sat on the top of a tower and flickered his fingers like that across his closed eyelids . . .[118]

Of course, it was too good to be true. For all that the "cosmonauts of inner space" of the Beat Hotel thought that the Dreamachine could be "the drugless turn-on of the 60s"[119] illuminating the world for the price of a light-bulb, it was never really going to have the kind of mass appeal they might have hoped for. It is fair to say that the device's undoubtedly impressive effects have intrigued a number of Burroughs-and-Gysin-inspired alternative rock musicians, such as Iggy Pop, Genesis P-Orridge, Kid 'Congo' Powers (the Dreamachine was included to great effect in the video for his single, 'Conjure Man'[120]) Lee Ranaldo from Sonic Youth, and DJ Spooky. Marianne Faithfull – who would meet Gysin for tea in Mayfair during her "lost years" and would later get to know Burroughs when Allen Ginsberg arranged for her to teach Song-writing at Naropa – recalled her first impressions of the Dreamachine, and her answer gives some sense of the associations that probably stopped the device from catching on commercially:

> I remember going to an exhibition of Brion Gysin, and there was the Dreamachine . . . I mean I knew it was really special 'cos I think I was tripping . . .

> Only a magical creature could think up something like that – it is like a wonderful idealistic idea, but you know it's never gonna fly . . .[121]

The other main addition to Burroughs' new circle at the Beat Hotel, and one who would become both a close personal friend and important creative collaborator, was the film-maker, Antony Balch. According to Gysin:

> Burroughs and I were forever saying we ought to be making movies but we had no contacts at all until I met Antony Balch at a party given just across our narrow alley.

> His mother worked in the movies and Antony grew up looking like a movie star but he wanted to make movies, produce them, direct them and distribute them . . . He made money by distribution which he spent on making three experimental shorts with us:

> *Towers Open Fire, The Cut Ups* and *Bill & Tony*. He then made a soft porn picture and a horror to get his hand in at a commercial film in the hopes of making *Naked Lunch* out of my

screenplay. It was not to be.[122]

The Third Mind collective around William Burroughs at The Beat Hotel was now complete with Brion Gysin, Antony Balch, and the addition of Ian Sommerville and Michael Portman. Allen Ginsberg, perhaps somewhat resentful of being displaced in his old friend-and-lover's affections, later wrote:

> Bill's all hung up with 18 yr. old spoiled brat English Lord who looks like a pale-faced Rimbaud but is a smart creep . . . Bill got some kind of awful relation with him and the kid bugs everyone so intimacy with Bill is limited and Bill absentminded all the time. . .[123]

Burroughs' first biographer, Ted Morgan, would describe Portman thus:

> . . . with the pouty lips and mischievous eyes of the Caravaggio Bacchus, the kind of face in which youthful self-indulgence is already tinged with decay.[124]

Born 15th October, 1943, the other Lost Boy, Michael William Berkeley Portman – to give him his full name – was young, good-looking, and infatuated with Burroughs, copying everything about him, from his preference for mint tea, Arab-style, and how he walked, to the way he took a fix – and at first Burroughs was flattered, writing to Brion Gysin:

> Miguel [*Michael*] Portman's beauty produce an aphrodisiac result. It's the principal of the thing you understand. If I could just get that guide alone . . .[125]

This last was a reference to the fact that, as well as his other, more obvious, attractions, young Portman was also highly suggestible, and prone to trancelike states. If Ian Sommerville was the Third Mind's Technical Sergeant, then Mikey was its Medium:

> "A much more beautiful and shining replica has materialised himself at 25 Lillie Road [*Burroughs' London address at the time*] . . .

Sixteen years old. Name Michael Portman . . .Turns into a
Tangier guide straight away and said: 'Me llama Meester. Que
quires?'[126]

The letters also give some insight into how relations between the Agents of
The Third Mind, emerging at that time as it was in anonymous, cheap
furnished rooms and hotels in London, Paris and Tangier, and the
correspondence between them, was by no means without its conflicts or
tensions. Two years later, still in the Empress Hotel and having established
an uneasy accommodation with his two young *amigos*, a letter to Gysin includes
this telling query:

> Some staff difficulties between Ian and Mikey – Ian is one head
> I can't walk in – Can you?[127]

Although there was an initial honeymoon period with his new *amigo*, Michael
Portman, in which Burroughs found the boy's youth, looks, and admiration
an obvious turn-on, the simple truth is that Mikey was an accident waiting
to happen. His father, Lord Portman, had died suddenly when Mikey was
still only a boy of 12, his widowed mother sought comfort in the arms of a
younger Greek playboy lover, and it was left to the family solicitor, Lord
Goodman, to dole out a not insubstantial allowance to the troubled teen.
Hurt, confused, and doubtless feeling abandoned all round, Mikey acted out
by being lazy, spoilt through and through, and unreliable. The poet and
actor Heathcote Williams, who was associate editor of the literary journal
Transatlantic Review when he met and befriended Burroughs in 1963, gives a
characteristic snapshot in a recent reminiscence:

> When I went round to Duke Street it often seemed that
> Burroughs attracted a coterie of characters very much like those
> whom he was satirizing in his work. One fictional character of
> his, for example, called the "Intolerable Kid" — a nightmarish
> creature of total appetite — sprang to life in the form of Mikey
> Portman, an epicene, voracious youth with a large mouth who
> would consume anything within reach and quickly turn the

whole of the Duke Street flat into his ashtray and needle depository.[128]

Mikey was also the main basis for the addict and virus carrier "Genial" in *The Ticket That Exploded.*Ian Sommerville *could not stand* Portman, feeling he had wilfully squandered all the opportunities his background, education, and family wealth had afforded him. Although Mikey had sought a kind of queer father figure in Burroughs, his true sexual preference was in Black rough trade. Before long, the honeymoon was over and the letters become a catalogue of paranoia, poltergeist disturbances, possession, and suspected psychic attack. During what would later become known as the "Psychedelic Summer," when Harvard professor and emerging psychedelic guru Timothy Leary descended on Tangier with a batch of powerful new psychedelics to try out on the Beat expats, a West Indian boyfriend of Mikey's famously remarked:

> "Oh Mikey, it is terrible what is going on. Here there is spirits fighting . . . all the time spirits fighting!"[129]

It is alleged that in 1961 Portman assisted Burroughs and Gysin in an act of ceremonial magic as they attempted to perform the Abra-Melin Working in an hotel in Marrakesh – although one has to wonder at this: conducted properly, the Abra-Melin is, in effect, a full-scale "magical retreat" – complete with complex devotions, fasting, and increasingly rigorous rituals, building in intensity over a six-month period, and as such aimed *exclusively* at the solo practitioner – so it is hard to imagine just how it would be adapted to a group working, even if one wanted to. In addition, although an integral part of the Abra-Melin procedure is the systematic conjuring and binding of *demons* – so that in the end the aspirant is suitably empowered and purified as to be able to attain to "the Knowledge and Conversation of the Holy Guardian Angel" – at no point does it involve the conjuring or "channelling" of *spirits*, so it is unclear quite what use a medium would be . . .

There are, in fact, various recorded practices that have come down from the magic of antiquity that *do* make use of children or youths to channel spirits – for instance, in the Greek Magical Papyri, a collection of texts gathering material ranging from the 2nd Century B.C. to the 5th Century A.D., which stand in relation to the Western magical tradition in much the same way as the Dead Sea Scrolls do to Christianity. A number of the spells given in these Papyri instruct the would-be magician to "make use of a boy" in acts of divination – in other words, employ a young, pre-pubescent male as a medium. The boys in question "should be uncorrupt, pure,"[130] and the nature of this purity is made quite clear:

> You should bring a pure youth who has not yet gone with a woman.[131]

Such young boys were chosen quite specifically to assist as mediums, particularly where a form of scrying was involved, as it was believed that their purity and absence of sexual desire or experience allowed them clearer perception of the spirit realms. Although it seems highly likely that Michael Portman, avowedly homosexual from a young age, had indeed "not yet gone with a woman" it is a stretch to imagine him as "uncorrupt" or "pure."

Both of these Lost Boys would come to unfortunate ends: Mikey Portman, as a member of the British aristocracy and the younger brother of Viscount Portman, had never wanted for money – but, more lethally, had never been asked or expected to *do* anything with his life. After realising his homosexuality at a young age, then becoming the first fully-fledged 'Burroughs groupie,' it was perhaps inevitable that he would succumb to a lifetime of alcoholism and drug-addiction. Later, he would also develop a fanatical Crowley fixation, and when I became friends with Brion's companion and collaborator Terry Wilson in 1980s London, he told me that when he visited Portman for the last time, he was scourging himself with a studded leather belt – crying out "Victory to Aleister Crowley!"[132] – his decorators not so much as batting an eyelid.

Mikey lived a short, pointless, fast, dissolute life, spiralling repeatedly between detox, short-lived recovery, and all-too-predictable relapse. He died of a heart attack on the 15th of November, 1983, just a month after his 40th birthday.

Ian Sommerville, on the other hand, was a young man of considerable intelligence and ability, who was more than a match for Burroughs – and probably also genuinely loved him. Things only really became estranged between them as a result of Burroughs' fascination with Scientology, which Ian just had no time for at all:

> When he fixes me with that Operating Thetan stare I just can't stand it . . . I can't get out of the room fast enough.[133]

Right from the start of their relationship, there had been a kind of slippery psychic symbiosis: the opening gambit on Burroughs' part had been to recruit Sommerville to help nurse him through detox, supervising a course of apomorphine as part of the cure for a codeine habit he had picked up. It is reported that Harold Norse called by to see how Burroughs was doing, and when the door was answered by Sommerville, tall, skinny and stripped to the waist, Norse addressed him as "Bill" – then immediately apologising that he had mistaken Ian for his friend. Sommerville replied: "Everybody does. I'm a replica." Although Sommerville turned out to be a strict but supportive nurse, efficiently doling out the precisely timed and calibrated regime of apomorphine shots, it was quite the baptism of fire for the young man, dealing with the agonies of his new friend's withdrawal, and clearly had a profound impact on him:

> "I can't tell you what it's been like, man, it's been fucking unbelievable . . . I never want to go through this again, man. Hallucinations, convulsions, freakouts, the edge of insanity. I had to hang on to *my* sanity by my fingernails, and they're bitten down to the moons. But it's worth it, man, Bill's getting better."[134]

Later, this "psychic fusion" had other consequences, turning the relationship into something of a see-sawing power-struggle. The poet and photographer Ira Cohen would report a particular incident that he was witness to, during a visit to Tangier: he was standing talking with Ian at the bottom of the hill in front of the Hotel Muniria, when all of a sudden Burroughs appeared at the top of the hill. Cohen did nothing to indicate Burroughs's presence to Sommerville, who had his back to the hill and could not have seen his lover's arrival anyway, when suddenly, still in mid-conversation, Ian began walking backwards up the hill to where Burroughs was standing, as if being pulled by a magnet, or reeled in . . .[135]

When Burroughs had considered returning to the States in the mid-1960s, Ian had felt abandoned, and not unsurprisingly had made what he probably thought was a fresh start with a young man nearer his own age, from his home-town of Darlington in the North of England, Alan Watson. Even though Burroughs *had* returned to London – and shortly thereafter he, Sommerville, and Watson, had lived together in a somewhat strained ménage at Duke Street – it had been the end as far as the potential for any future relationship between the two was concerned. Unsure how to try and reclaim what might well have been the love of his life, Burroughs felt powerless, and, to his eternal regret, let Sommerville slip away – and although they would remain friends and even occasional lovers, it was over. Due to his ability with mathematics, after some confusion and uncertainty, Ian was able to pursue a career-path that took him into the newly emerging world of computers:

> He was a very talented young man. I mean he understood things that I could just grasp, like probability theory and floating equations, physics. It all came naturally . . . Then he got into computer programming.[136]

He relocated to Bath, in the West of England, where for a while he would share a house with John Michell, author of *The View Over Atlantis* (a book about ley-lines, among other things, described by Professor Ronald Hutton as "almost the founding document of the modern earth mysteries movement."[137])

Burroughs relocated definitively to the USA in 1974, and two years later he received a telegram from Ian in respect of his 62nd birthday on the 5th of February, 1976, which read:

HAPPY BIRTHDAY, LOTS OF LOVE. LOTS OF PROMISE. NO REALISATION.

Later that day Burroughs received a second message, this time from Antony Balch: it seems that on his way back from sending the telegram, Ian – who had only recently passed his driving-test, and bought himself a car – had been hit by a drunk-driver, and killed instantly. He was not yet 36.

It was typical of the mind-set and world-view under which Burroughs and Gysin were operating that they considered both their young *amigos* to have been the victims of curses at one point or another:

Always weak-willed and self-indulgent, Mikey's heroin use all-too-predictably escalated, until he was juggling alcoholism, detox, and drugs at an alarming rate. Still a firm believer in the apomorphine treatment, Burroughs of course had wanted to take Mikey to register with Dr. Dent – but found himself opposed by Portman's godfather, Lord Goodman, who instead wanted the boy treated by a friend of his, Lady Isabella Frankau. At the time, Dr. Frankau was considered to be offering a discreet and enlightened treatment option from her exclusive Harley Street practice, but the simple truth is that she was a "writing doctor" – only too happy to give out Private prescriptions for heroin, methadone or morphine to her wealthy clients. Understandably, she was opposed to any alternative, such as Dr. Dent and his apomorphine treatment, as the last thing she wanted was for prospective patients to be cured – and for a while Burroughs was unwittingly drawn into a battle-of-wills with Frankau, it seemed over the very soul of poor hapless Mikey Portman.

For all that he was wilful and stubborn, Portman could also be curiously passive, suggestible, and easily lead. Indeed, it was a key part of what had attracted and interested Burroughs in the first place, Mikey's potential as a "medium" – but now his apparent lack of clearly-defined identity caused Burroughs to worry that the young man was at risk of possession. This came to a head on one occasion when Lady Frankau attempted what would nowadays be called an "intervention" where Portman was concerned, showing up announcing that she had arranged for him to be admitted to a sanitarium for "emergency treatment" – although Burroughs had little doubt it was just a ploy to get Mikey away from him and Dr. Dent, and enrol him on the equally addictive methadone program. One of Burroughs' newly-emerging superstitions at that time was that a cold sore could be a "point of entry" for hostile possessing forces, maybe even The Ugly Spirit: Mikey had just such a cold sore on his lip, and shortly after the confrontation with Frankau, Burroughs was convinced he saw something like a silvery light slip off of Mikey's shoulder and hit him in the chest:

> I not only felt it, I saw it, it was something slid off his shoulder
> like silver, silver light. You could see it very clearly.[138]

Whatever it was, it gave him a sudden sense of the "dying feeling", and causing him to pass out. When he came round, he knew that he had been hit by a curse that Lady Frankau had placed on Mikey . . .

With regard to Ian, Burroughs was even more convinced that he had been cursed, and that it had very definitely caused Ian's death. Sommerville had been a confirmed homosexual until quite recently, when, for the first time in his still-young life, he had slept with a woman. A Dutch girl, Susan Janssen, who had been visiting Ian in Bath, made a definite play to seduce him, and was successful: the only problem was that her regular boyfriend, Bill Levy – an American, living in Amsterdam, where he edited a counter-culture magazine called *The Fanatic* – developed a terrible grudge against Sommerville as a result. Levy would "dedicate" an issue of *The Fanatic* to Ian, featuring an article *Electric Ian: Portrait of a Humanoid – A Tawdry Brief Life*, in which he heaped scorn, ridicule, and personal insult against him, stating that he was an "electric-razor queen who shaves his genitals" with a deformed penis, and that he had been Burroughs' "kept lover" with a "fascination with rough trade."[139] To add insult to injury, Levy included quotes from the likes of Burroughs, the poet Heathcote Williams – and even Susan Janssen – taken out of context in such a way as to make it seem they were all belittling him. When Burroughs later found out that Ian had just heard about the magazine and its content on the same day he was involved in the accident that killed him, he was totally convinced that Levy had cursed him, and was responsible for his death.

Both Ian and Mikey would continue to appear in Burroughs' dreams – and thus his writings – for the rest of his life.

As for the rest of the available correspondence, all the usual obsessions and preoccupations are there: cut-ups loom large, as well as endless iteration of their possible applications; drugs, of course – although sometimes more *against* than *for*, as numerous letters promoting the apomorphine treatment for addiction attest; film – both the experiments with Balch and various projected adaptations of *Naked Lunch* involving Mick Jagger, Dennis Hopper, and, uh, a former CIA hitman (!), that all-too-predictably amount to nothing; and the strange dance with Scientology, deserving a book all of its own . . .

Also included are diplomatic appeals to his long-suffering mother, too-little-too-late attempts to reach out to his "cursed from birth" son, Billy Jnr. – who, despite showing some promise as a writer, would eventually succumb to his own alcohol and drug excesses, necessitating a liver transplant, which only really managed to give him a brief extension on his frustrated and unhappy life before he died of complications at the age of 33 – and endless struggles with publishers (mostly over money, it has to be said).

It is ironic that as his concerns become ever more internalised – and at times quite literally occult – and the work he is producing is amongst his most 'difficult,' that the model of 'William Burroughs' as icon of counter-culture cool is born. His engagement with experimental methods, non-literary forms, and the Underground Press seems strangely at odds with his recurring hope that the next project will be a commercial breakthrough: it is nothing short of hilarious when he reports, regarding *The Wild Boys*, that:

> Antony *[Balch] swears* it will be a best seller . . .[140]

There is plenty among the second volume of the *Collected Letters* to support the engagement of Burroughs and Gysin with what they called "the Magical Universe". Tim Cummins, in his review for English newspaper *The Independent*, characterises how "the two worked at the centre of a web of occult and artistic actions"[140] – and the order of emphasis he gives is indeed appropriate.

Within the wide body of occult theory that forms the framework for practice within the Western magical tradition, one concept that has come to be of almost central significance is that of the Knowledge and Conversation of the Holy Guardian Angel. This is a Rite – or even series of Rites – aimed at connecting the practitioner with what may be considered as anything from a "Higher Self" to, quite literally, the intermediary or even embodiment of whatever deity he or she chooses to engage with. No lesser an authority than "the Wickedest Man In The World" and self-professed "Great Beast 666" Aleister Crowley wrote to one of his disciples:

> It should never be forgotten for a single moment that the central and essential work of the Magician is the attainment of the Knowledge and Conversation of the Holy Guardian Angel.
>
> Whether it be thought of as the Genius of the Hermetic Order of the Golden Dawn, the Augoeides of Iamblichus, the Atman of Hinduism, the Daemon of the ancient Greeks – or indeed, either a literal messenger from the Divine or the idealised embodiment of all that is highest and best in one's True Self – the seeking of Contact with this entity is considered by many to

be the central most important Work in Magic, which should not only come above and before any other, but of which success (or failure!) is a key determinant as to any further progress.[142]

It occurs to me that there is a point in the progress of William S. Burroughs into his own particular "Magical Universe" – whether aided and abetted by cut-up revelations, drug-visions, the E-meter of Scientology, friends and mentors like Brion Gysin and Jacques Stern, or just guided by his own dreams, hallucinations, and imaginings – that he knowingly and willingly embraced, in the words of Rimbaud, a "complete and systematic derangement of all of the senses"[143] with much the same goal. Like the famous "paranoiac-critical method" of the Surrealist painter, Salvador Dali – which he described as a "spontaneous method of irrational knowledge based on the critical and systematic objectivity of the associations and interpretations of delirious phenomena"[144] – Burroughs also sought to exploit the ability of the brain to perceive *apparent* connections or resemblances between things which, rationally speaking, are *not* linked – which is in itself a kind of *magical thinking*.

Interlude:
William S. Burroughs,
Scientologist

> L. Ron Hubbard, the founder of Scientology, says that the secret of life has at last been discovered – by *him*. The secret of life is *to survive* . . . To survive what, exactly? Enemy attack, what else?

> We have now come full circle . . . back to the magical universe, where nothing happens unless some force, being, or power wills it to happen. He was killed by a snake? Who murdered him? He dies of a fever? Who put the fever curse on him?[145]

It is perhaps as well at this point to say a few words on William Burroughs' engagement with Scientology. When Scientology was first created by former pulp sci-fi writer and self-styled explorer and adventurer, L. Ron Hubbard, for a while – at least in certain more radical, forward-thinking circles – it was considered to be a potential breakthrough into a kind of self-empowering, liberating, accelerated analysis, and was not initially perceived of as the "mind control cult" that it is seen as now as a consequence of endless tabloid speculation about troubled Hollywood celebrities. It is, perhaps, this present image of the movement that has caused a number of Burroughs commentators to overlook its significance to his life & work from the late 1950s and, on-and-off, throughout the whole of the 1960s – the most common objection being, in effect, something along the lines of *"how could somebody of Burroughs' obvious intelligence and originality of thought fall for such a thing?"* – with many concluding that *if* Burroughs paid any attention to Scientology *at all*, it was simply to gain material for his later satirical routines. Indeed, as Brion Gysin once remarked in concerning his old friend's literary use of material drawn from his involvement with Scientology:

> "He must be one of the few people who has made more money from them than they made from him."[146]

The simple truth, however, is that Burroughs was ripe for something like Scientology. Taking into account his curious openness to contested knowledge and "fringe science" – a susceptibility doubtless influenced by his childhood introduction to the magical universe of strange and malevolent forces – and building on his belief in the significance of Korzybski's General Semantics, yet total dissatisfaction with conventional Psychoanalysis, but most importantly of all, his continuing hunger to ease the pain of the psychic trauma and wounds that he carried with him over his drug addiction, failed relationships, homosexuality (over which his feelings remained conflicted and unresolved well into middle age), possible childhood abuse, and shooting of Joan Vollmer, despite initial appearances to the contrary, William Seward Burroughs was, in fact, an ideal candidate for what Hubbard's "modern science of mental health" initially claimed to offer.

I will not attempt to offer a full-length, in-depth account or examination of Burroughs' history with Scientology here, partly because it falls somewhat outside the immediate remit of this book – but also because such an excellent job has only recently been done by my friend and colleague, David S. Wills, in his superb study *Scientologist! William S. Burroughs and the "Weird Cult."* Wills has written a marvellous, thoroughly researched, and well-written book that should be of interest to fan and scholar alike. Highly readable, it takes us through Burroughs' involvement with Scientology all the way from first vicarious encounter via the myth-making Brion Gysin, then sudden enthusiasm for the efficacy of auditing and the E-meter, to his increasingly see-sawing relationship with the Church of Scientology – from zealous convert to "squirrel" (one who uses the methods and techniques for their own ends, without approval or supervision), then outspoken critic, and sometimes back again – and, finally, self-appointed personal nemesis for the movement's initially charismatic but increasingly despotic founder, L. Ron Hubbard.

Drawing on both published and unpublished sources – including material from the Berg Collection of papers from the Burroughs Estate, and previously unseen essays by Burroughs written during his time as an active Scientologist – David S. Wills corrects many of the errors and misapprehensions of previous authors, in particular with regard to the origins of Burroughs' interest, length of involvement, degree of commitment, and amount of inspiration he derived and influence that Scientology and the ideas of L. Ron Hubbard had over his work at one of the most prolific periods of his life.

As well as a careful reading of the articles, essays, and novels for their use of images and references pertaining to Hubbard and Scientology, Wills provides a lively and informative account of Burroughs' life and work both before and after his involvement with the Church – accessible enough for the newcomer, and with enough new information to keep even an old hand like myself happy. For example, the fact that Wills discovered press-clippings Burroughs had taken from a newspaper exposé linking Hubbard to infamous "black magician" Aleister Crowley – which included a photo of his potential successor, rocket-scientist Jack Parsons, on which Burroughs had written "a dream come true"[147] – is priceless!

Intersection
Reading & Time

This foreword . . . is an essay in 'intersection reading' right
where you are sitting standing walking now.[148]

One extension of the cut-ups, and other applications such as the fold-in,
was what Burroughs began to call "intersection reading" or "intersection
writing" – somewhat cryptically explained in the three-column *Foreword* he
wrote for *Rules Of Duel*, an experiment in just such techniques by his friend
Graham Masterton:

When you read look listen think precise intersection points right
where you are reading now <u>look round</u> . . . Now

The Moving Times was a preliminary experiment in what I called intersection
reading right where you are sitting standing walking now.[149] *The Moving Times*,
written by Burroughs as a regular insert for a small circulation mimeographed
magazine, *My Own Mag*, edited by Jeff Nuttall in London, was inspired by
his experiments with cut-ups from various different newspaper sources, which
were often collaged into his scrapbooks. As such, it was designed in a three-
column format to look as much like an actual newspaper as possible,
sometimes with added headlines and photos torn from real papers:

Start with newspapers like this: Take today's paper. Fill up three
columns with selections. Now read *cross* columns. Fill a column
on another page with cross column readings. Now fill in the
remaining columns with selections from yesterday's papers and
so on back. Each time you do this there will be less of present
time on the page. The page is 'forgetting' present time as you
move back in time through word columns. Now to move
forward in time. Try writing tomorrow's news today . . .[150]

Graham Masterton, who had been a trainee newspaper reporter when he first wrote to Burroughs in Tangier in 1964, is eminently qualified to explain "intersection writing" as the initial exchange of letters between the two had revealed just such an intersection:

> . . . when I first wrote to him, from a neighbourhood where I lived called Gossops Green, he wrote back to say that he had been reading *The Power and the Glory* by Graham Greene. *Graham* Masterton, Gossops *Green, Graham Greene*. Get it? Because of that, he felt that a writer could follow the clues given to him by his own words, shuffle them and rearrange them and look for any messages that evoked more intense and descriptive feelings – feelings outside the normal reading of a text.[151]

Masterton had already been working on "a scattering of chaotic notes and poems"[152] under the intended title *Rules Of Duel*. After much discussion and encouragement from Burroughs, it began to take new shape as an example of intersection writing, which he explained:

> . . . depended on the writer to look for ways in which to interchange words and phrases to bring out new meanings. You would look for coincidences in names and places. You would look for a way to take half of one sentence and attach it to another, to give a totally different or a more descriptive view of the same event. It was shaking up words like the particles in a kaleidoscope, and creating constantly new patterns.[153]

By the time Burroughs had relocated to London, Masterton was deputy editor for the newly-launched "Men's magazine" *Mayfair*, as a result of which he was able to commission a whole series of articles from his friend in which Burroughs holds forth about all manner of his "fringe science" and "underground" interests: from the apomorphine treatment to E-meters and engrams, hieroglyphic silence to Korzybski's General Semantics, the use of Deadly Orgone Radiation and infrasound as possible weapons, a positive review of *The Mind Parasites* by Colin Wilson, and a veritable one-man campaign against L. Ron Hubbard's Scientology – in short, all the preoccupations of the "radical" late 1960s-to-early-1970s that surface in *The*

Job, Exterminator!, and, to a lesser extent, *The Wild Boys* and later *Ah Pook Is Here* – all will get their first airing in the series of articles titled *The Burroughs Academy*.

An even more radical experiment that was undertaken by Burroughs where the subject of "time" is concerned was his attempt to free himself from the Control Machine, inspired by his comparison of the modern media of *Time*, *Life*, etc., with the interlocking Sacred Calendars of the Maya:

> The Ancient Mayans possessed one of the most precise and hermetic control calendars ever used on this planet, a calendar that in effect controlled what the populace did thought and felt on any given day . . .[154]

This is not perhaps that surprising, when you consider both the desire for absolute freedom evinced in Burroughs' work – and also the prevailing wish to escape from Past Conditioning, or make up for "mistakes too monstrous for remorse / To tamper or to dally with."[155] The same impulse that drove him to explore the promise of Scientology, that the method of "auditing" and use of the "E-meter" could erase "engrams" – in other words, free you from the pain of unhappy memories, all the negative associations of unwanted feelings – also inspired him to create storylines in which his libertarian freedom fighters would travel in time in an attempt to alter history in such a way that would, hopefully, allow for more favourable outcomes.

One of the few critics who seemed to really understand this aspect of what Burroughs was attempting was Angela Carter, who would later write about how this "derailment" of regular chronology had the effect of "shattering the sense of cause and effect" on the part of the reader:

> The method is eclectic and discrete and it is important, and essential, because Burroughs is doing something peculiar with the reader's time. He's stopping it. Or, rather, stop-starting it. Taking it out of the reader's hands, anyway, which is where we tend to assume it ought to be . . . Burroughs' project is to make

time stand still for a while, one which is more frequently that of religion than of literature . . .[156]

The significance of Time was revealed in a revolutionary agenda Burroughs proposed in *The Revised Boy Scout Manual*, an unpublished work written at the height of the counter-cultural upheaval of the radical 1960s, released in a small edition as two spoken-word tapes:

> To consolidate revolutionary gains, five steps are necessary:
>
> 1. Proclaim a new era and set up a new calendar.
>
> 2. Replace alien language.
>
> 3. Destroy or neutralise alien gods.
>
> 4. Destroy alien machinery of government and Control.
>
> 5. Take wealth and land from individual aliens. Time to forget a dead empire and build a living republic.[157]

Perhaps mindful of his readings in Dunne's *An Experiment With Time* about non-linear, even parallel, time-streams – and doubtless influenced by the disruption of conventional chronology apparently revealed by the various cut-up experiments – he wrote:

> The Colonel decides to make his own time. He opens a school notebook and constructs a simple calendar consisting of ten months with 26 days in each month to begin on this day February 21, 1970, Raton Pass 14 in the new calendar. The months have names like old Pullman cars in America where the Colonel had lived until his 18th year . . .[158]

This is not, in fact, the Dream Calendar that Burroughs employed himself. Over the years I have tried to clarify the actual Dream Calendar Burroughs devised and used, and have attempted to piece together the often confusing – at times even conflicting! – data emerging from different sources, both published and unpublished. Matters are complicated by Barry Miles telling us that "the system began with only eight separate months, and they came around in a little different order the second time, with a new month, Wiener Wald, added."

Miles gives:

1.   Terre Haute

2.   *Marie Celeste*

3.   Bellevue

4.   Seal Point

5.   Harbor Beach

6.   Niño Perdido

7.   Sweet Meadows

8.   Land's End

. . . and Wiener Wald was added after Seal Point from the second time round onwards.[159]

Some clarification came with the publication of the collection *Rub Out The Words*, in which we were given perhaps the clearest outline of the scheme, in a letter dated Wednesday January 21, 1970 ("Bellevue 6") to his erstwhile friend and collaborator Brion Gysin:

Dear Brion,

THE DREAM CALENDAR

1.   Terre Haute

2.   *Marie Celeste*

3.   Bellevue

4.   Seal Point

5.   Wiener Wald

6.   Harbor Beach

7.   Cold Spring

8.   Great Easter

9.   Sweet Meadows

10.   *Land's End* [160]

So we see that by the time Burroughs writes to Gysin, the Dream Calendar has evolved to become the 10-month system above, with Niño Perdido replaced by Cold Spring, and another new month added, Great Easter. A system of 10 months of 23 days each, repeating from a start-point known as The Creation, which was Tuesday, December 23, 1969 – which in the new Dream calendar became Tuesday, Terre Haute 23, 1969.

Burroughs explains further:

> The above idea came to me one night December 22, 1969, which would be Terre Haute 22 . . .

> The starting date used is December 23, 1969 which is Terre Haute 23 in this calendar. Calculations from this date can be made into the past or the future. We could for example calculate on what date Terre Haute 23 fell on 77,000,000,000 years ago . . . . nodding listlessly in doorways on a mild gray day they died of an overdose of time. [161]

Clearly the main inspiration and point-of-reference for this has to be the elaborate system used by the Mayans: the interlocking 365-day Solar Calendar called the *Haab*, and the 260-day sacred calendar called the *Tzolkin* – as well as further Lunar cycles, a 584-day Venus cycle, and something known as

The Long Count, that dated events in mythological time from the Creation. Burroughs had studied the Ancient Maya at Harvard in the 1930s, sowing the seeds of a lifelong fascination; he also discussed them with his common-law wife, Joan Vollmer, and, interestingly, it was she who first suggested to him that the Mayan priests might have been using some kind of mind-control. Later, when he lived and travelled extensively in Mexico, Central and South America in the 1950s, he began to construct a theory of the various interlocking calendars used by the Maya as an elaborate Control Machine:

> . . . the priests could calculate into the future or the past exactly what the populace would be doing hearing seeing on a given date . . . they could determine what conditioning would be or had been applied on any given date . . .[162]

At the time of the French Revolution, a radical experiment in the application and measurement of time was attempted. Starting at the end of 1793 the New Calendar of the French Republic was introduced – and although with its 10-day-weeks (each made up of 10 hours, in turn comprising 100 minutes), it could be thought of as part of the wider movement towards the total decimalisation of France, its greater purpose was to ruthlessly expunge any-and-all religious or royalists influences from the day-to-day life of the people. For nearly twelve years it ran its course, until it was finally abolished by Napoleon, with effect from 1st January 1806.

In the same spirit that weapons of oppression are often appropriated to become tools of liberation, Burroughs clearly felt that the construction of a calendar of one's own would be a valuable deprogramming tool. Firstly, you would be freeing yourself from the codified and predictable system of the Control Machine – its main Operating Program, in effect. Secondly, you would be replacing it with one of your own devising, with associations and symbolism – whether individually meaningful, or totally arbitrary – that would replace the apparatus of conditioned response: the Reactive Mind, and its contents and associations, which had previously been programmed by the Control Machine calendar.

In George Orwell's dystopian classic *1984*, the powers-that-be attempt to introduce "NewSpeak" in the belief that unwanted concepts the authorities oppose will be eradicated if the people simply no longer have the words to be able to think about them with: subversive thoughts will become literally *unthinkable*. The founder of General Semantics and author of *Science and Sanity*, Count Alfred Korzybski, whose lectures Burroughs attended in the 1930s and was profoundly influenced by, had once declared that "Man is a being naturally endowed with time-binding capacity"[163] – in which case, those who dictate the terms by which time is measured impose their will on the very medium of history, and set the beat to which we must all march. In much the same way as the French Republic introduced a New Calendar as a way of breaking from the Old Order, through protagonists such as Colonel Sutton Smith – and indeed his own efforts – Burroughs was in effect declaring a New Order of Time, distinct from that of the Dominator-Culture, and in doing so was drawing a line of separation from all that it stood for . . .

. . . perhaps drawing a line in the very sands of time.

Out Of Time
And Into Space

> I'm primarily concerned with survival, with the question of
> Nova conspiracies, new mythologies possible in the Space Age,
> heroes and villains with regard intentions toward this planet . .
> .[164]

Increasingly, as the 1960s gave way to the 1970s, new preoccupations were
emerging in the thinking and writing of William Burroughs: it seems it was
no longer enough to just "create a new mythology for the space age," as he
had proclaimed to Eric Mottram in 1964 – rather, it was becoming ever
more readily apparent that, for Burroughs, the Spiritual Destiny of Man was
in Space:

> We postulate that man is an artifact designed for space travel.
> He is not designed to remain in his present biologic state any
> more than a tadpole is designed to remain a tadpole.[165]

Although the idea and the way it was talked about changed and evolved over
time – no doubt taking its initial inspiration from his youthful engagement
with science fiction, and gaining momentum parallel to the accelerating Space
Race during the 1960s – right from the beginning, it was pretty clear that, as
far as Burroughs was concerned, this was not a conventional scenario
concerned solely with advances in technology:

> To travel in space you must leave the old verbal garbage behind:
> God talk, country talk, mother talk, love talk, party talk. You
> must learn to exist with no religion no country no allies. You
> must learn to live alone in silence. Anyone who prays in space is
> not there.

> The last frontier is being closed to youth. However there are
> many roads to space. To achieve complete freedom from past

conditioning is to be in space.[166]

The separation of the physical body from a soul or spirit – or, latterly, consciousness – has often been described as the fundamental "split" at the heart of Western thought, the Cartesian duality of mind and matter. In many ways, this is simply a hangover or restatement of the division insisted upon by Christian thinkers, the divide into spiritual and physical – with the obvious emphasis being that the exalted *spiritual* was preferable and superior to the lowly *physical*, mired as it was in a world of sin, with a similar preference of the *mental* surviving into modern, more secular times. Count Korzybski, whose *Science and Sanity* and classes in General Semantics had been such an influence on the young Burroughs, had categorised this as the "Aristotelian straightjacket" – with its absolute insistence on either/or, and no room for both/and, or other alternatives.

> The hope lies in the development of non-body experience and eventually getting away from the body itself, away from three-dimensional coordinates and the concomitant animal reactions of fear and flight, which lead inevitably to tribal feuds and dissension.[167]

It is timely at this point to reflect on the fact that when Burroughs was asked by an interviewer in 1984 about his "religious position," he replied without hesitation:

> An Ishmalian and Gnostic, or a Manichean . . . The Manichean believe in an actual struggle between good and evil, which is not an eternal struggle since one of them will win in this particular area, sooner or later. Of course, with the Christians there was this tremendous inversion of values where the most awful people are thrown up as this paragon of virtue for everyone to emulate . . .[168]

Gnosticism is a fairly broad term, covering the various competing forms of early Christianity – many more informed by and open to pagan thought, oriental beliefs, and magic, than the "official" version – condemned as heresy by the orthodox Church of Rome, which won out ultimately by its ruthless and systematic eradication of the competition. Manicheanism, on the other hand, is a more specific belief system, which although sharing much with other broadly Gnostic systems of thought, is clear in its belief that the universe is the battlefield of equally balanced and opposing forces of darkness and light, good and evil, in which the outcome is by no means certain.

> All of my work is directed against those who are bent, through stupidity or design, on blowing up the planet or rendering it uninhabitable.[169]

Like most Gnostics, followers of Manicheanism also believed that the true creator God is remote, and largely unknowable and unattainable. The world of matter is a Fallen one, in which Spirit has the misfortune to be trapped, as if in a prison ruled over by a blind, mad god, the demiurge – and various sub-beings who claim a counterfeit divinity, referred to as Archons, or "rulers" – all of whom are likewise delusional, and seek to fool Man that they are in fact the true creator(s.) Burroughs presents the composite figure of Mr Bradley-Mr Martin, an avatar of duality who appears throughout the cut-up "Nova Trilogy" and related works of the 1960s, as just such a figure:

> Mr Bradley-Mr Martin, in my mythology, is a God that failed, a
> God of conflict in two parts, so created to keep a tired old
> show on the road, The God of Arbitrary Power and Restraint,
> Of Prison and Pressure, who needs subordinates, who needs
> what he calls his "human dogs" while treating them with the
> contempt a con man feels for his victims . . .[170]

For the Gnostic, the one hope is not in a passive salvation or by trusting in received wisdom, but through direct personal experience or knowledge, hence "gnosis." It is only the remembering of your true nature as a spiritual being that might enable you to escape this prison of flesh, sin, and suffering, and ultimately transcend the limitations of a physical body in a fallen world of illusion, and return to the real freedom of pure spirit. In this light, Scientology can be thought of as a kind of "Sci-Fi Gnosticism" – which may also have been part of its appeal to Burroughs. Scientology, like Gnosticism, also emphasised direct personal experience of the phenomena being explored, which doubtless would have appealed to the man from the "show me" state of Missouri. There was a great deal of emphasis on Man's essential nature as an immortal, indestructible being of pure spiritual energy, and the practice of various techniques for achieving exteriorisation of consciousness, independent of the physical body. Although he was not a writer to address his spiritual longings in terms of conventional religion by any means, over time Burroughs began to show a marked concern with "astral projection" and "out of the body experience" – both in his fiction and non-fiction work, as witnessed by literary scholar Gregory Stephenson:

> . . . Burroughs' writing, in the manner of the ritual practices and mythological systems of the Gnostics, serve to effect self-knowledge, internal transformation, and transcendence. In this sense his work occupies a position in that zone of contemporary culture that is still being defined, where anthropology, philosophy, religion, psychology, and literature overlap and merge into a single discipline: human liberation.[171]

With the first volume of his last major trilogy, *Cities of the Red Night* in 1981, Burroughs re-introduced a major preoccupation with just such "liberation." An early chapter has an agent of *Academy 23*, Yen Lee, employ such methods for a potentially hazardous reconnaissance:

> Yen Lee sat down and looked once again at the town through his field glasses. There were still no villagers in sight. He put his glasses down and conducted an out-of-body exploration of the village-what westerners call "astral travel." He was moving up the street now, his gun at the ready. The gun would shoot blasts of energy, and he could feel it tingle in his hands . . .[172]

As well as more serious considerations of consciousness exchange and soul-transference, the theme of astral projection is played somewhat for laughs in a scenario featuring gay incestuous male twins, which draws on Monroe's *Journeys Out of the Body*:

> They had to be careful about sex in the navy, so Jimmy and
> Jerry got a book on astral projection and decided to learn to do
> it in the "second state," as the book called it, and they finally
> succeeded though they never knew exactly when it would
> happen or who was going to visit whom until it happened and
> this was sometimes under embarrassing circumstances, like in
> the shower room or during a physical examination. One twin
> lets out an eerie high-pitched wolf howl and turns bright red all
> over as the hairs on his head and body stand up and crackle.
> Then, as if struck by lightning, he falls to the floor in an erotic
> seizure ejaculating repeatedly in front of the appalled and
> salacious tars . . .[173]

Not long after, Burroughs gives more serious consideration to the theme when discussing Man's possible evolutionary next step:

> The human body is much too dense for space conditions.
> However, we have a model to hand that is much less dense in
> fact almost weightless: the astral or dream body. This lighter
> body, a 'body of light,' as Crowley called it, is much more suited
> to space conditions.[174]

His friend, Brion Gysin, had once declared rather grandly:

> "Of course the sands of Present Time are running out from
> under our feet. And why not? The Great Conundrum: 'What
> are we here for?' is all that ever held us here in the first place.
> Fear. The answer to the Riddle of the Ages has actually been
> out in the street since the First Step in Space. Who runs may
> read but few people run fast enough. What are we here for?
> Does the great metaphysical nut revolve around that? Well, I'll
> crack it for you, right now. What are we here for? We are here to
> go!"[175]

But that may not have been enough for Burroughs: to go *where*, exactly? And to what end? He concluded:

I consider that immortality is the only goal worth striving for:
immortality in Space. Time is that which ends, and Man is in
Time. The Old Man of the Mountain discovered that
immortality is possible in Space, and this is the Western Lands
of the Egyptian Book of the Dead . . .[176]

In the goal of non-body freedom from past conditioning in space, he may
have thought that he had found both a solution and an escape.

The Invisible Generation

> All tape recorder tricks are useful: speed up, slow down, overlay running contradictory commands simultaneously, echo chambers for stations and airports. Effects are obtained by persistence and exposure – by getting as many operators in the street as possible. For wide coverage use a car cutting-in your suggestions with popular tunes and street sounds . . .[177]

Gradually, then, as the Sixties progressed, it was clear that the cut-ups were an idea whose time had come. Perhaps it was just the next inevitable progression in what was to become the dominant form in 20th Century Art, starting with collage and montage: the Cubists had attempted to show different viewpoints on the canvas simultaneously – with its parallels in literature, first with stream-of-consciousness allowing Joyce to put the inside of people's heads on the page; then Eliot and his appropriation providing the textual equivalent of Duchamp's found object or readymade, and beginning to question the very notion of originality. Or perhaps it was that modern life was increasingly fragmented, disconnected, and accelerated, and increasingly art and forms of expression were required that could reflect this. Helped by Burroughs and Gysin's gradually emerging status as counter-culture gurus, their ideas and influence began to spread. It didn't hurt that Burroughs' image had appeared on the cover of *Sgt. Pepper* by The Beatles, or that rock bands started naming themselves from his work: first there would be The Insect Trust, The Mugwumps, Soft Machine, and Steely Dan, and later Clem Snide, Dead Fingers Talk, Nova Mob – even *Naked Lunch* . . .

It has also been claimed that the rock music term "Heavy Metal" – first appearing as "Heavy metal thunder" in Steppenwolf's anthemic *Born To Be Wild* – originates with Burroughs: *The Soft Machine* (1962) includes the character "Uranian Willy, the Heavy Metal Kid" – and, subsequently, *Nova*

Express (1964) develops the use of Heavy Metal as a sci-fi metaphor for addictive drugs:

> With their diseases and orgasm drugs and their sexless parasite
> life forms – Heavy Metal People of Uranus wrapped in cool
> blue mist of vaporized bank notes – And The Insect People of
> Minraud with metal music.[178]

By the 1970s William Burroughs was the epitome of hip as far as drug savvy musos with literary pretensions were concerned: a coked-out David Bowie explained how he used "the Burroughs cut-up method" in Alan Yentob's 1974 BBC profile *Cracked Actor*, and then demonstrated (*badly*); his friend Brian Eno would name a track *Dead Finks Don't Talk* as a nod to Burroughs' novel *Dead Fingers Talk*, but would also look for ways to introduce chance with his *Obliques Strategies*, a set of cryptic aphorisms intended to encourage creative solutions by lateral thinking, such as:

> Honour thy error as a hidden intention.[179]

There would also be a number of meetings in the pages of the music press, not so much "interviews" as Burroughs being paired with some musical artist or other by well-meaning rock journalists, who would then document the encounter and (hopefully) any interesting conversation. The first, and probably best known, was in February 1974 with David Bowie – then at the height of his "Ziggy Stardust" fame – but by all accounts the meeting was ill-prepared, with Burroughs having heard only two of Bowie's songs and Bowie only really glancing at *Nova Express*. Although Burroughs would later reply to Genesis P-Orridge's query, "Why did you do that ridiculous interview with David Bowie?" with the quip "Advertising!"[180] after being prompted by the sight of the life-size cut-out of Mick Jagger from the film *Performance* at Duke Street, in fact Bowie and Burroughs seem to have genuinely hit it off. About halfway through the interview, after an exchange about dreams as a source of inspiration, Burroughs suddenly answers Bowie's query "What are your projects at the moment?" with what reads almost like a definitive statement of intent:

> At the moment I'm trying to set up an institute of advanced studies somewhere in Scotland. Its aim will be to extend awareness and alter consciousness in the direction of greater range, flexibility and effectiveness at a time when traditional disciplines have failed to come up with viable solutions. You see, the advent of the Space Age and the possibility of exploring galaxies and contacting alien life forms poses an urgent necessity for radically new solutions. We will be considering only non-chemical methods, with the emphasis placed on combination, synthesis, interaction and rotation of methods now being used in the East and West, together with methods that are not at present being used to extend awareness or increase human potentials.

> We know exactly what we intend to do and how to go about doing it . . . Basically, the experiments we propose are inexpensive and easy to carry out. Things such as yoga-style meditation and exercises, communication, sound, light and film experiments, experiments with sensory deprivation chambers, pyramids, psychotronic generators and Reich's orgone accumulators, experiments with infrasound, experiments with dream and sleep.

> Expansion of awareness, eventually leading to mutations . . .[181]

Clearly a connection was made: Bowie would visit Burroughs again in the late Seventies, when he was living in the Bunker, taking a four-foot-high vase of flowers in tribute. He had been working on a painting of Burroughs, with a burning red sky as background. Bowie could not have known that Burroughs was working on *Cities of the Red Night*, a pleasing coincidence to both of them. Victor Bockris observed:

> When David Bowie came by for a drink . . . he was the model of gentlemanly courtesy and his entire demeanour conveyed respect . . .

When we left to take a cab uptown . . . Bowie graciously took Burroughs by the arm and carefully escorted him across the wide streets.[182]

In June 1975, Burroughs would meet with Led Zeppelin guitarist Jimmy Page for a feature in *Crawdaddy* magazine – an article for which Burroughs penned what is surely one of his definitive statements where belief in The Magical Universe is concerned:

> Since the word 'magic' tends to cause confused thinking, I would like to say exactly what I mean by 'magic' and the magical interpretation of so-called reality. The underlying assumption of magic is the assertion of 'will' as the primary moving force in this universe–the deep conviction that nothing happens unless somebody or some being wills it to happen. To me this has always seemed self-evident. A chair does not move unless someone moves it. Neither does your physical body, which is composed of much the same materials, move unless you will it to move. Walking across the room is a magical operation. From the viewpoint of magic, no death, no illness, no misfortune, accident, war or riot is accidental. There are no accidents in the world of magic. And will is another word for animate energy.[183]

Not so dissimilar to Aleister Crowley's abiding definition that:

> Magick is the Science and Art of causing Change to occur in conformity with Will.[184]

According to the *Rolling Stone* journalist and later Led Zeppelin chronicler, Stephen Davis, who orchestrated the meeting between Burroughs and Page, Crowley inevitably cropped up in the conversation between the two, which ranged far and wide:

> Over margaritas at the nearby Mexican Gardens restaurant, Burroughs asked about Page's house on the shores of Loch Ness in Scotland, which had once belonged to Aleister Crowley. Was it really haunted? Page said he was sure it was. Does the Loch Ness monster exist? Page said he thought it did. Skeptical,

Burroughs wondered how the monster could get enough to eat.
The conversation continued over enchiladas. Burroughs talked
about infrasound, pitched below the level of human hearing,
which had supposedly been developed as a weapon by the
French military. Then on to interspecies communication, talking
to dolphins via sonar waves. Burroughs said he thought a
remarkable synthesis could be achieved if rock music returned
to its ancient roots in ceremony and folklore, and brought in
some of the trance music one heard in Morocco. Jimmy Page
was receptive. "Well, music which involves [repeating] riffs,
anyway, will have a trancelike effect, and it's really like a mantra.
And, you know, we've been attacked for that."[185]

As the clarion call of Punk was heard in New York, Patti Smith was the first
to cheer the return of the Beat Godfather to his native land in 1974 – Victor
Bockris describes how she announced ("as if it were a move of military
significance") from the stage at a reading for the St. Mark's Poetry Project:

Mr. Burroughs is back in town. Isn't that great![186]

Patti had long been vocal about her enthusiasm for the Beats, especially
Burroughs and Allen Ginsberg, adding them to the roll-call of heroes and
inspirations she would celebrate through her rock 'n' roll poetry of "three
chords merged with the power of the word." She would later describe the
importance and influence of the artists and poets she would meet in New
York, from her early days living at the Chelsea Hotel, where she would meet
New York's answer to Jean Genet, storyteller Herbert Huncke ("the first
Beat"), and archivist, film-maker, and vagabond occultist Harry Smith, to
performing alongside Gregory Corso, John Giorno, and Peter Orlovsky at
St. Mark's Poetry Project and the like:

I was very privileged to know these people and I had different
relationships with them all . . . But William was the one I was
most attached to. I just adored him. I had sort of a crush on
him when I was younger and he was very good to me. He really
liked my singing and encouraged me to sing. He used to come

to CBGBs to see us and, of course, his work inspired me. *Horses*, the opening of *Horses*, with Johnny's confrontation in the locker room, was very inspired by William's *The Wild Boys*. In *The Wild Boys* there is also a 'Johnny.' My 'Johnny' is a continuation of William's 'Johnny.' William really taught me a lot about how to conduct myself as a human being, you know? Not to compromise and to do things my way. What William always said was, "The most precious thing you ever have is your name, so don't taint it. Build your name and everything else will come. Keep your name clean." I learned a lot from William.[187]

Burroughs would later return the compliment by penning the following for a volume of her *Collected Works*:

Patti Smith is not only a great performer, she is a shaman – that is, someone in touch with other levels of reality. Her effect on the audience is electric, comparable to voodoo or umbanda rituals, where the audience members become participants and are literally lifted out of themselves.[188]

Burroughs would get to know a number of the other key figures in the New York Punk and New Wave scene during his time at the Bunker – the account given by Victor Bockris in *With William Burroughs* includes visits for drinks and dinner from the likes of Lou Reed, Richard Hell, and Jean Michel Basquiat, as well as Debbie Harry and Chris Stein of Blondie, near neighbours on the Bowery with whom Burroughs bonded over discussions of assassinations and weaponry, and psychic phenomena such as hauntings and poltergeists – but it seems to have been Patti Smith that he was always genuinely closest to. In her memoir, *Just Kids*, Smith recalls meeting Burroughs in the lobby of the Chelsea Hotel – "He comes stumbling out of the El Quixote a bit drunk and dishevelled. I straighten his tie and hail him a cab. It's our unspoken routine." – and later gives an affectionate snapshot of how she remembers him from those days:

William Burroughs was simultaneously old and young. Part sheriff, part gumshoe. All writer. He had a medicine chest he kept locked, but if you were in pain he would open it. He did not like to see his loved ones suffer. If you were infirm he would feed you. He'd appear at your door with a fish wrapped in newsprint and fry it up. He was inaccessible to a girl but I loved him anyway.[189]

Despite Patti's great affection for that other Chelsea Hotel resident, Harry Smith, it is curious that, despite an initial period of interest in his work, Burroughs could never take to him. He may have been impressed by Harry Smith's pioneering work archiving American Folk Songs, his early experimental collage films, such as *Heaven and Earth Magic* – even his not inconsiderable knowledge of matters esoteric and ethnic, with his collections of Native American Indian and Eskimo relics – but Burroughs was appalled that Smith was such a "shameless moocher" and ultimately concluded:

Harry Smith another wrong number. He fancies himself a black magician and does manage to give out some nasty emanations. Was it William the Second who said in regard to black magic, "Whether their spells are effective or not they deserve hanging for their bad intentions"??[190]

As a footnote to this, there are amusing anecdotes about the apparent enmity and rivalry between Smith and Burroughs fellow "cosmonaut of inner space" and former Beat Hotel associate, Jacques Stern: at one point, the pair of them were both resident at the Chelsea, their natural tendencies toward irascibility and paranoia exacerbated by their chemical intakes and occult preoccupations, both clearly feeling that New York's premier bohemian refuge was not big enough for two magi such as themselves. When Stern, in a fit of alcohol-and-cocaine-fuelled rage, came to the conclusion that Smith had to be responsible for the theft of a priceless Fifteenth-Century alchemical manuscript from his private collection, it was *war*: magickal and psychic war. In her fascinating account of the history of the Chelsea Hotel and its colourful occupants, *Inside the Dream Palace*, Sherill Tippins quotes Barry Miles, describing how residents were:

. . . amazed to see the rival wizards conducting magical battles in the lobby, "frantically twisting their fingers into obscure mudras and snarling at each other," oblivious to the tourists trying to check in. [191]

"Is This Machine Recording?"

> Riot sound effects can produce an actual riot in a riot situation. Recorded police whistles will draw cops. Recorded gunshots, and their guns are out.[192]

After working exhaustively through the various applications and derivations of the cut-up method with words on paper, it was inevitable that William Burroughs would turn his attention to the possibilities of film and tape-recorders. After all, a big part of the appeal of the cut-up breakthrough in the first place was that it would allow writers to actually *get to grips* with their material, words, in the same way that painters and sculptors had always taken for granted. Burroughs describes the ease with which cut-ups can be performed on tape in his novel *Nova Express*, as well as giving some indication of where he thought it might all be going:

> This is machine strategy and the machine can be redirected –
> Record for ten minutes on a tape recorder – Now run the tape
> back without playing and cut in other words at random – Where
> you have cut in and re-recorded words are wiped off the tape
> and new words in their place – You have turned time back ten
> minutes and wiped electromagnetic word patterns off the tape
> and substituted other patterns – You can do the same with
> mind tape after working with the tape recorder – (This takes
> some experimentation) – The old mind tapes can be wiped
> clean – Magnetic word dust falling from old patterns[193]

Burroughs felt the exploration of what could be achieved through the actual manipulation of words should be taken *even further*, though. If, as he theorised, all writing and art was a form of magic, the purpose of which was to *Make Things Happen*, what effects might be realised by taking the word *off the page altogether?*

Get it out of your head and into the machines. Stop talking stop arguing. Let the machines talk and argue. A tape recorder is an externalized section of the human nervous system. You can find out more about the nervous system and gain more control over your reaction by using a tape recorder than you could find out sitting twenty years in the lotus posture.[194]

The systematic experiments with tape-recorders would point a startling new way forward: at first Brion Gysin made some simple cut-up recordings with a reel-to-reel tape, but then things were taken further by William's companion and lover, mathematician Ian Sommerville:

He was an expert model-maker, handy with tools. We made the first Dreamachines together. He was as fascinated by taperecorders as I was. Together we put on a lightshow with my sound poetry sounds in 1962-63 that got catalogued later by Fluxus as "expanded cinema."[195]

Due to practical turn of mind and natural facility for gadgets, Ian quickly became known as the "Technical Sergeant" of The Third Mind: running Gysin's Permutation Poems through a computer, coming up with the design and building the first prototype Dreamachine, and approaching tape-recorders with awe and a fascination but that was part spiritual, part erotic. Ian believed that all the tape-recorders of the world were connected on some level, and many of the Routines that later appear in Burroughs' *The Ticket That Exploded* about lovers splicing each other's recordings in together no doubt have their origins at this time. When the novel was published in 1962 it included an *Acknowledgment* to:

Mr. Ian Sommerville of London pointed out the use and significance of spliced tape and all the other tape recorder experiments suggested in this book.[196]

Ian was the one to introduce Brion and William to the various potentials of the tape-recorder for multi-tracking, overdubbing, speeding up and slowing down – but perhaps his most important suggestion was that these experiments should be extended to actual street recording and playback on location. Soon Burroughs was carrying a small portable tape-recorder with him everywhere, and encouraging young friends to do likewise:

> you need a Philips compact cassette recorder handy machine for street recording and playback you can carry it under your coat for recording looks like a transistor radio for playback playback in the street will show the influence of your sound track in operation of course the most undetectable playback is street recordings people don't notice yesterday voices phantom car holes in time accidents of past time played back in present time[197]

The small-press publisher, poet, performance artist, painter, and all-round counter-culture Renaissance man, Jeff Nuttall, editor of the mimeographed *My Own Mag*, had been corresponding with Burroughs in Tangiers since the end of 1963 and become an enthusiastic student of all things cut-up. Later, he would give an account of their first meeting, when Burroughs came to London during the bitter Winter of 1964, and was "stopped at customs and his visit was limited to fourteen days, no reason given." Nuttall describes visiting Burroughs at the Empress Hotel – encountering "a pale boy . . . ill with junk" who is presumably Mikey Portman, and meeting "Tony Balch"[198] – while the whole time:

> Through the casual drift of the conversation Bill interspersed testing, hinting remarks, nudging me towards an understanding of what he was doing with cutup . . .[199]

Nuttall invited Burroughs to contribute to his magazine, which would also showcase such fellow practitioners as Mary Beach and Claude Pelieu in San Francisco, and Carl Weissner in Heidelberg, and his response was enthusiastic:

> '– Innarested in – Mag – noospaper format – columns – juxtaposition – headlines. Could take a walk – recording – what I call *innersection point* – an' y'have a little picture – Might be – uh – streetcorner – name of the street. On y' go – get on a bus –

Little picture, number of the bus – Recording, recording. Then cut it up, grid it, shuffle it, fold it in. Feed it back.'[200]

Burroughs' contribution, a mock newspaper-style insert called *Moving Times*, would showcase some of his most radical experiments with cut-ups, extended into fold-in, intersection writing, and three-column layouts. Nuttall would later write of their encounter:

> Two short months later it dawned on me what Burroughs was attempting. It was like the earth opening under your feet.[201]

The following year, Burroughs would write to his young New York acolyte, Bruce Holbrook – who would later appear as "Baby Zen" in Antony Balch's film *The Cut-Ups*, being 'examined' by Burroughs as "The Doctor" – giving quite specific instructions:

> I hope you have been able to buy one of the Norelco Carry-Corders 150. I have been using this machine and it is the only practical machine for use in the field. It uses tape cartridges which can be slipped in and out instantly weighs only three pounds can easily be carried under a coat the recording on or off controlled from the mike. . . The important things is to play the recordings back on location . . . The mere act of playing a street recording back in the street makes a hole in reality since people are hearing yesterday or whenever . . .[202]

The German writer and translator, Carl Weissner, who began corresponding with Burroughs in 1965, later told Victor Bockris of an encounter when he visited him at home in Heidelberg at this time:

> He put his hands into his pockets and in one smooth movement brought out two reels of mylar tape and put them on the table.
>
> "Got your tape recorder?" he asked.
>
> "Yes."
>
> "Let's compare tapes."

We played his tapes, then some of mine. Nothing was said . . .

Then we put a microphone on the table and took turns talking to the tape recorder switching back and forth between tracks at random intervals. We played it all back and sat there listening to our conversation.[203]

When *Esquire* magazine sent Burroughs on assignment to cover the Chicago Democrat Convention in 1968, his low-key appearance – usually described as a cross between a retired mortician and a minor bank official – enabled him to move anonymously through the crowds, recording the Protestors, and also the Riot Police. Over lunch at the Sheraton hotel, he explained his new tactics to *Esquire*'s John Berendt:

Look, man, what you do is this: You tape about ten minutes of someone talking, then you reverse back to the beginning and go forward again, cutting in every few seconds to record bits and pieces of something else. You keep on doing it until you've made a complete hash of it all. Then you walk around with the damn thing under your jacket, playing it at low volume. It flips people out. I do it in London all the time.[204]

With his young friend, writer Graham Masterton, editor of the newly-launched *Mayfair* (the UK's first "men's magazine" – launched as a competitor to *Playboy* and *Penthouse* – for which, curiously enough, Masterton was able to commission a regular column from Burroughs), he made covert recordings and tried to take surreptitious photos when they visited the Church of Scientology's HQ at Saint Hill in East Grinstead along with the film-maker, Antony Balch:

. . . I am doing a job on Scientology. We called and asked for an interview . . . No dice as I expected. "We want to hear your side of the story," produced no effect. So we are going down to St. Hill this Sunday with photographers . . . will ask the villagers what they think about scientology. Knock on the door at St. Hill. Take pictures etcetera and Antony *[Balch]* will be there with a movie camera and of course recorders. Should be fun and games.[205]

Later, in July 1970, Burroughs attended the *Phun City* Sci-Fi Conference outside Worthing, along with writer friends Alex Trocchi, Jeff Nuttall, and J. G. Ballard. The organiser, Mick Farren of *International Times*, observed:

> William Burroughs stalked the night in his FBI man's hat and raincoat, requiring hippies to talk into his portable tape machine while he baffled them with instant cut-ups.[206]

Years later, as the 1960s gave way to the 1970s, in hotel rooms in London, and again in Paris, in Brion's tiny Rue de St Martin apartment, a similar role would be fulfilled by new seekers such as Udo Breger, and in particular the aforementioned Terry Wilson:

> . . . I found Burroughs' phone number in London, he was living in Duke Street, and Brion was also living there, on and off . . . So I just phoned up, and it happened to be Brion who answered the phone and said to come round, so I did . . . And that story where he asked me to bring something that I was writing so I was standing there with Green Base in the doorway and he just opened the door and took it out of my hand like I was the postman and shut it! Then I received a letter from William a couple of months later saying to come round so eventually I did . . . Just like that![207]

He would become (in Brion's words) "an Apprentice to an Apprentice," and enable Gysin to distil his final and perhaps most enduring statement, *Here To Go: Planet R-101* – a guidebook to "The Other Method," as it is said magic is described in Morocco. It sits alongside *The Job* by Burroughs, and their joint venture, *The Third Mind*, as veritable manuals of psychic exploration and resistance.

Later, I would get to know Terry Wilson myself, in 1980s London. Right from the start it is made clear that Terry feels that his friendship with William and Brion – and, most particularly, his time spent with Brion in Paris – was indeed a kind of apprenticeship, even an initiation . . .

But initiation into *what*, exactly?

> Phony magicians and phantom intelligence agents move in on rue St Martin, on the track of psychic power, while 'predatory hustlers' and 'bloodsuckers' emerge from under the floorboards, eager to grab a good-sized chunk of a dying artist's estate . . . [The apprentice's] initiation demands both risky out-of-the-body experiences and hazardous dealings with 'CREEPS', the con artists of a malign conspiracy . . .

> There was a conspiracy to wipe out Bedaya *[Brion Gysin]* and myself . . . Of course they intend to do everything they can to stop me getting any of that money. But the whole thing is part of a bigger scene – a big power battle, to neutralise and assimilate a lifetime of psychic power into three-dimensional financial manipulative areas.[208]

He likes to talk about Charles Fort, the researcher into "anomalous phenomena" and author of such handbooks of the weird and strange as *The Book of the Damned* and *Lo!*, says that Burroughs was more aware of – and influenced by – him than he would admit. He reads Buchan, *The Power-House*, draws some strange comfort from the famous lines:

> You think that a wall as solid as the earth separates civilisation from barbarism. I tell you the division is a thread, a sheet of glass.[209]

I got the distinct impression that he was wary, to say the least, of those who actively identify as occultists, the seeming ubiquity of post-Crowleyan Theory and Practice. At one point he cautions me about "the company of predatory 'magical' thinkers"[210] – "What, 'magick' with a 'k'?" I ask – "Yeh . . ." he sighs. This is perhaps inherited from Brion, who was pretty dismissive of Aleister Crowley as a "queen bee," and the "drones" who are such eager followers. He was *not* impressed with Kenneth Anger's "box of tricks," for instance, when he met him as part of the "Swinging London" circles around

Robert Fraser, Christopher Gibbs and The Rolling Stones in the 1960s. Besides, he preferred an older, wilder magic, whose passing he still mourned:

> It was almost closing time for Magical Morocco. Electronic mind control was moving in and the Djnoun forces would soon be in full retreat gems to be snapped up before they disappear forever. Spells and curses. Dance and trance. The Other Method was up for grabs.[211]

Burroughs, for all his Harvard education and celebrated intellect, was also possessed of a worldview that was informed – you might even say overshadowed – by a fear and fascination with the supernatural that had been shaped in childhood, and had stayed with him ever since. He had a particular sensitivity to what he saw as *meaningful* coincidences, a veritable mantra of his being "there is *no such thing* as a coincidence." Instead, Burroughs asserted that "writers operate in the magical universe" – later writing:

> I will speak now for magical truth to which I myself subscribe. Magic is the assertion of *will*, the assumption that nothing happens in this universe (that is to say the minute fraction of the universe we are able to contact) unless some entity *wills* it to happen.[212]

Such claims lead his first biographer, Ted Morgan, to state that the single most important thing about Burroughs was this frequently professed belief in what he referred to as "the Magical Universe." Gysin himself was naturally inclined to intrigue and mystery, and had come back from Morocco full of tales of black magic, curses and possession, and Burroughs was an all-too-eager audience for the spellbinding storyteller. He felt that his own travels in exotic parts had opened his eyes to a Bigger Picture:

> Now anyone who has lived for any time in countries like Morocco where magic is widely practiced has probably seen a curse work. I have.[213]

With regard to curses, Brion Gysin had told Burroughs the story of how he believed he had been the target of a curse intended to oust him from the restaurant, the Thousand and One Nights, which he had run in Tangier:

> . . . while getting the restaurant ready I found a magic object, which was an amulet of sorts, a rather elaborate one with seeds, pebbles, shards of broken mirror, seven of each, and a little package in which there was a piece of writing, and the writing when deciphered by friends who didn't even want to *handle* it, because of its magic qualities, which even educated Moroccans were not anxious to get in touch with, but it said something like, an appeal to one of the devils of fire, the devil of smoke – to take Brion away from this house: as the smoke leaves this chimney may Brion leave this house and never return . . .[214]

When Gysin, apparently in trance, told Burroughs "The Ugly Spirit shot Joan because" he thought he finally had the answer that no amount of psychoanalysis or self-examination had been able to provide: the unforgiveable slip that had caused the death of his common-law wife, Joan Vollmer (when the "drunken insanity" of their infamous "William Tell Act" resulted in Burroughs accidentally killing Joan by a gunshot to the head) had come about because he was literally *possessed* by an evil spirit.

This was indeed a War Universe, as the Indian mystic Sri Aurobindo had said. The price of existence was eternal conflict, apparently. If Brion had identified The Enemy, The Ugly Spirit, then William instinctively knew the only solution available to him:

> I live with the constant threat of possession, and a constant need to escape from possession, from Control. So the death of Joan brought me in contact with the invader, the Ugly Spirit, and manoeuvred me into a lifelong struggle, in which I have had no choice except to write my way out.[215]

If the Word was indeed the basic mechanism or unit of Control – the "virus" by which The Ugly Spirit, or its agency Control, exerted its malevolent influence – then surely a real understanding of the Word, what words are and what can be done with them – was essential. All these explorations and obsessions were not merely diversions, experiments for artistic or literary amusement, or the creation of novelty, but part of a deadly struggle with unseen, invisible – perhaps even evil – psycho-spiritual enemies. The only hope for deprogramming and self-liberation was to subvert the methods of Control and its various agencies, understand the tools used so that they could become weapons to turn back on the Control Machine – or ultimately The Ugly Spirit itself.

Many years later, in London for *The Final Academy* series of events in 1982, when Burroughs was asked about these early experiments with tape recorders – a hot topic with nearly all of the *avant garage* "Post-Industrial" experimental musicians taking part – he actually described them with a chuckle as "Sorcery!"[216] He has also explained how the tape-recorder can be used as a tool for deconditioning:

> As soon as you start recording situations and playing them back on the street you are creating a new reality. When you play back a street recording, people think they're hearing real street sounds and they're not. You're tampering with their actual reality.[217]

Subsequently, in an interview I conducted with him in 1988, Brion Gysin's "apprentice-to-an-apprentice" Terry Wilson responded to questions about his interpretation of the *intent* behind such experiments:

> MS: You are quoted as talking about the cut-ups – and writing generally – as a form of exorcism
>
> TW: That simply came from one of my observations in *Here To Go* where I was saying that William's texts – once they brought the cut-ups into the tape-recorder area, cutting up tapes and whatnot – William's texts increasingly became like spells and very much exhibited a preoccupation with exorcism.[218]

An illustration of the way that these preoccupations had begun to filter through to every area of the lives of Burroughs and his circle at that time is a somewhat sinister incident concerning a young man called Alan Watson. During a cooling-off period in the relationship between Burroughs and Ian Sommerville, the younger man had found a new boyfriend from his hometown of Darlington, in the North of England, and nearer his own age, Alan Watson. Later, in a perhaps misguided attempt at reconciliation, Burroughs had invited Sommerville and Watson to move in with him when they were stuck for somewhere to live, but it was soon all-too-apparent that the older, reserved Burroughs just *could not stand* the younger man who, as far as he was concerned, had come between him and Ian. To make matters worse, with his dyed blond hair and painfully tight hipster trousers that left little to the imagination, Alan Watson was very camp, all limp wrists and hands-on-hips – described by Burroughs as "100% swishy queen" – who would respond to the jeers of workmen on building sites by calling out "Score a goal for me, boys!"[219] and blowing kisses, and liked nothing better than to shriek along to the opera of Maria Callas at full blast. Burroughs, unable to concentrate to write or get any work done, and feeling increasingly sorry for himself, began to drink heavily and sulk – which Ian had no patience with *at all*, his already diminished affections dwindling even further. An eerie expression of the underlying tensions came to light one day when Watson went to sunbathe in Hampton Court, taking along a cassette of what he thought was one of his favourite Opera tapes to listen to, but which instead turned out to be a recording Burroughs had made of himself impersonating Watson, grotesquely caricaturing his voice and repeating his favourite expressions mockingly. Shocked, he tore the tape from the player and threw it into the nearby canal – but he had no doubt that Burroughs had tried to put a curse on him.

Returning to the more serious occult applications of street-recording and playback, Terry Wilson would later further refer to a discussion he had recorded with Brion Gysin on this very subject in the *Ports of Entry* section of *Here to Go: Planet R101*:

> TW: The cut-up techniques made very explicit a preoccupation with exorcism – William's texts became spells, for instance. How effective are methods such as street playback of tapes for dispersing parasites?

> BG: We-e-ell, you'd have to ask William about that, but I do seem to remember at least two occasions on which he claimed success . . .

> Uh, the first was in the Beat Hotel still, therefore about 1961 or '2, and William decided *(laughing)* to take care of an old lady who sold newspapers in a kiosk . . .

> Now the other case was some years later in London when he had perfected the method and, uh, went about with at least one I think sometimes two tape recorders, one in each hand . . .[220]

Gysin continues by describing one of the chants that Burroughs would frequently employ for such purposes, the enigmatic rhyme described as an "anti-curse" which he can be heard reciting to great effect in the voiceover recorded for his friend, film-maker Antony Balch, to use with a print of the film *Häxan* (a black & white, silent, Swedish-Danish horror film from 1922, loosely based on a study of the 15th Century German Witch-Hunter's Guide, the *Malleus Maleficarum*) that Balch was distributing in the U.K. as *Witchcraft Through the Ages*:

> Lock them out and bar the door.

> Lock them out forever more.

> Nook and cranny, window, door,

> Seal them out forevermore.Curse go back, curse go back,

> Back with double fear and flack.Curse go back, curse go back,

> Back with double pain and lack.

Silver arrow through the night,

Silver arrow, take thy flight.

Silver arrow, seek and find

Cursing heart and cursing mind.[221]

Later, Burroughs would narrate a short film, called simply *Ayahuasca*, about a *curandero* on the Putumayo River in Colombia, and his desire to pass on knowledge of plant medicine to the next generation before it is lost. He is also one of the narrators for *Shamans of the Blind Country*, an epic four-hour documentary on magical healing among the pre-Buddhist Bön practitioners of the Himalayas, filmed by German professor of Ethnology, Michael Oppitz, and released in 1980.

As well as the obvious step of cutting-up street recordings, following Ian's example Burroughs also began to splice in what he called "trouble noises" – recordings of alarm bells, breaking glass, fire engines, as well as sound effects of explosions, machineguns, and riots recorded from TV. This procedure could also be accompanied by the taking of photographs, which could then be collaged or *cut-up* in some way – for example, by cutting out the image of the intended target, quite literally *removing* it. These symbolic manipulations, via captured image or soundtrack, opened up a whole new realm of possibility:

> I have frequently observed that this simple operation making
> recordings and taking pictures of some location you wish to
> discommode or destroy, then playing recordings back and taking
> more pictures – will result in accidents, fires, removals, especially
> the last. The target moves . . .[222]

Probably the definitive statement on the subject appears in *The Job*, a book of interviews by Daniel Odier, with commentary and added text by Burroughs (originally published in French in 1969 as *Entretiens avec William Burroughs*, but released in English the following year.) In the opening section, *Playback From Eden To Watergate*, Burroughs states:

Here is a sample operation carried out against the Moka Bar at
29 Frith Street, London, W.1, beginning on August 3, 1972.
Reverse Thursday. Reason for operation was outrageous and
unprovoked discourtesy and poisonous cheesecake. Now to
close in on the Moka Bar. Record. Take pictures. Stand around
outside. Let them see me. They are seething around in there...
Playback would come later with more pictures. I took my time
and strolled over to the Brewer Street Market, where I recorded
a three-card Monte game. Now you see it, now you
don't...Playback was carried out a number of times with more
pictures. Their business fell off. They kept shorter and shorter
hours. October 30, 1972, the Moka Bar closed. The location was
taken over by the Queen's Snack Bar.[223]

In addition to the campaign waged against the Moka Bar, Burroughs also
made similarly sorcerous attempts that same year against the London HQ
of Scientology at 37 Fitzroy Street. Although he considered it another success
when they closed down, he seemed unable to bring any 'playback' influence
to bear on their new location in Tottenham Court Road, which remains the
Dianetics and Scientology Life Improvement Centre to this day.

As well as Burroughs' own writings, further insights into these methods can
also be found in *Playback: My Personal Experience of Chaos Magic with William
S. Burroughs, Sr.*, by Cabell McLean (aka Cabell Hardy.) A student at Naropa
College in Boulder, Colorado, in the late 1970s, McLean met Burroughs
while he was teaching there. He soon moved in with him to become his
lover and companion (c.1976-1983), also acting as an assistant during
completion of *Cities of the Red Night* and the commencement of writing
what would become its sequel:

> I collaborated with him on instructive experiments, learned
> research techniques, went with him to scout locations he wished
> to use in his work, did 'walk-throughs' of scenes, and so
> forth.[224]

Indeed, the very first excerpt from what would eventually see print as *The*

Place of Dead Roads was published with the working title *"From Gay Gun"* under *both* their names in the *Washington Review* for Summer-Fall 1977:

> At 17 Audrey is handsome at first glance. Tap of boot heels on the wooden sidewalk long red hair on buckskin shoulders, yellow hair and blue eyes dancing. Joey's hair is tied back to keep it out of his eyes thin hands drawn up into his V-coat gray bolo tie and boots of black lizard. On closer inspection there is something furtive and feral and sad in this face a Black Irish face with red hair.[225]

Cabell enlarges upon the Moka Bar incident:

> [*William*] continued going to the bar for a few more days, enduring their abuse, while he tape recorded the sounds inside. Later, he would stand outside and film or photograph the premises from outside. Then he went back in and began to play the tape recordings at low or subliminal levels, and continued to take photographs on his way in and out of the place. This he did for several days. The effects were remarkable: accidents occurred, fights broke out, the place lost customers, the subsequent loss of income became irredeemable, and within a few weeks, the bar was permanently closed.[226]

He continues with an account of his own about an experience he and a girlfriend "Poppy" had in a deli in the Mall in Boulder, which when related to Burroughs gives rise to a similar operation, the account of which serves as a particularly fine object lesson in the power – and perils! – of what was by now being referred to as *Playback*.

Originally published in the *Ashé Journal of Experimental Spirituality* (and currently still available in the aptly named anthology *Playback: The Magic of William S. Burroughs*), an enjoyable, thought-provoking account that gives a valuable insight into Burroughs' continuing engagement with such techniques – as well as his sometimes quite direct teaching methods:

"You know Cabell, sometimes the best weapon is *no weapon at all...*"[227]

A further spooky connection that came out of Burroughs' continuing exploration of cut-ups, the question of *just how-random-is-random*, and obsessive experimentation with tape-recorders, as well as his preoccupation with the occult and parapsychological research, was his fascination with the infamous "unexplained voices on tape" of Latvian psychologist Konstantin Raudive. Writing in 1968 – but translated into English in 1971 as *Breakthrough: An Amazing Experiment in Electronic Communication with the Dead* – Raudive described his experiences with what have since come to be known as Electronic Voice Phenomenon (EVP for short.) Put simply, EVP are sounds allegedly resembling human speech which turn up on various recording media – initially the experiments were conducted with reel-to-reel audio tape – but with no apparent or intentional input source, which advocates claim are of supernatural origin.

Speaking to a Class of his students at the Kerouac School of Disembodied Poetics at Naropa, Burroughs explained:

> These voices are in a number of accents and languages, often quite ungrammatical... "You I friends. Where stay?" sounds like a Tangier hustler. Reading through the sample voices in *Breakthrough*, I was struck by many instances of a distinctive style reminiscent of schizophrenic speech, certain dream utterances, some of the cut-ups and delirium voices like the last words of Dutch Schultz.[228]

Although there are a number of quite rational possible explanations (even disallowing for fraud or wishful thinking), the majority of claimants believe they are, quite literally, voices of the dead. Burroughs was not so sure – he was more in favour of the explanation that:

> They are somehow imprinted on the tape by electromagnetic energy generated by the unconscious minds of the researchers

or people connected with them.[229]

And no doubt remembering his time exploring Scientology, he added:

> Remember that your memory bank contains tapes of everything you have ever heard, including of course your own words.[230]

But as with all his other sources and studies, Burroughs the Writer would get his money's worth: strange and evocative phrases from Raudive's book would turn up as source material for later cut-ups, and even chapter titles in his 1981 novel, *Cities of the Red Night*, such as *Are you in salt, Cheers here are the nondead*, and *We are here because of you* all originate with the "unexplained voices on tape."

Another enigmatic and perhaps portentous phrase that recurs throughout Burroughs' oeuvre – including *Cities of the Red Night*, where it is likewise used as the title of a chapter – is *Horse hattock to ride to ride*. Quite where or when this phrase originated, or indeed *what* it is meant to mean, is uncertain – but, interestingly, the associations are undoubtedly with the folklore of witchcraft. The "founding father" of the Modern Witchcraft Revival – or "Wicca" – Gerald Gardner left behind his own personal collection of magical recipes and spells, or "Book of Shadows" as it is known in the trade, which includes the couplet: "Horse and hattock! Horse and go! Horse and Pellatis, Ho Ho!" One possible origin is that in Scottish folklore, the fairies are said to pronounce the phrase "Horse and Hattock!" when they wish to go off on their nightly escapades, or else to leave a place and return to their own realm. This practice then became associated with Witchcraft thanks to one Isobel Gowdie, a Scottish woman tried for Witchcraft in 1662. In her detailed confessions, she spoke of how she used the phrases "Horse and Hattock in the Devil's Name" or "Horse and Hattock, Horse and go, Horse and Pellatis, Ho Ho!" in order to fly by mounting a broomstick:

> "Then they would put a strae between their legs, cry — 'Horse

and hattock in the Devil's name!' and flee awa owre the muirs and fells."[231]

To my mind there are two possible means by which William Burroughs may have encountered this rather colourful piece of folklore: firstly, researching references or sources for the phrase, I discovered that "Now horse, and hattock, cried the laird . . . Now horse and hattock speedily"[232] appears in Sir Walter Scott's 18th Century Romance of sinister goings-on at the Scottish Borders, *The Black Dwarf,* and remembered we are told in *The Place of Dead Roads* that the author's alter-ego, Kim Carsons, had read Scott as a boy. Then, secondly, that "Horse, hattock, To ride, to ride" is mentioned by Dion Fortune in *Psychic Self-Defence* as an example of the kind of formulae – apparently nonsensical – recited by witches as "aids to concentration."[233]

Tape-recorder magic of another kind also occurs in *Cities of the Red Night,* when Clem Snide the private investigator's attempts to trace a Missing Person take him to the Greek island of Spetsai – a location that Burroughs had in fact visited in the early 1970s, and which was also the setting for *The Magus* by John Fowles. In a deliberate blurring of art and life, Burroughs has his psychic detective protagonist read *The Magus* during his visit, also travel out to the other side of the island to see the villa and beach that are used as key settings in the novel – just as he had done himself on his visit to the island.

Earlier, Snide's Client, Mr. Green, who has retained him to look for his missing son, Jerry, asks him "It's true then that you use uh psychic methods?" and is told:

> "I use any methods that help me to find the missing person. If I can locate him in my own mind that makes it easier to locate him outside it."[234]

The description of Snide's taping and playback as part of his use of "psychic methods" clearly mirrors Burroughs' own experiments, as he makes recordings of the ambient sounds and takes photos in the missing person's various last-known locations, also reading selections from *The Magus* into the recorder:

> I will explain exactly how these recordings are made. I want an hour of Spetsai: an hour of places where my M.P. has been and the sounds he has heard. But not in sequence. I don't start at the beginning of the tape and record to the end. I spin the tape back and forth, cutting in at random so the *The Magus* may be cut off in the middle of a word by a flushing toilet, or *The Magus* may cut into sea sounds. It's a sort of *I Ching* or table-tapping procedure. How random is it actually? Don Juan says that nothing is random to a man of knowledge: everything he sees or hears is there just at that time waiting to be seen and heard.[235]

10. William S. Burroughs with Genesis P-Orridge, at the time of their first meeting, Duke Street, St. James, 1973. Photo taken by WSB's "Dilly Boy" companion, Johnny Brady.

11. *Black Sun Bill*, recreation of collage for Wild Fruits fanzine, 1988. Incorporates portrait of WSB, original photo by Ruby Ray, San Francisco 1980, reproduced with her kind permission.

12. *Wild Boys: Zimbu Xolotl Time* – original artwork copyright Emma Doeve, reproduced with her kind permission.

reproduced with her kind permission, and with thanks to Anthony Blokdijk, Maldoror Stichting/Den Haag.

13. Geff Rushton (aka 'John Balance') & Peter 'Sleazy' Christopherson of Coil with
WSB. Taken in Lawrence, Kansas, 1992, at the time of the filming of the video for
Ministry's *Just One Fix*, which featured WSB and was directed by Sleazy.

14. *The Electronic Revolution* (Dutch language edition, 1988.) Cover design and image treatment by Peter 'Sleazy' Christopherson. Reproduced with the kind permission of Anthony Blokdijk, Maldoror Stichting/Den Haag.

16. Original artwork by Billy Chainsaw, reproduced with his kind permission.

17. Original artwork by Billy Chainsaw, reproduced with his kind permission.

18. The author, outside Dalmeny Court, 8 Duke Street, St. James. Photo by C. J. Bradbury Robinson, August 2013, reproduced with his kind permission.

Uncle Bill
& The "Wreckers
Of Civilization"

Burroughs, and Gysin, both told me something that resonated with me for the rest of my life so far. They pointed out that alchemists always used the most modern equipment and mathematics, the most precise science of their day. Thus, in order to be an effective and practicing magician in contemporary times one must utilize the most practical and cutting-edge technology and theories of the era. In our case, it meant cassette recorders, Dream Machines and flicker, Polaroid cameras, Xeroxes, E-prime and, at the moment of writing this text, laptops, psychedelics, videos, DVDs and the World Wide Web . . .

Basically, everything that is capable of recording and/or representing "reality" is a magical tool just as much as it is a weapon of *control*.

- Genesis Breyer P-Orridge, *Magick Squares and Future Beats*.[236]

Around the same time that Punk was emerging here in the U.K., another home-grown genre that was drawing inspiration from Burroughs, Gysin and the cut-ups was the "Industrial Music" of Throbbing Gristle and related bands like Cabaret Voltaire, and later 23 Skidoo. Richard H. Kirk, founder-member of Cabaret Voltaire, and later a key player in the Sheffield Electronic Music/Dance underground, said:

A lot of what we did, especially in the early days, was a direct application of his ideas to sound and music. One book in particular, *The Electronic Revolution*, was an influence on us . . . It was almost a handbook of how to use tape-recorders in a crowd, to promote a sense of unease or unrest by playback of

riot noises cut in with random recordings of the crowd itself.
That side was always very interesting to us . . . Cut-ups might
have lost some of their potency through mainstream use, but as
an idea it is still very valid, at least on a personal level . . . I do
believe by cutting up certain texts you can read into the future
to a certain extent.[237]

TG prime-mover Genesis P-Orridge had actually met Burroughs while he
was living at Duke Street in London in the early 1970s, and he and band-
mate Peter 'Sleazy' Christopherson had been directly inspired by the outsider
stance of the "Literary Outlaw" as much as they were influenced by his
theories. Along with Chris Carter and Cosey Fanni Tutti, P-Orridge and
Christopherson would help to invent a new genre of music that they dubbed
"Industrial" – stripping down music even further than the back-to-basics of
Punk to create a kind of Garage musique concrete, in which the processing
and manipulation of found sound was a key part of the semi-improvised
mayhem that was as often sonic assault as it was about the alchemy of
sound. Their launch at the Institute of Contemporary Arts in London's
The Mall saw an unprecedented backlash in the press in response to their
confrontational shock-tactics and uncompromising "anti-music" – with the
Daily Mail of 19th October 1976 infamously quoting the Tory MP Nicholas
Fairbairn that "These people are the wreckers of civilization!"

When P-Orridge had first visited Burroughs at Duke Street in 1973, he
asked him "Tell me about magick?" and whether or not he still used cut-ups
in writing? Burroughs replied "No, I don't really have to anymore, because
my brain has been rewired so it does them automatically." He cracked open
a bottle of Jack Daniels, poured them both a stiff drink, then put on the TV
to watch *The Man From U.N.C.L.E.*, explaining "Reality is not really all it's
cracked up to be, you know . . ."[238] and began hopping through the channels
on the TV with the remote – at the same time mixing in pre-recorded cut-
ups from the Sony tape-recorder:

what we see is determined to a large extent by what we hear

you can verify this proposition by a simple experiment turn off
the sound track on your television set and substitute an arbitrary
sound track prerecorded on your tape recorder street sounds
music conversation recordings of other television programs
you will find that the arbitrary sound track seems to be
appropriate and is in fact determining your interpretation of the
film track on screen[239]

P-Orridge was experiencing a demonstration of cut-ups and playback in
Real Time, Right There, Where He Was Sitting.

> I was already being taught. What Bill explained to me then was
> pivotal to the unfolding of my life and art: Everything is
> recorded. If it is recorded, it can be edited. If it can be edited
> then the order, sense, meaning and direction are as arbitrary and
> personal as the agenda and/or person editing. This is magick.[240]

Burroughs went on to describe his theories about the pre-recorded universe,
quoting Wittgenstein, and describing with obvious relish his experiments
with tape-recorders at both the Chicago Democrat's Convention in 1968
and, closer to home, on the streets of London: using playback to wage
psychic warfare against the Scientology HQ and the infamous Moka Coffee
Bar.

In addition to the street-recordings, cut-up with the "trouble sounds" of
police sirens, screams, sound effects of explosions and machine-gun fire
taped from the TV, Burroughs had also taken photographs of his targets.
As part of his explanation, he showed P-Orridge one of his journal
scrapbooks in which he had posted two photos: a simple black & white
street-scene, with the relevant building clearly visible, and then another
beneath it from which he had carefully sliced out the "target" with a razor-
blade, gluing the two halves of the photo back together so as to create an
image of the street with the offending institution removed. The same
principle could clearly be applied to photos of people that you wanted to
"excise" from your life, he said.

These ideas would have a profound effect on P-Orridge and Christopherson, as well as many of the "anti-musicians" and sound-artists that they would collaborate with or inspire in their turn. But it wasn't just the *sonic* application of the cut-ups with tape-recorders that spoke to them, rather the whole approach to challenging conventional wisdom and deprogramming the self from the imposed beliefs and values of mainstream society. Of the family tree that reaches from Industrial pioneers Throbbing Gristle through Psychic TV and ultimately to Coil, much fruit has been borne relating to Burroughs and Gysin, the cut-ups, The Other Method (a term Burroughs adopted from Gysin, who had told him "Magic calls itself The Other Method for controlling matter and knowing space"[241]) and The Third Mind.

A further anecdote from P-Orridge that demonstrates Burroughs' lingering interest in the "unexplained voices on tape" is given in his account of an experiment conducted during a visit to Burroughs at his home, the former YMCA Locker Room nicknamed The Bunker, on August 6th, 1981 – a date that always had mythic significance for Burroughs as a "dividing line in history" as it was when the Americans had dropped the atomic bomb on the Japanese, bringing the Second World War to an abrupt close:

> Given that we were meeting on 'Hiroshima Day,' as Burroughs designated it, there was a feeling that perhaps quite a large number of souls might wish to breakthrough. We set up an old tape recorder on the kitchen table where many a dinner soiree was held over his New York years and hit record. Each of us took turns listening. . . Final report from the Bunker? Nothing! Oh, how we hoped for evidence, but we just got the expected hiss and short-wave *Twilight Zone* type sounds. Regardless – and Crowley was fastidious in reminding the initiate of this – we did not fall into the trap of 'lust of result.'[242]

After TG had split, P-Orridge and Christopherson went on to form "Psychic Television Limited" – with its attendant conceptual art gag masquerading as fan-club pretending to be a cult, "Thee Temple ov Psychick Youth" [sic], or

TOPY as it was known – and for a while there was an inner circle that revolved around a strange hybrid of the ideas of occultists Aleister Crowley and Austin Osman Spare regarding consciousness alteration, dream control, and sex-magic. TOPY ran curiously parallel – and at times fed into – the then-emerging Chaos Magic scene in much the same way as Industrial had Punk, and the life and work of Burroughs and Gysin and their associates, with their Cut-ups, Dreamachine, Playback, and Third Mind, equally offered a kind of toolkit for similar ends. It looked like *if* the Revolution *was* going to be televised *after all*, then Psychic TV were going to be first in line to put in their bid for the franchise. . .

Highlights of the creative cross-fertilisation between Burroughs and the Industrial pioneers have included the release of the album *Nothing Here Now But The Recordings*, and *The Final Academy*. Organised by David Dawson, Roger Ely, and Genesis P-Orridge and Peter Christopherson, *The Final Academy* consisted of a series of main events over four days at The Ritzy Cinema, Brixton, in which William S. Burroughs and Brion Gysin would be celebrated in film, music, performance and readings. The famous experimental films shot by Antony Balch in the 1960s would be shown each night. There would also be performances by the experimental music groups that had been inspired by their example: 23 Skidoo, Last Few Days, Cabaret Voltaire and the debut of Psychic TV (recently formed from the ashes of Throbbing Gristle), as well as a variety of other poets and performance artists. Some, like John Giorno and Terry Wilson, were of course friends with Burroughs and Gysin; others, like Anne Bean, Paul Burwell and Ruth Adams, were associates of Roger Ely. His B2 Gallery ran an exhibition of Brion Gysin paintings, complete with Dreamachine, collages from *The Third Mind*, and scrapbook material. There were also book-signings, with a whole host of new publications – such as new paperback editions of *A William Burroughs Reader* and *Cities of the Red Night*, Victor Bockris' seminal collection of after-dinner conversations, *With William Burroughs: A Report From The Bunker*, as well as *Here To Go: Planet R101*, the definitive statement from Brion Gysin, with the help of Terry Wilson, and the Burroughs/Gysin/TG special, both from RE/Search Publications – and also other regional events in Liverpool, London, and Manchester, including additional performances by Marc Almond, Jeff Nuttall, and Heathcote Williams, and films by Derek Jarman and Cerith Wyn Evans.

In the press at the time of *The Final Academy*, P-Orridge had this to say about the influence of Burroughs and Gysin:

> William, Brion and the poet John Giorno used writing because in their day writing was the most vital, living form for propaganda. They got hold of tape recorders and made films with (the late) Antony Balch, always trying to reapply what they discovered through writing to other media. Now you've got groups like Cabaret Voltaire, 23 Skidoo, Last Few Days and Psychic TV who have followed through and used tape, cut-ups, random chats and sound in the way they've read or at least been inspired in Burroughs' and Gysin's books. They've put it, though, into popular culture, i.e. music, which happens at the moment to be the most vital form.[243]

All too soon though cracks began to show, and P-Orridge and Christopherson parted company: Genesis would develop PTV in the direction of Rave music – applying the cut-up methods of sampling, cut-and-paste and appropriation to the development of a Techno Psychedelia, and TOPY increasingly concerned with New Age, Merry Prankster-style utopian tribalism. His role as figurehead for these disparate anti-movements, and the cultural memes he was engineering – from cut-ups and sex-magick, to tattooing, piercing, and body modification – inevitably lead to conflict with the authorities, and P-Orridge had to flee England for a life of exile in the United States. Eventually he would come to perhaps the most radical application of all of his interpretation of the ideas of Burroughs and Gysin: Pandrogyny, in which P-Orridge and his spouse, Lady Jaye, would literally try and cut-up gender.

When Peter Christopherson broke with P-Orridge, PTV and TOPY, it was to join forces with his then life-partner, another "graduate" of *The Final Academy* and former "psychick youth", Geff Rushton (aka 'John Balance'), to concentrate on the magickal and musical entity that was Coil. They continued to hold Burroughs and Gysin in the highest regard as role models and teachers, and find new ways to apply their lessons through the newly emerging computer technologies that allowed for the sampling and manipulation of sound like never before – whilst at the same time acknowledging the inspiration of the more 'hands on' original experiments:

> The original intentions of cut ups were, if we go back to Burroughs and Gysin, to allow the future to leak through. They were spells, rituals and magical maps with which to break up reality. That was their intention and their result. On *Love's Secret Domain* we made a deliberate attempt to get back to magical cut ups . . .[244]

Another more direct acknowledgment of their debt was when they were instrumental in producing the new Dutch edition of the key Burroughs text, *The Electronic Revolution*, in collaboration with Maldoror Press of The Hague. Christopherson created the layout and cover-design, and Balance provided the introduction, in which he wrote:

> This book is the original handbook of possibilities. It is both 'user' and 'misuser' friendly. The true danger lies in denial. It is intended to be used, to be used and applied. Experimentation is of vital importance.[245]

Peter 'Sleazy' Christopherson had also known Burroughs from the early days of Throbbing Gristle, operating in a defiantly "non-musician" capacity – his own use of pre-recorded sound and tapes in TG had been directly inspired by Burroughs. Certain from a very young age that he was homosexual but feeling stifled by his academic family background in the North of England, his discovery of Burroughs' *Naked Lunch* at the back of W. H. Smith's one rainy Saturday afternoon had been a revelation to the 13 year old boy. "It changed my life!"[246] he said later, continuing that:

> My perception of Burroughs' work is that things that happen in his books happen in a spirit world where there isn't really any self-consciousness, intellectualisation or present time really. The time they take place in isn't the annihilating reality of now. It is some other space altogether . . .[247]

A talented photographer who helped to design high-profile rock album covers as a day-job, in his spare time Christopherson delighted in taking photos of young male friends in what appeared to be compromising situations, carefully staged. One particular set of images was for his friend John Harwood's boutique *Boy*, which appeared to show youths beaten and bloodied by Skinhead thugs; another was an early set of promo photos for the Sex Pistols, taken in the public toilets of a YMCA – apparently declined by Malcolm McLaren because they made the band look "too much like psychotic rent-boys."[248] These kinds of extra-curricular interests had earned Christopherson the affectionate nickname "Sleazy" from his band-mates (one that would endure with friends – and, later, fans alike – throughout his life.) When it came to Industrial Music, his role in Throbbing Gristle completely bypassed conventional instrumentation of any kind. Inspired by Burroughs, he would enthusiastically apply and develop such ideas as he had read about in *The Job* and *The Electronic Revolution* with found-sound and loops – frequently cutting up recordings live, from prepared tapes and treated radio and TV sources.

In 1977, Christopherson was in New York on business and visited Burroughs at The Bunker, taking with him a portfolio of his "boy" photos. Burroughs was really enthusiastic about the images, and talked about wanting to incorporate them in a book alongside the text he was the working on, *Blade Runner* (Sleazy made clear: "Nothing to do with the film!"[249]) – but regrettably the publisher wouldn't run to the expense. Nonetheless, they bonded over a bottle of vodka, Christopherson later recalling:

> I remember getting very, *very* drunk with him . . . and it was one of those times where you could sit for a long time and not say anything and feel OK about it. Maybe that has something to do with the place, which is a converted YMCA . . .[250]

But he also had a more practical suggestion:

> . . . I suggested that it would be great to release a record of his original cut-up recordings . . . we really wanted people to be able to hear what they *actually* sounded like.[251]

Genesis P-Orridge had also been suggesting the same idea for a while:

> I thought of doing the LP in 1973, it was about the first thing I suggested to him when I met him. And I wrote him letters suggesting it again and again and again for the following eight years, and suddenly one day James Grauerholz wrote back and said "Okay." Just when I thought he was never going to do it![252]

So eventually it was agreed, and arrangements were made for P-Orridge and Christopherson to go over to Lawrence, Kansas, where, in the middle of the Summer heat, they spent a frantic and humid week in a motel room with inadequate air-conditioning, a rented Revox tape-recorder, going through a shoebox full of old tapes. By all accounts the actual tapes were in a pretty poor condition, and it sounds like they were duplicated for posterity not a moment-too-soon. As P-Orridge later told Vale in an interview for *RE/Search*:

> He just agreed to us taking the tapes away, fifteen hours of them, and editing them down to an LP. It's a good job we got them, 'cause they were recorded over twenty years ago and the oxide was actually crumbling off the tapes as we held them.[253]

The album, titled *Nothing Here Now But The Recordings*, came out in May 1981 on Throbbing Gristle's own Industrial Records label, serial number IR0016.

It was a significant release: there had been previous records of Spoken Word from William S. Burroughs, starting with the classic *Call Me Burroughs* issued by the English Bookshop in Paris in 1965, and reissued the following year on the ESP label; and then in 1971 a recording of Burroughs reading a draft of *Ali's Smile* was released in a very limited edition of only 99 copies – but this was the first time that recordings of the actual cut-up experiments with tape would be made available.

It would also be the final release on the Industrial Records label, followed by the demise of Throbbing Gristle later that year. Notifying their fans and followers with a simple postcard, reading "Throbbing Gristle: The Mission Is Terminated", in many respects things had come full circle for the Wreckers of Civilization: passing on the baton to the next generation with the challenge, example and inspiration of the cut-up experiments of William S. Burroughs and Brion Gysin.

Something would come full-circle in 1992, when Peter Christopherson was approached in the capacity of his 'day job' as a director of promo videos by the members of Ministry, an American hardcore-industrial-rock band, whose *Just One Fix* was about to be released as a single. According to Christopherson's partner, John Balance:

> . . . they had used some Burroughs samples and their record company made them take them off as they were scared of copyright infringement and William heard and he said "Oh no, put them back on." So we went over and filmed them all, William shooting and stuff and while we were there we also did some recording with him for Coil.[254]

Among the spoken word samples of Burroughs used by Ministry, the phrase "Bring it all down" seemed to offer an appropriate comment and counterpoint to their pounding anthem of drug-addled desperation, at least in part inspired by frontman Al Jourgenson's own battles with crack and heroin addiction. As fans of Throbbing Gristle and Coil, Ministry were well aware of Sleazy's previous connections with Burroughs, and so asked if it would be possible to make arrangements for the writer to appear in the video. Christopherson made the call to Lawrence, asking Burroughs if he would be willing to consider the project? When Burroughs named a fee, Christopherson winced, "William, that's a *lot* of money!" – to which the Old Writer allegedly replied "Well, I got a *lot* of fuckin' cats to feed . . ."[255]

Clearly a mutually satisfactory arrangement was arrived at, however, as the artwork for the eventual release features an original painting by Burroughs, titled appropriately enough *Last Chance Junction and Curse on Drug Hysterics*. In Christopherson's finished promo clip, we see both footage of Burroughs at target practice, and also a more formal sequence, in which the High Priest of Junk is seen making passes back and forth with his hands like a conjuror. This is clearly a reference to a sequence in the early experimental film shot with Antony Balch, *Towers Open Fire*, where a close-up of Burroughs' hands passing back-and-forth over a stack of old film cans – apparently causing them to disappear, "as if by magic'" – is juxtaposed with the chant "Curse go back, curse go back" on the accompanying soundtrack.

The visit to Lawrence, Kansas in 1992 would turn out to be Coil's last encounter with Burroughs. While filming for *Just One Fix*, they observed first-hand how he incorporated a form of sigil magic into his shooting practice – drawing images or phrases which were stuck on to the targets, before being blasted with his favourite handguns. They would also record him for use in a sadly unrealised project, named after a haunting phrase that appeared in his work, *Wounded Galaxies Tap At The Window*. Balance told an interviewer:

> . . . I'm fed up of hearing him speak over other people's work so we got him to say a load of words, from which we'll do an original cut-up . . .[256]

Speaking later, he also confirmed "We got him to speak some words to do a magical cut up"[257] – adding mischievously "We did hot knives with him . . .

He's always sort of in a netherworld even when you meet him"[258] – before going on to explain:

> If you got him on Thursday afternoon when he gets back from the clinic in Kansas where he had his methadone . . . he'd be dancing around like a kid, singing songs about falling in love with astronauts . . . He was brilliant on that day. His level of extrovertness [*sic*] was in direct proportion to the amount of time it was since Thursday afternoon.[259]

One can only assume that Balance and Christopherson were treated to an impromptu performance along the lines of this "astronaut serenade" from the Introduction Burroughs had written for a collection of the poems of his friend, John Giorno:

> As the poet says:
>
> You reckon ill who leave me out –
>
> When me you fly, I am the wings!
>
> Yes, maybe we will go along into space, invited or not:
>
> Heavily muscled Randy Scott,
>
> You're my favourite astronaut.
>
> Hunky Scotty, oh yooo-hooooooooooo –
>
> I'm going to hitch a ride with youuuuuu![260]

They also discussed the possibility of using ketamine, a dissociative substance more typically used as a veterinary anaesthetic, but which was starting to attract attention on the rave scene as a "post-club" drug believed to induce a plausible approximation of the famed Near Death Experience. As psychologist Todd Girard wrote in a joint paper in 2011, "Ketamine may disrupt patterns of brain activation that coalesce to represent an integrated body and self, leading to out-of-body experiences,"[261] but in the end the ageing psychonaut thought it might be too much of a risk to his health, and erred on the side of caution. Burroughs then signed a copy of *The Cat Inside*, reaching down to pick up a stray cat-whisker, which he affixed to the title-page as part of the dedication, just above his signature. Christopherson later summed up this last visit with Burroughs as follows:

> He was charming . . . He was like us in that he's not particularly sociable and quite happy to invite you to his house and make sure you've always got a drink in your hand but not actually talk that much, just sit for hours watching the cats. But he wasn't an unfriendly person; he was more shamanic in his demeanour. I'd have conversations with him on occasion but that was always an exception.[262]

Interlude:
The Moka Coffee Bar
(Slight Return)

By the time I was living in London in the late 1980s, the site of what had once-upon-a-time been the infamous Moka Coffee Bar in Frith Street had become The New Maxim's – one of those curious Soho establishments that sells porn upstairs and operates as a 'Hostess Bar' downstairs. The original Maxim's had been round the corner in Old Compton Street, until it was closed down after pressure from the Police and raids by the Vice Squad. Curiously, *that* Maxim's had originally started life as the "World Famous Maxim's Revue Bar" – originally located *next door* to the Moka, as can be seen from the photos William Burroughs took during his Playback Operations in 1972 – so by The New Maxim's setting up in Frith Street, *something* had clearly come full circle . . .

Although it is not actually mentioned in the account given in *The Job*, Burroughs alleged privately that the proprietors of the Moka Bar were Maltese: over 15 years later, despite the radical change in the nature of business conducted on the premises at 29-30 Frith Street, London W1, it was known to be in the hands of *Maltese gangsters*. Coincidence, or . . . ?23 years after I saw it last, The New Maxim's was still there – but at the time I tried to visit, at least, it was closed for business.

Perhaps somewhere there lurked a disgruntled former customer, flitting among the shadows like an Undercover Agent as he moves into Present Time, making his furtive recordings, as he takes his photos – only, these days probably on a mobile . . . ?

Once again, Playback stalks Frith Street – and the Ghost of William S. Burroughs

SMILES . . .

A Progressive Education

> From the diary of a six year old boy at the American School in Tangier Morocco: "I get up at 8.30. I eat my breakfast. Then I go to the job."
>
> When asked what he meant by the job he said, "school of course."[263]

September, 1982, and William S. Burroughs is in London for *The Final Academy*. Everybody wants to get their books signed, or have their photo taken with him. I choose to do neither, deliberately. Eventually I am in just the right place at just the right time. When I get a chance to speak to William in person, I ask him about magic – a common interest for most of the artists involved, one way or another – and whether he would care to recommend any books on the subject? Without hesitation he mentioned Dion Fortune's *Psychic Self-Defence*, even though he qualified it as "a bit old-fashioned." To break the ice, I talk about books: he is delighted to discover that I have read his beloved Denton Welch, also J. W. Dunne's *An Experiment With Time*. I have found them in my old school library, and know both have been a tremendous influence on him in different ways.

On something of a roll, I mention *Real Magic* by Philip Emmons Isaac Bonewits to Burroughs, and he acknowledges that it has "some good information"[264] – but is much more enthusiastic about *Magic: An Occult Primer* by David Conway. Many years later, I would discover from Conway himself that he and Burroughs had corresponded back in the early 1970s – but *that* is another story . . .

Knowing of his interest in Reich's Orgone Accumulator, I mention also that I have just read Colin Wilson's *The Quest For Wilhelm Reich*, published the year before. Burroughs likes Wilson, he says, jokes that "The Colonel" with his cottage in Wales in Wilson's *Return of the Lloigor* and his own "Colonel

Sutton-Smith" (also equipped with a cottage in Wales) from *The Discipline of DE* are one and the same. He had also taken the trouble to write an extensive and largely positive review of Wilson's *The Mind Parasites* when it had come out in 1967:

> Mind parasites, malignant beings who lurk in the deepest layers of the unconscious... (in precise physiological terms this would correspond to the back brain or hypothalamus) ...sapping the very life force of mankind, cutting him off from his natural capacity for self renewal... It was all so unsettling that I broke the habit of a lifetime and drank a bottle of champagne at lunch time.
>
> The means are at hand to conquer inner space but they are not being used. Despite impressive technical advances the planet is still in the stone age psychologically. Who would profit from turning the clock all the way back to the stone age and keeping man out of space? A parasitic entity that lives in the human body and could not survive space.[265]

Regrettably, the feeling was not mutual. Wilson once remarked to an interviewer:

> ... somebody rang me and said Bill Burroughs is in London and we're giving a party for him, and would you come along? And I said, honestly I can't see any point, because I don't like his work; I hate his work![266]

(The aforementioned David Conway also informed me that Colin Wilson once referred to Burroughs as "that *dreadful* man!"[267])

As Burroughs began to talk of Black Magic and Curses in North Africa, travelling with Medicine Men up the Amazon, and describing his experiments with tape-recordings and playback on the streets of London's West End and in the midst of the 1968 Chicago Democrat's Convention and ensuing riots, I realised that for Burroughs this was UTTERLY REAL. He talked about different kinds of perception, and I heard for the first time his famous remark that the purpose of all art and writing is "to make people aware of what they know but *don't know* that they know." He described the "Walk Exercise," in which you try to see everybody on the street before they see you:

> I was taught this by an old Mafia don in Chicago . . . sharpens your 'Survival IQ' . . . It pays to keep your eyes and ears open.

He told me about a dream that he had as a young man, working as an exterminator in Chicago: of watching from a helpless out-of-body point of view, floating above the bed, as his body got up and went out with some unknown and sinister purpose that he was powerless to influence . . . with a shudder, he told me that possession was "still the basic fear."[268]

In 1991, the writer Victor Bockris visited his old friend at home in Lawrence, Kansas, to talk with him for *Interview* magazine. During a discussion about author Whitley Strieber's alleged 'Alien Contact' experiences – and how Burroughs was finding the nineties "a very un-funny . . . very grim decade" – at one point Bockris was very upset about a "sense of being invaded", and the reply shows that for William S. Burroughs the old concerns had *not* gone away:

> You are no more invaded than the rest of us. When I go into my psyche, at a certain point I meet a very hostile, very strong force. It's as definite as somebody attacking me in a bar . . . What you have to do is confront the possession. You can do that only when you've wiped out the words.[269]

In later years, William Burroughs became increasingly preoccupied with different notions of immortality, one in particular being the immortality a writer may have through his work. In *The Place of Dead Roads* he writes:

> "Whenever you use this bow I will be there," the Zen archery master tells his students. And he means there quite literally.

The obvious comparison is with the writer:

Whenever anyone reads his words the writer is there. He lives in his readers.

And on a more personal note, speaking through his "Shootist" alter ego, Kim Carsons:

My saga will shine in the eyes of adolescents squinting through gunsmoke.[270]

Increasingly, however, as Burroughs moved toward Old Age he began to express himself more and more through a newfound love of painting, to the extent that it practically became a second career. With *The Western Lands*, the final volume of his acclaimed 'Red Night' trilogy, it seemed as if Burroughs was taking stock of his long life and looking back over his varied career. Many critics, fans and general readers alike found it hard not to take the book as his "farewell to literature" when they read the closing lines:

The old writer couldn't write anymore because he had reached the end of words, the end of what can be done with words . . . How long can one hang on . . . clinging always to less and less.

In Tangier the Parade Bar is closed. Shadows are falling on the Mountain.

"Hurry up, please. It's time."[271]

It was not to be the case, however. Although there is certainly a sense of taking stock, of settling scores and putting one's affairs in order about *The Western Lands*, it was by no means the last book from William S. Burroughs. No sooner had it been published, and the author taken time out to promote his newly developing "second career" as a painter, than he was telling interviewers:

. . . *Western Lands* is just the end of a cycle. But I'm already writing another, a short novel – *Ghost of Chance* . . . *[About]* Jesus Christ. And lemurs, and Captain Mission and the pirates – set in Madagascar. And then there's the Museum of Lost Species – or

Extinct Species, rather. There's a lot in there to do with magic, and miracles . . .[272]

As well as the slim novella, *Ghost of Chance* – illustrated with a collection of his own smeared inkblot calligraphies – there was a steady trickle of literary material: *The Cat Inside*, a meditation on what his adoption of cats had meant to him, not so much as domestic pets but more as psychic familiars:

> Evidence indicates that cats were first tamed in Egypt. The Egyptians stored grain, which attracted rodents, which attracted cats. (No evidence that such a thing happened with the Mayans, though a number of wild cats are native to the area.) I don't think this is accurate. It is certainly not the whole story. Cats didn't start as mousers. Weasels and snakes and dogs are more efficient as rodent-control agents. I postulate that cats started as psychic companions, as Familiars, and have never deviated from this function.[273]

Burroughs described how the various cats he had begun to gather around him served just such a function, reminding him of loved ones from his past:

> I have said that cats serve as Familiars, psychic companions. "They certainly are company." The Familiars of an old writer are his memories, scenes and characters from his past, real or imaginary. A psychoanalyst would say I am simply projecting these fantasies onto my cats. Yes, quite simply and quite literally cats serve as sensitive screens for quite precise attitudes when cast in appropriate roles. The roles can shift and one cat may take various parts: my mother; my wife, Joan; Jane Bowles; my son, Billy; my father; Kiki and other amigos; Denton Welch, who has influenced me more than any other writer, though we never met. Cats may be my last link to a dying species.[274]

Whether they came from dreams, borrowed from the work of other writers, or based on people he had actually known, characters were all-important to Burroughs. C. J. Bradbury Robinson – who knew him well during his years in Duke Street, London, when Burroughs was something of a mentor to the younger writer – has written that although Burroughs seemed to live a life of quiet solitude, he never felt that the older writer was lacking for company:

> He once said to me: I'm never alone, Brad – I have my characters . . . And one could sense they were there *in the room* . . .[275]

Burroughs himself had described on a number of occasions just how "alive" his characters were to him, sometimes in no uncertain terms:

> . . . any writer who hasn't jacked off with his characters, those characters will not come alive in a sexual context. I certainly jack off with my characters . . .[276]

The Cat Inside was also a final expression of the "Third Mind" with his old friend and collaborator, Brion Gysin, who provided simple elegant brush-stroke calligraphies of cats by way of illustration, even though he was dying slowly from inoperable cancer.

Then there was *My Education: A Book of Dreams* – partly inspired by Jean Genet's *Prisoner of Love*, and partly a meditation on themes that had recurred throughout the writer's long and often troubled life, as they came to him in his dreams. Burroughs had often stressed "dreams are a fertile source of material for writing . . . at least forty percent of my material derives from dreams"[277] – and now his dreams, painting, and writing were all influencing and feeding back into each other:

> And so dreams tell stories, many stories. I am writing a story, if it could be so called, about the *Mary Celeste*. I am painting scenes from the story I am writing. And I am dreaming about the *Mary Celeste*, the dreams feeding back into my writing and painting . . .[278]

A poignant development is that Burroughs experiences a number of dreams that took place in a consistent "afterlife" setting that he starts to refer to as

"The Land of the Dead" – these dreams become a roll-call of all the lost loved-ones from down the years:

> The Land of the Dead can be recognised by certain signs: The people are all dead and known to me, Mother, Dad, Mort, Brion Gysin, Ian Sommerville, Antony Balch, Michael Portman (Mikey), Kells Elvins. There is always difficulty in obtaining breakfast or any food for that matter . . .[279]

In addition, there was the first collection of *The Letters of William S. Burroughs, 1945 to 1959*, which allowed us to follow the life of Burroughs the Man after WWII – charting the development and increasing desperation of his addiction, his travels both inner and outer, and the inevitable consequences of his shooting Joan – as well as opening an at times eye-wateringly candid window onto the emergence of Burroughs the Writer, leading up to completion of *Naked Lunch* and the discovery of the cut-ups . . .

"Hurry Up, Please.
It's Time."

It was a hectic, portentous time . . . We all thought we were interplanetary agents involved in a deadly struggle . . . battles . . . codes . . . ambushes. It seemed real at the time. From here, who knows? We were promised transport out of the area, out of Time and into Space. We were getting messages, making contacts. Everything had meaning. The danger and the fear were real enough . . .

Remember when I threw a blast of energy and all the light in the Earl's Court area of London went out, all the way down to North End Road? There in my five-quid-a-week room in the Empress Hotel, torn down long ago. And the wind I called up, like Conrad Veidt in one of those sword-and-sorcery movies, up on top of a tower raising his arms: *"Wind! Wind! Wind!"*

It all reads like sci-fi from here. Not very good sci-fi, but real enough at the time. There were casualties . . . quite a number. So here I am . . . like the honorary agent for a planet that went out light-years ago. Maybe I am. Who will ever know?[280]

William S. Burroughs engaged with a number of methods & systems down the years, in the search for some method, special knowledge, or technique, which would free him to be whom he wanted to be, to live how he wanted to live – and, perhaps most important of all, liberate him from the ever-impending threat of possession by The Ugly Spirit. James Grauerholz, his companion and collaborator for 23 years from 1974 until Burroughs' death in 1997, said of him:

Burroughs often wrote about his belief in a "magical universe." He studied anthropology and comparative religions at Harvard and at Mexico City College, and he developed a view of the world that was based primarily on Will: nothing happens unless someone wills it to happen. Curses are real, possession is real. This struck him as a better model for human experience and psychology than the neurosis theories of Freud, in the end. But it also fit neatly into his personal experience of "Self and Other." For him, the Other was a deadly challenge to the Self, and never worse than when it manifested as "the Other Half," an Other *inside* . . . he did pursue a lifelong quest for spiritual techniques by which to master his unruly thoughts and feelings, to gain a feeling of safety from oppression and assault from without, and from within. The list of liberational systems that he took up and tried is a long one . . .[281]

As Burroughs himself would write in his journal, barely a couple of months before his death:

Do I want to know? I have tried psychoanalysis, yoga, Alexander's posture method, done a seminar with Robert Monroe (the *Journeys out of the Body* man), EST in London, Scientology, Sweat Lodges and a *yuwipi* ceremony.

Looking for the answer?

Why? Do you want to know *the secret?*

Hell, no. Just what I needed to know, to do what I can do.[282]

This was not all that different to the kind of concerns he had expressed to his friend, the editor and writer Graham Masterton, all those years ago at Duke Street:

To paraphrase a little what he said to me one evening (because I can't recall his exact words) "If there are procedures or rituals which we can use to communicate with the dead, what we need to discover is, how do they work? Belief, in itself, is not enough."[283]

In the early 1950s travelling in South America he took Yagé (now better known as Ayahuasca), a brew made by Medicine Men from the "Vine-of-the-Soul" that was said to induce telepathy and put you in touch with the

Ancestors – at one time quite literally being fellow traveller with the father of modern ethnobotany, and fellow Harvard man, Richard Evans Schultes.

Later, in Brion Gysin's Thousand and One Nights restaurant in Tangier, he would meet "the first rich hippies", John and Mary Cooke, who were key early supporters of L. Ron Hubbard. After hearing more about them and their methods from Gysin at The Beat Hotel in Paris, there was an intensive period with Scientology: first in London and then at Saint Hill, East Grinstead (which was the World HQ for a while in the 1960s, before 'Ron' took to the High Seas.) Burroughs was on board long enough to be declared "Clear" before falling foul of the Church's party line and deciding that Scientology was "a wrong number" – but even in the late 1980s he still spoke emphatically of the efficacy of some of their techniques, the uses of Auditing and the E-meter, while deploring what he saw as the crypto-fascist, religious aspects of the cult. His friend, the Scottish Beat writer and fellow addict, Alex Trocchi, was probably only half-teasing when he later told me, echoing Ian Sommerville, that "Bill was only interested in Scientology because he thought it would give him power over people."[284]

Burroughs had also dipped into Erhard Seminars Training, and the Silva Mind-Control Method, and was enthusiastic about research into Parapsychology and Sensory Deprivation. For a while in the 1960s in London he took a course called 'Mind Dimensions' that promised deep relaxation in a waking state, and attended workshops given by the psychic healer, retired army officer Major Bruce MacManaway:

> . . . saw group concentration lift a piano into the air. Piano weighed like 300 pounds at least. It was in London.

He gave a very convincing demonstration of White Magic:

> "You are going up through a tunnel of light. You will be met by kind guides and friends."[285]

The group of about twenty would use trance and visualisations of a pillar of light – Burroughs felt that the Major had definite ability, though, and after asking for help with a bout of sciatica compared the laying-on-of-hands to the tingling he had experienced in Reich's Orgone Accumulator.

American Return

> America is not a young land: it is old and dirty and evil before the settlers, before the Indians. The evil is there waiting . . .[286]

After his return to the United States in 1974, Burroughs began to re-engage with more traditional styles of writing such as the picaresque, as a way of combatting the writer's block that he felt was a dead-end almost inevitably brought about by his over-zealous commitment to non-linear, non-narrative – and even non-literary – experimentation. Using the tentative return to episodic, magical realist-style narrative that had characterised works such as *The Wild Boys* and *Port of Saints*, Burroughs began to work on what would eventually become his "comeback" novel, *Cities of the Red Night*, which would also be the first volume of his last great trilogy.

In June 1976, Burroughs moved into what had been the locker-room of a former YMCA at 222 Bowery – a large, bare, almost windowless space of concrete walls, floor, and ceiling, which became known affectionately as "The Bunker." Described by Victor Bockris as a "totally white, starkly lit cavern"[287] it was in the middle of a rundown area of bums and junkies in New York's Lower East Side, but the three locked gates and bulletproof metal door between Burroughs and the street were enough to make him feel secure. Apart from its security, The Bunker had other attractions, which Burroughs, as ever, would 'borrow' for a setting in his writing:

> More advanced and detailed incantations are carried out in the locker-room gymnasium of an empty school . . . "All that young male energy, so much better than a church my dead I mean my dear, all those whining snivelling prayers . . ."[288]

There was also the fact that Burroughs and some of his friends and visitors felt the place to be haunted, which doubtless prompted a number of his discussions at that time regarding ghosts and incubi and succubi, as well as various psychic experiments. As he would write in explanation regarding *Fear and the Monkey*, one of the very few of his texts that Burroughs identified as a *poem*, which revisits a number of familiar literary preoccupations:

> August 1978
>
> This text arranged in my New York loft, which is the converted locker room of an old YMCA. Guests have reported the presence of a ghost boy. So this is a Oui-Ja board poem taken from Dumb Instruments, a book of poems by Denton Welch, and spells an invocations from the Necronomicon, a highly secret magical text released in paperback. There is a pinch of Rimbaud, a dash of St.-John Perse, an oblique reference to Toby Tyler with the Circus, and the death of his pet monkey.FEAR AND THE MONKEY
>
> Turgid itch and the perfume of death
>
> On a whispering south wind
>
> A smell of abyss and of nothingness
>
> Dark Angel of the wanderers howls through the loft . . .[289]

Ever since his youth William Burroughs had been intrigued by magic and the occult, reading the Egyptian and Tibetan Books of the Dead and Eliphas Levi's *History of Magic* while he was at Harvard. Evidently, with his return from the Old World to the New, he had not left such interests behind. In 2007, Malcolm Mc Neill visited Ohio State University Archives to examine correspondence between himself and Burroughs in connection with *Ah Pook Is Here*, and later wrote:

> Most of the material in the box was familiar to me, but amongst the paperwork, I found one folder entitled "WSB Desk Scraps" that turned out to be especially enlightening. It was described as a collection of "newspaper clippings and odds and ends" that Bill had brought over from London. Amongst his little hoard of photos, bon mots, and aphorisms were several catalogues, business cards, and flyers from theosophist, spiritualist, and

occult societies. Otherworldly reference he'd considered important enough to bring with him across the Atlantic.[290]

Apart from the radical geographical shift of returning to his Native Land, Burroughs also found unexpected stimulation via the teaching positions that his old friend Allen Ginsberg had secured for him – which, although they started badly with bored, disinterested students who had no idea who he was, and were just expecting a minimum pass grade, would eventually bring him into contact with a new audience of young people who were inspired by his ideas, life, and writings, and would in turn inspire him. One in particular was a young man from the American Mid-West, James Grauerholz, who would become Burroughs' assistant, companion, and manager for the next 23 years, arranging lucrative Reading Tours and enabling him to be left alone just enough to get on with the work that he needed to do, while efficiently and respectfully taking care of the day-to-day business side of things.

In this new atmosphere, Burroughs would meet many young people, some of whom would become particularly close friends, even "amigos" – his usual designation for young men who, as well as assisting with household, routine, and even "secretarial" chores, were companions and also on-and-sometimes-off lovers. One of the first of these, who Burroughs had run into in a grocery store and again on the underground, was Steven Lowe, the son of an undertaker, who would become an important companion during his years at the Bunker in New York, being instrumental in providing the research about pirates that would eventually help catalyse and feed into *Cities of the Red Night*.

The writing of *Cities* infamously ran aground of a terrible writer's block: begun shortly after Burroughs' return to the U.S in 1974, it was not completed until 1981 – without doubt the longest time he had ever taken completing a book. The simple truth is that sometime in the late 1970s, living at the infamous Bunker on New York's Bowery, William Burroughs began fooling around with junk again and inevitably became re-addicted. A number of contributing factors can be considered, and have been proffered as explanations of a sort: that New York City at the time was awash with what has been described as a veritable tsunami of good quality, reasonably priced smack (the world heroin market became flooded with new supplies from Middle Eastern poppy fields after the fall of the Shah of Iran) – that the New York Punk culture, which had adopted Burroughs as its totem "Beat Godfather" enthusiastically mixed chemically-assisted hedonism and drug-fuelled nihilism – that the stream of fans and well-wishers who began to make the counter-cultural pilgrimage to the Bunker would bring offerings, only too happy, as Burroughs' Personal Assistant, James Grauerholz, would later put it, to "get high with the Pope of Dope"[291] – that the steady decline of his son, Billy Jnr., as a result of his own life of alcohol and drug abuse, and the unbridgeable emotional distance between them, was more than the usually cool and detached Burroughs could bear; and that Billy, despite considerable help and support from the likes of Ann Waldman, Allen Ginsberg, and Burroughs Senior, and displaying some talent as a writer, would die aged only 33, from complications following a liver-transplant . . .

Perhaps it was all of these, or none of these. Burroughs himself had said on a number of occasions that asking *why* somebody becomes an addict is about as much use as asking why somebody catches malaria, the implication being that addiction is simply "a disease of exposure."[292] Whatever the reason, by the late 1970s Burroughs had become re-addicted, and despite the inevitable costs, his needs could be taken care of pretty easily in New York. There were always younger friends like the writer Stewart Meyer or film-maker Howard Brookner who were prepared to take care of actually copping the dope, an increasingly risky proposition for Burroughs as a man in his sixties, despite blackjack, pepper-spray and swordstick (as former Hüsker Dü drummer and fellow junkie, Grant Hart, once remarked: "An old man with a cane is still just an old man."[293]) Elsewhere, however, it could be a major logistic problem. At more or less the same time, Burroughs' newfound career as Spoken Word performer was being managed by James Grauerholz to bring in some much-needed money for the aging writer. Although rewarding, both financially and in terms of recognition and reaching out to a new audience, going on tour meant going away from easy access to the street supplies of home.

A particularly vivid snapshot of this period in the life of William S. Burroughs, both junkie *and* writer, is given by the Dutch photographer, Gerard Pas. In a lengthy account he describes being along for the ride on a Reading Tour that took Burroughs to Brussels and Amsterdam in 1979, on the sole understanding that he was there to help take care of the author's drug needs. From connecting him to the local scene so he can score, to even helping him to shoot up ("On how I injected William Seward Burroughs 65 year old feet"[294]), and full acknowledgement of the "Devil's Bargain" that it could require to have access to or be a part of Bill's world, Pas gives a pretty unflinching glimpse behind-the-scenes.

At the same time that all this was happening, Burroughs had begun a regular teaching assignment at the first fully accredited Buddhist College in America, Naropa University in Boulder, Colorado, at the instigation of his old friend Allen Ginsberg, who was intimately involved with the setting up and organising of the college in association with his Tibetan Guru, Chögyam Trungpa Rinpoche. Also at the urging of Ginsberg, Burroughs would go on one of Trungpa's Spiritual Retreats, but could not agree to the stipulation that he should not take along writing materials, objecting:

> . . . a writer has to take it when it comes and a glimpse once lost may never come again, like Coleridge's *Kubla Khan*. Writers don't write, they read and transcribe. They are only allowed access to the books at certain arbitrary times. They have to make the most of these occasions. Furthermore I am more concerned with writing than I am with any kind of enlightenment, which is often an ever-retreating mirage like the fully analysed or fully liberated person. I use meditation to get material for writing.[295]

Burroughs kept a journal of the experience, later published as *The Retreat Diaries*, in which he explored his thoughts and feelings about Tibetan Buddhism, and the *tonal* and *nagual* of Carlos Castañeda's Don Juan, which leads to an attempt at something like a statement of position:

> As far as any system goes, I prefer the open-ended, dangerous and unpredictable universe of Don Juan to the closed, predictable karma universe of the Buddhists . . .
>
> I am not looking for a master; I am looking for the *books* . . .
>
> I will endeavour to summarise the highly complex and sophisticated system of spiritual training outlined by Don Juan . . . The *tonal* is the sum of any individual's perceptions and knowledge, everything he can talk about and explain, including his own physical body. The *nagual* is everything outside the *tonal*: the inexplicable, the unpredictable, the unknown . . .
>
> . . . the role of the artist is to make contact with the *nagual* and bring a part of it back into the *tonal* in paint or words, sculpture, film, or music. The *nagual* is also the area of so-called psychic phenomena . . .[296]

He also writes of his attempts at astral projection ("by the method outlined in Monroe's *Journeys Out of the Body*"[297]) in the hope of visiting significant friends who occur in his dreams, for example:

> I was thinking about Bradbury Robinson, an English friend who was then going in for Mystical Christianity . . .[298]

These considerations lead Burroughs to make an unequivocal statement of his ultimate divergence from Buddhism:

> Telepathy, journeys out of the body – these manifestations, according to Trungpa, are mere distractions . . . *[they]* are all means to an end for the novelist. I even got copy out of scientology . . . Any writer who does not consider his writing the most important thing he does, who does not consider writing his only salvation, I – "I trust him little in the commerce

of the soul."[299]

While he was teaching at Naropa, Burroughs also met a young student, Cabell McLean aka Cabell Lee Hardy, who would become another significant part of his inner circle. At first glance, Cabell could almost have stepped from the pages of one of Burroughs' novels. As artist Emma Doeve, who has illustrated his Burroughs-inspired prose, has commented:

> Cabell McLean was one of William Burroughs' "Wild Boys"
> but maybe a lone wolf separated from the pack.[300]

Cabell was descended from and named for the American literary innovator, James Branch Cabell, author of the epic fantasy classic, *Jurgen*.[301] He was a cross-dressing drug-taking gender-bending Wild Boy who also had an academic background in History, Literature & Medicine – having studied Elizabethan and Jacobean Drama, Fitzgerald, and his namesake, Cabell; reading Chaucer in the original and speaking Mandarin Chinese. After attending the University of Virginia, McLean first met Burroughs when he attended Naropa College as a Graduate in the late 1970s. Cabell came to the attention of Larry Fagin, who told him: "Where you need to be is with William. You're writing stories here, not poetry. Bill's the one you should be talking to." Anne Waldman and Michael Brownstein gave similar advice: "Go see Bill."[302] He decided to attend one of Bill's classes before making up his mind about approaching him, perhaps understandably more than a little awestruck and wary. As he would later describe:

> Although I had seen many images of William, I have to say I
> was unprepared for the real thing when I went to his class. I was
> completely taken aback by the ancient power that emanated
> from him. He simply amazed me, and I found myself almost
> speechless (a most unusual state for me, I can assure you!) I had
> the overwhelming impression of ancient wisdom. I realize now
> that I was seeing the sheer weight of the Ugly Spirit on him.
> The spirit he had carried for so long, the spirit that had been
> trying to write his way out of since his wife Joan's death . . . I

was hardly conscious of what he said during the class. I was too involved in watching his face, listening to the sound of his voice. I felt I was absorbing his words as one does the rays of the sun.[303]

Between 1977 and 1983, McLean benefited from the direct tutelage of Burroughs in his literary endeavours. He collaborated with Burroughs on *Gay Gun* – which was the starting point for what would become first *The Johnson Family* and, ultimately, *The Place of Dead Roads* – and the first-ever excerpt was published as "From Gay Gun" in the *Washington Review* volume 3 number 4, December-January 1977-78, and attributed to William Burroughs *and* Cabell McLean.

As well as sharing a flat with Burroughs Senior, McLean also hung out, fought, and was friends with his ill-fated son, Billy Jnr., was published alongside Jim Carroll, Gregory Corso, and Allen Ginsberg, and over time became close to Herbert Huncke and his long-term companion, Louis Cartwright. Another mutual friend of Huncke *and* Burroughs, who would hang out at The Bunker and also met Cabell, was Leslie Winer – the tall, androgynous supermodel that everybody thought was a boy, who recorded what would later become the proto-Trip Hop cult album, *Witch*, and lived with Jean-Michel Basquiat for a year before turning her back on the world of Fashion:

> for me he was just someone i knew. a kind human i enjoyed spending time with. i met him when i was 17 (late 70s nyc) – introduced by a mutual friend – he asked for my phone number, called me the next day & i spent 4 or 5 years going over there in the afternoons & so forth. if i had to characterize our relationship i would say it was more like a grandfather granddaughter dynamic. our friendship wasn't based upon the fact that he was 'william burroughs' . . .[304]

The film-maker and poet, Marc Olmsted, who was a companion to Allen Ginsberg in the late 1970s, has written a vivid account of meeting with Burroughs and telling him of a dream in which he had seen him with a face covered in tattoos, like the character Quequeg in *Moby Dick*, and been told that Burroughs was a master of Peruvian magic. On hearing this, Burroughs replied:

"I *am* a master of Peruvian magic, my dear."[305]

Olmsted also mentions that Burroughs appeared to have a new "cool queer secretary" from Naropa, Cabell, who for the time being at least had somewhat displaced James Grauerholz – which perhaps goes some way to explaining the "sibling rivalry" between them. Cabell McLean gets a pretty bad rap when he is mentioned at all in the "official" Burroughs biographies, painted as little better than a cross-dressing, drug-taking, groupie rent-boy. His surviving long-term partner of 18 years, artist and Santeria priest, Eric K. Lerner – and others that knew him as part of the inner circle around Burroughs at the Bunker, such as the aforementioned Stewart Meyer and Leslie Winer – are quick to acknowledge that, although Cabell was certainly no saint, his bad behaviour was pretty typical of the scene at that time. Some sources have suggested – usually *off the record*, of course – that the negative portrayal of Cabell that has lingered in certain circles is nothing short of old-fashioned jealousy, plain and simple, because of his intimacy with and access to Burroughs. You do have to ask, *if* McLean really *was* quite the pain-in-the-ass that is suggested, *why* Burroughs continued any kind of relationship with him at all – beyond, say, a casual fling – yet alone such a close and creative one as lasted for the best part of seven years? *Something* clearly meant enough to both men for them stay in touch for another fourteen years after they ceased to be romantically or sexually involved, and they stayed friends for the remainder of Burroughs' life until he died in 1997. Cabell McLean tragically died of complications of Hepatitis and being HIV+ in 2004, after several years of largely unacknowledged work trying to assist and educate about HIV and AIDS. He remained a prolific writer right up until his death, producing two novels, screen treatments, short stories, poems, essays and numerous technical articles and a book on AIDS treatment and activism, the 302-page *ARIC's AIDS Medical Glossary*. In a memoir that he was working on right up until his death, he wrote:

> . . . I lived with Bill Burroughs between late 1976 and early 1982. For aficionados of Bill's work, that means I was with him during much of the work on what is perhaps his greatest endeavour, the *Red Night* trilogy. I came into his life just before the final edits of *Cities of the Red Night* were completed, was with him throughout the writing of *The Place of Dead Roads*, and the beginnings of work on what would eventually become *The Western Lands*.
>
> I came to Bill originally because I wanted to learn how he wrote those absolutely incredible books. Our relationship was based on a simple arrangement: I helped out when I could, kept him company, paid my share of expenses, and so forth, and he taught me all he could. From Bill I learned, really, how to write all over again, from scratch. That wasn't his idea, but mine. As soon as I saw Bill work at close range, it became painfully clear that everything I thought I knew about writing was completely *bass ackwards*.
>
> Under Bill's tutelage, I learned to be a "workmanlike" writer, to use his phrase. I collaborated with him on instructive experiments, learned research techniques, went with him to scout locations he wished to use in his work, did "walk-throughs" of scenes, and so forth. We travelled, entertained friends (both famous and not so famous), and always, always we talked and laughed and drank together. I felt then I was the most fortunate person in the world, and I still feel that perhaps these were the best days of my life . . .[306]

Whatever their difficulties together, long after they had parted Cabell would remain present for William Burroughs, being mentioned in both *Last Words* – in which a footnote confirms "Cabell Lee Hardy was Burroughs companion in Boulder, Colorado in the late 1970s, and they remained friends thereafter"[307] – and, somewhat more enigmatically, in several of the dreams recorded in *My Education*, such as:

Boulder at sunrise . . . .36-caliber pistol . . . It was me all the time of course . . . Cabell was me . . . the curse came down from me . . .[308]

McLean's surviving partner, Eric K. Lerner, informs me that James Grauerholz sent both a contribution towards funeral expenses and a wreath when Cabell died.

In his many articles and interviews, during his time teaching at Naropa, and in person, William S. Burroughs could be remarkably consistent as to the books he recommended – such as the poetry of his beloved Rimbaud or St. John Perse, or the prose of Jane Bowles or Denton Welch: "Both writers are masters of the unforgettable phrase that no one else could have written"[309] – as well as Jack Black's hobo confessional, *You Can't Win*, or Joseph Moncure March's 1928 book-length narrative poem of Prohibition Era melodrama, *The Wild Party* ("It's the book that made me want to be a writer" Burroughs enthused on the dust-jacket of the 1994 reprint.)

As well as the early literary inspirations, Burroughs was equally quick to acknowledge the books that had influenced his more esoteric thinking, from the oft-cited Carlos Castañeda, Dion Fortune, and books about the Assassins, to the later impact of Norman Mailer's 1983 epic, *Ancient Evenings*, with its exploration of Ancient Egyptian beliefs about the afterlife and system of seven souls, and the splendidly titled *The Origin of Consciousness in the Breakdown of the Bicameral Mind* (1976) by psychologist Julian Jaynes, which Burroughs felt explained much about the nature and origin of imaginary voices and verbal hallucinations, the possibility of telepathy – and perhaps even the location and function of 'Word' within the human brain.

There was also the enduring interest in those books, like the Egyptian and Tibetan Books of the Dead, which he had first encountered in college at Harvard, which combined both an earlier form of picture-based writing, and were also intended as manuals for spiritual survival out-of-the-body and navigation of post-mortem states. Later, Burroughs would add the picture-books of the Ancient Maya, comparing and contrasting what he considered the essential difference in their function and intent:

> The Mayan codices are undoubtedly books of the dead ; that is to say, directions for time travel. If you see reincarnation as a fact then the question arises : how does one orient oneself with regard to future lives ? Consider death as a dangerous journey in which all past mistakes will count against you . . .
>
> For this reason I consider the Egyptian and Tibetan books of the dead, with their emphasis on ritual and knowing the right words, totally inadequate. There are no right words . . .[310]

Burroughs had always spoken consistently of the importance of dreams and the influence of psychic factors in his work, for instance:

> When I was writing *The Place of Dead Roads*, I felt in spiritual contact with the late English writer Denton Welch . . . whole sections came to me as if dictated, like table-tapping.[311]

Maurice Denton Welch (1915-1948) was an English writer, now sadly overlooked, who produced a handful of novels, poems and short-stories in the 1940s. At the age of 20, a motorist knocked from his bicycle, leaving him an invalid and in great pain, apparently only finding occasional relief thereafter when given a pain-killing injection of morphine:

> At first Denton did not believe in the power of the syringe, 'but the moment she pricked me so heartlessly, pushing the needle right in with vicious pleasure, I had faith; I knew that it was magic'.[312]

For the rest of his short life he would be crippled, and often bed-ridden. The product of an upper-class English background, Denton was homosexual and about as repressed as it was possible to be by almost all the circumstances of his sad young life, but his writing was the one place in which he could find a kind of freedom. Burroughs had first been introduced to Welch's writings in the late-1940s, when Jack Kerouac had loaned him *Maiden Voyage*, a coming-of-age tale of travelling from a relatively carefree colonial childhood in Hong Kong to the unhappiness of boarding school in cold, dull, grey Home Counties England. Many people find Welch's writing far too precious and mannered – apparently Brion Gysin just could not *stand* him – but Burroughs continued to remember his reading of Welch fondly, enthusing about him to friends in London like C. J. Bradbury Robinson in the late 1960s and Jim Pennington of Aloes Press in the early 1970s. Later, back in the States, Burroughs was re-introduced to his work, and experienced it as a revelation:

> It was not until I reread Denton in 1976 that I realized the full extent of his influence. My Kim Carson (the hero of *The Place of Dead Roads*) *is* Denton Welch. In 1976 I spent the winter in Boulder, Colorado. Cabell Hardy, with whom I shared an apartment, managed to borrow *Maiden Voyage*, *In Youth Is Pleasure*, *A Voice Through a Cloud*, *The Journals*, a book of short stories called *Brave and Cruel*, and a volume called *A Last Sheaf*. These constitute almost the whole of Denton's literary output written over a ten year period. Denton Welch makes the reader aware of the magic that is right under his eyes . . .[313]

The "Priest"
They Called Him

I must Create a System, or be enslav'd by another Man's;

I will not Reason and Compare: my business is to Create.

William Blake, *Jerusalem.*

What of those identifying themselves as magicians or occultists? What have they made of Burroughs and his work? Phil Hine, an early innovator and leading light of Chaos Magic, as well as an exponent of Freestyle Shamanism and Tantra, had this to say:

> I'm greatly indebted to Burroughs' writing for enabling me to discover the 'nightmare culture' of sexuality, drugs and magick. Though I was first turned on to magick through the drawings of Austin Osman Spare, I realised that it was the work of Burroughs that awoke in me the desire to visit alien landscapes, and cross in to the various 'zones' forbidden by society in general . . . Over the years I have come to regard Burroughs' work as an 'astral grimoire'; or launch pad from which to explore male sexuality and magick.[314]

At the time of the 30th anniversary of *The Final Academy* series of events, I interviewed Phil Hine for the "unofficial celebration" *Academy 23*, and he talked openly about how his first encounter with Burroughs had been the fairly predictable interest in sex and drugs and rebellion of the "angst-ridden teenage outsider"[315] – but that when he began to engage with magic more seriously in his late teens-early twenties, he came to re-examine Burroughs and his Work more seriously:

> . . . mid-to-late-80s that I came back to Burroughs with a specific 'magical eye'. And I think one of the things that interested me in what Burroughs was saying about magic is that

he was very much writing from a queer gay man's attitude to magic – and at that time there was very little that allowed homosexuality into magic in any kind of positive way.[316]

He also agreed that there is a continuing ambivalence and denial about various aspects of Burroughs' Life and Work – for instance the number of straight readers, occultists or not, who are "a bit wary of the sexuality angle. It's almost as if they want Burroughs to be straight"[317] – as well as a comparable squeamishness about his engagement with the occult. Phil Hine is certain in his assessment, however:

> Well I think it's pretty clear from his writings that he was an occultist. I think the other problem with Burroughs and the occult is he's not an obvious occult writer. A lot of occultists will tend to only read occult writing, and anybody who doesn't have a pentagram on the cover of their book is not thought of as being relevant. And I think that kind of mentality has perhaps prevented him getting people looking at him as an occultist. His occultism is just a feature of his life, rather than a major raison d'être of his work. I mean he's not like Crowley for example – but he's no.netheless interesting because he's somebody whose experimented with occult forms quite openly in his life, and brought them into his fiction – and discusses them quite openly in his interviews.[318]

Of the 'family tree' that reaches from Industrial pioneers Throbbing Gristle through Psychic TV and ultimately to Coil, much fruit has been borne relating to Burroughs and Gysin, the cut-ups, and The Third Mind – more than I will attempt to document here, in fact – but highlights have included a Dutch edition of the key Burroughs text, *The Electronic Revolution*, for which John Balance provided the introduction and Peter Christopherson the layout and cover-design. Also, towards the end of his life, while visiting with him in Lawrence, Kansas, they observed how Burroughs incorporated sigil magic into his shooting practice, and also recorded him for use in the sadly unrealised project, *Wounded Galaxies Tap At The Window*. Balance explained:

. . . we asked him to recite certain key words and phrases for us. This material has a shamanic quality to it, really it is a magickal spell. This is where we connect with William; he describes the invisible world, he documents the hidden mechanisms. This is what we also seek out; the secret mechanisms, the occult . . .[319]

Peter 'Sleazy' Christopherson knew Burroughs from the early days of Throbbing Gristle, and his own use of pre-recorded sound and tapes in TG had been directly inspired by him. He visited Burroughs in New York at his Bunker, where they would discuss the possible use of Christopherson's photos for an edition of *The Wild Boys*, and conduct Raudive-style tape experiments. He would be instrumental in the release of an LP from Burroughs' audio archive, *Nothing Here Now But The Recordings*, on TG's Industrial Records, and later still Burroughs would acknowledge Coil as the main successors to his and Brion's work at The Beat Hotel. Christopherson said:

My perception of Burroughs' work is that things that happen in his books happen in a spirit world where there isn't really any self-consciousness, intellectualisation or present time really. The time they take place in isn't the annihilating reality of now. It is some other space altogether . . .[320]

More recently, Genesis Breyer P-Orridge has written a lengthy, in-depth text all about his encounter with Burroughs, Gysin, and the cut-ups, *Magick Squares and Future Beats*, in which he concludes:

I believe that a re-reading of their combined body of work from a magical perspective only confirms what they themselves accepted about themselves, that they were *powerful modern magicians.*[321]

He also stresses:

I strongly advise any reader who has been inspired to reconsider their picture of both the Beats and their world picture to look for an essay by William S. Burroughs titled *The Discipline of Do Easy* or *The Discipline of DE* which is part of the book

Exterminator! In my own private, alchemical life, a rigorous and continual application of this idea has been as central to my uncanny achievement of countless goals as the Austin Osman Spare system of sigilization.[322]

The film-maker and self-professed magician Kenneth Anger has recently spoken of the Occult activities of Burroughs and Gysin in the 1960s: in particular their scrying experiments, and also how at the time of the moon landings, they would clip newspaper photos of the astronauts to place spells on them, in the hope that they would make contact with non-human intelligences!

It is perhaps somewhat ironic that Anger makes this revelation appearing in Nic Sheehan's documentary, *FlicKeR*, a film in celebration of Brion Gysin and the Dreamachine, if one takes into account the obvious antipathy that apparently existed between the two. In his recent "definitive and official" biography, *Call Me Burroughs: A Life*, Barry Miles describes an incident in which Burroughs, dining with Gysin and Sommerville at one of his favourite restaurants, the otherwise deserted *Renommé*, feels himself subjected to a sudden case of psychic attack:

> Bill had gone upstairs to the lavatory, when he was suddenly hit by a wave of hostility. He leaned against the wall, gasping, "I'm dying, I'm dying, I'm dying!" At that moment the Yugoslavian owner came up the stairs and said something and the sensation disappeared. Bill returned to Brion and Ian, who were downstairs . . . Brion said, "Kenneth Anger, very definitely." Bill agreed. Anger was noted for throwing curses all over the place, even threatening his best friends like the Rolling Stones.[323]

In their excellent and ground-breaking book, *Demons of the Flesh: The Complete Guide to Left Hand Path Sex Magic*, Zeena and Nikolas Schreck make several references to the writings of Burroughs. In fact, just after the title page, a quotation from Burroughs sits alongside one from Andre Breton ("Desire is the great force") and another from Goethe's *Faust* ("The Eternal Feminine draws us onwards") to welcome us to the book:

> Let's talk about the most mysterious subject of all, sex. Sex is an
> electromagnetic phenomenon.

Zeena and Schreck refer to Burroughs, Gysin and the "third mind" in their
Introduction (titled *Foreplay*, appropriately enough) and make reference to
his exploration of Scientology. There is also a discussion of his interest in
astral projection and dream states, mentioning Robert Monroe's *Journeys Out
Of The Body* – a firm favourite with Burroughs – which goes on to examine
"demon lover" phenomena:

> If we are going to investigate incubi and succubi seriously, I
> really feel that we must begin by admitting that psychiatrists
> have no more objective proof that they come from our
> imaginations than priests have that they come from the devil . .
> .[324]

They also include his novel, *Cities of the Red Night*, and the book of interviews,
With William Burroughs: A Report From The Bunker, by Victor Bockris, in their
extensive bibliography – but the key statement made about Burroughs in
Demons of the Flesh surely has to be:

> One of the most useful and practical approaches to sex with
> daemonic entities has been provided from a perhaps unexpected
> source: the author William S. Burroughs, whose writings and
> interviews consistently reveal a perception and working
> knowledge of erotic initiation rarely observed in more
> traditional magical specialists.[325]

Zeena and Nikolas Schreck are both former associates of the Church of
Satan and the Temple of Set, with a lifetime's experience of Left Hand Path
practices ranging from Western "Black Magic" to Tibetan Buddhism; they
now head their own Sethian Liberation Movement, in which they seek to
combine devotion to the Ancient Egyptian god-against-the-gods, Set, with
Tantric Shakti, so it is surely worth noting also when they describe the

"homosexual sex magic rite which begins with an invocation of Set" from Burroughs' 1981 novel, *Cities of the Red Night*, as "credible."[326]

The ritual in question takes place in the chapter *Are you in salt* (a phrase deriving from the "unexplained voices on tape" of Konstantin Raudive's *Breakthrough*) – in which the private investigator, Clem Snide, is trying to decide how best to proceed with a Missing Person case that has begun to look like Ritual Murder:

> Back at the loft we decided to try some sex magic. According to psychic dogma, sex itself is incidental and should be subordinated to the intent of the ritual. But I don't believe in rules. What happens, happens.
>
> The altar is set up for an Egyptian rite timed for sunset, which is in ten minutes. It is a slab of white marble about three feet square. We mark out the cardinal points. A hyacinth in a pot for earth: North. A red candle for fire: South. An alabaster bowl of water for water: East. A glyph in gold on white parchment for air: West. We then put up the glyphs for the rite, in gold on white parchment, on the west wall, since this is the sun-down rite and we are facing west. Also we place on the altar a bowl of water, a bowl of milk, an incense burner, some rose essence, and a sprig of mint.
>
> All set, we strip down to sky clothes and we are both stiff before we can get our clothes off. I pick up an ivory wand and draw a circle around our bodies while we both intone translations of the rite, reading from the glyphs on the wall.
>
> *"Let the Shining Ones not have power over me . . ."*
>
> We pay homage to the four cardinal points as we invoke Set instead of Khentamentiu, since this is in some sense a black ritual . . . It is time now for the ritual climax, in which the gods possess our bodies and the magical intention is projected in the moment of orgasm and visualized as an outpouring of liquid gold.[327]

It seems highly likely that this ritual in Burroughs' work of fiction is largely based upon what is described as "The Egyptian Master Ritual" in David Conway's early-1970s bestseller, *Magic: An Occult Primer*. There are a number of quite specific details that can all be found in the ritual in Conway's book, from the many sensory and visual cues – such as "a flower at each cardinal point . . . an ivory wand . . . a small bowl of milk . . . a bowl of water . . . mint" – to the caution that "works of discord, destruction or death . . . have to be confined to sunset."[328] It is not hard to imagine that Burroughs is drawing his inspiration from Conway's advice that:

> For kliphothic intentions the name of Seth (Set) is generally substituted for that of Khentamentiu. Seth, the slayer of Horus *[sic]*, has rightly or wrongly become the patron of 'black' rituals based on the Egyptian tradition.[329]

Apart from the fact that Burroughs referenced Conway's work a number of times with remarkably consistency, there may have been a more personal connection. Writing to David Conway after the launch of his memoir, *Magic Without Mirrors: The Making Of A Magician*, I broached the subject of Burroughs' "endorsement" of his earlier book, and he revealed that there had, in fact, been a correspondence between them. Although no mention is made of this in his otherwise quite candid and rather vivid memoir, David suggests that Burroughs initially approached him via a mutual acquaintance at Jonathan Cape Ltd – who had been the publisher of the first edition of *Magic: An Occult Primer* in 1972, as well as a number of titles by Burroughs:

> . . . we pledged that our exchanges would remain secret. That was his suggestion. He feared all manner of psychic repercussions, potentially harmful (but largely paranoid), were what we discussed to get "out." (And by "out" he had in mind more than just out into public knowledge.)[330]

True to his word, Conway would not divulge the actual content of his correspondence with Burroughs – explaining "in the event each of us burned the other's letters"[331] — but did offer:

> What I can mention is that of common concern to us was the access magic gives to a wellspring of power – a whole universe almost – which, in terms of conventional morality, is staggeringly evil yet ineffably beautiful. In confronting it, the magician becomes less the knightly hero that slays the dragon than the damsel who succumbs to its depravity. Here of course is the ugly-beautiful complementarity found in so many folk tales.[332]

He concluded:

> WSB was a man with the voracious curiosity of a precocious, if undisciplined, child. But he craved to experience things rather than merely to know them. In other words he sought to commit his total – not just cerebral – resources to that goal. Knowing one must lose oneself to find oneself, he feared this all-or-nothing approach might bring loss without deliverance. More specifically it might lead to the disintegration of his precarious selfhood rather than its emancipation. Those were the concerns he expressed to me (not always coherently) in our correspondence – and it explains why *[Dion Fortune's] Psychic Self-Defence*, as well my own approach, appealed to him. He was not first and foremost a "magician", any more than I am, but a human being for whom magic (among other techniques) might lead not just to enlightenment but to a glorious (and liberating) apotheosis of the self.[33]

"Nothing Is True, Everything Is Permitted. . ."

I say unto you: one must still have chaos in oneself to be able to give birth to a dancing star. I say unto you: you still have chaos in yourselves.

Friedrich Nietzsche, *Thus Spake Zarathustra.*

Even towards the end of his life, William S. Burroughs' engagement with The Magical Universe did not wane. The magical, psychic, spiritual and occult appear in his later fiction like never before, from depictions of astral travel and "sex in the Second State" to descriptions of actual rituals, referencing everything from Aleister Crowley and The Golden Dawn, to the Myths of Ancient Egypt, and even the dreaded, mythical *Necronomicon* of H. P. Lovecraft:

> This book is dedicated to the Ancient Ones, to the Lord of Abominations, *Humwawa,* whose face is a mass of entrails, whose breath is the stench of dung and the perfume of death, Dark Angel of all that is excreted and sours, Lord of Decay, Lord of the Future, who rides on a whispering south wind, to *Pazuzu,* Lord of Fevers and Plagues, Dark Angel of the Four Winds with rotting genitals from which he howls through sharpened teeth over stricken cities, to *Kutulu,* the Sleeping Serpent who cannot be summoned . . .[334]

All of this was interwoven with increasingly neo-pagan concerns for the Environment, the impact on Man and Nature of the Industrial Revolution with its emphasis on "quantity, not quality" and standardisation – as well as perceived turning points in History. His adoption of the Ancient Egyptian model of the Seven Souls, continuing development of a very personalised myth of Hassan-i Sabbâh and the Assassins of Alamut, and resistance to

Christianity ("the worst disaster that ever occurred on a disaster-prone planet . . . virulent spiritual poison . . ."[335]) made him of increasing interest and relevance to the new occultists who were emerging from successive generations of counter-culture that Burroughs had helped to shape through the example of his life and work.

In the early 1990s, the elderly Burroughs was initiated into the Illuminates of Thanateros, the leading Chaos Magic group, which had been founded in the late 1970s by pioneering English occultists, Peter J. Carroll and Ray Sherwin. Perhaps this was not such a surprising development. Many Chaos Magicians clearly felt a debt to Burroughs and his peers, and shared many of the same concerns as Thee Temple ov Psychick Youth: demystifying magic, yet at the same time distilling the best from Aleister Crowley and Austin Osman Spare, while taking advantage of the latest ideas emerging in computers, maths, physics and psychology. With the experiments started at The Beat Hotel, that he then took out onto the streets of London, Paris, and New York, William S. Burroughs was recognised as a definite pioneer and precursor: and with the later connections established through a younger generation of artist-occultists, the link from "cosmonaut of inner space" to "psychonaut" was assured.

It is suggested that William Burroughs' introduction to Chaos Magic had originally been via "Australasian Chaos Sorcery" practitioners, the Templum Nigri Solis. According to their own history, TNS formed in Australia as "an independent Magickal Temple" in the 1970s, drawing together members from a diverse range of backgrounds and practices. After meeting, comparing notes, and working with IOT co-founder (and then Head) Peter J. Carroll, during his "Grand Tour" of the 1980s, TNS agreed to affiliation and began "operating within the Pact of the Illuminates of Thanateros"[336] [although this connection would later be severed, around the time that Carroll stepped down from the Pact in 1995.] In due course, Burroughs would contribute an Introduction to the limited edition anthology, *Between Spaces: Selected Rituals*

& Essays From The Archives Of Templum Nigri Solis, which he described as "a working manual . . . a how-to book to guide the spiritual quest of Everyman" and enthused "the exercises described here are immediately workable."[337] Although relatively short, the Introduction is something of a showcase – including old favourites such as "It is necessary to travel. It is not necessary to live" and a slight misquoting of his old friend Alex Trocchi's famous "I am an astronaut [sic] of inner space" – as well as a virtual Statement of Position:

Science should be more Magical and intuitive, Magic more factual and scientific. This book is a step towards achieving such a synthesis and refuting some of the implicit dogmas of science that are quite as absurd as those of fundamental religion.

> Dogma One: The human will can never influence physical processes. This dogma is contradicted by common observation and common sense. People are wished to death every day . . . [338]

He continues by advising:

> Now the outer and the inner must merge – or more precisely re-merge, for they once were one. It is the task of the Magician, the Artist and the Scientist of varied disciplines to heal this ancient split . . .[339]

And then repeating the Buddhist warning that the Heaven Worlds may well be more dangerous to the seeker than the Hell Worlds – "Nothing is more dangerous to the spirit than security" – before signing off with "Keep moving, Pilgrim."[340]

Burroughs would establish a more personal connection with members of the IOT in the United States, as might be expected, as well as other Chaos Magicians visiting from the United Kingdom. Douglas Grant was North American Section Head for the IOT at the time Burroughs became involved, and oversaw his initiation as "Frater Dahlfar.23." Apparently:

. . . Douglas went shooting with him *[WSB]* – .45s at targets and shamanic paintings made by an American Indian shaman/ Vietnam vet . . .[341]

They bonded over a shared interest in the Old Man of the Mountains, Hassan-i Sabbâh, with his infamous Assassins of Alamut and credo, "Nothing is True, Everything is Permitted" – allegedly his Last Words – which had been adopted as an unofficial motto by the Chaos Magicians, and had also exercised considerable fascination for Burroughs, who had utilised him as a source after being introduced to the legend by Gysin, all those years ago at the Beat Hotel. He had even incorporated him as a character in *The Western Lands*, trying to imagine details of Sabbâh's life, the evolution of his ideas, and how he had gathered and communicated with his followers – going as far as to identify with him, through the similar struggles of his protagonist William Seward Hall, writing as Kim Carsons:

> What did Hassan i Sabbah find out in Egypt? He found out that the Western Lands exist, and how to find them. This was the Garden he showed his followers. And he found out how to act as Ka for his disciples.[342]

For his part, one of the contributing factors in Douglas Grant's interest in the possible relationship between photography and magick had been discovering the infamous "Playback" operation that Burroughs had conducted against the Moka Bar:

> Burroughs utilized Polaroid technology to cast a spell upon a coffee house that had wronged him. He theorized that by taking a Polaroid snapshot, the magician was taking the subject (be it person, place or thing) out of time and space. The person/ place/thing was then more malleable to an act of sorceric enchantment.[343]

Through Grant, Burroughs was introduced to fellow IOT USA initiates Robert F. Williams, Jr (better known as "Bob") and his wife, Stephani. They would later play host to visiting IOT members from the UK, such as Phil

Hine, Dave Lee, Ian Read and Ingrid Fischer, who all went on the pilgrimage to Lawrence, Kansas, for an audience with the new "Elder of Chaos." They also recorded an interview, *William S. Burroughs Addresses The Magickal Pact of the Illuminates of Thanateros*, which was shown as a video-presentation to an international gathering of IOT members at Lockenhaus, Austria, in August 1994. A transcript was also included in the first issue of the new *Kaos Magic Journal* of the IOT USA that same Summer. When asked whether there was "Any one incident in your life that confirmed the magical nature of the universe?" Burroughs replied:

> . . . oh yes, as a child – I don't know how old I was, just about 4 years old – I was sleeping or I had been sleeping, I woke up, it was dawn and I'd made a little block house the previous afternoon and I saw these little grey men playing in the block house, flickering and then gone – and they're gone through a sort of medium, a sort of invisible medium – it was something very definite, so I realized that there was this other reality just beyond that medium . . .[344]

There followed a wide-ranging discussion about "the State of the World Today" and the views of William S. Burroughs, which took in AIDS, Brion Gysin and painting, Colin Wilson's Space Vampires, Dr. Duncan Harvey and Einstein's brain, Iran, John Wheeler's Recognition Physics, so-called "luck" and the dangers of wishing, possession, Rwanda, Santeria and Yagé, and the question of "voluntary drug withdrawal as a self-induced initiatory state" – to which he remarked:

> Well, I've heard people talk about it but I've never seen it happen. I've never known of anyone who voluntarily would completely abstain from drugs that were available to him . . . Crowley made such a claim, but I doubt very much if it was valid. It's too painful . . .[345]

Interestingly, his framing message pulled no punches in identifying an enemy that was, perhaps, more than a little unexpected:

It seems to me that our deadliest enemy at the present time is not organized religion but the scientist . . . you see in the magical universe the underlying principle is that nothing ever happens unless some person, some being, wills it to happen – and this is absolutely the flat opposite of the scientist's assumption that the will has no effect whatever. Well . . . they're trying to deprive us of our Will, exactly what they're trying to do, they're deadly enemies.[346]

As we have seen, British occultist Phil Hine admits to having had a longstanding admiration for Burroughs, a figure he both looked up to in his youth as a role model for the Outsider Queer Gay Man, and also cites as an influence and inspiration for some of his own early experiments in Chaos Magic. He has written a number of articles on the subject, including *Bitter Venoms: The Magic of William S. Burroughs*, *Cacodemonic Copulations*, and *Zimbu Xototl Time*, in which he makes the following statements:

William S. Burroughs' 1969 novel *The Wild Boys* introduces several themes into the author's magical universe: the struggle to escape the mechanisms of social control; the search for transcendence of the biological trap of duality, and the narrator's ability to rewrite (and thereby destroy) his own past . . .

In his later works such as *Port of Saints*, *Cities of the Red Night*, and *The Place of Dead Roads* the wild boys continue their subversion by rewriting identity and history. In these works, Burroughs also returns to developing and articulating a magical technology based on sexuality in order to deconstruct social control mechanisms which prevent the evolution of the human artefact.[347]

When Bob Williams of IOT USA brokered the deal for Hine's book, *Condensed Chaos: An Introduction to Chaos Magic*, with American publisher New Falcon, through contact with James Grauerholz he was able to arrange to show the text to Burroughs, which resulted in the following endorsement:

Phil Hine's book is the most concise statement . . . of the logic of modern magic. Magic, in the light of modern physics, quantum theory and probability theory is now approaching science. We hope that a result of this will be a synthesis so that science will become more magical and magic more scientific.[348]

Subsequently, when Hine was over in the States in 1995, it was arranged that he would be taken to visit Burroughs. Bob Williams and his wife, Stephani, collected Phil Hine and his partner, Maria, for the drive to Lawrence, Kansas, where they met with the Old Man for a long afternoon of talk which took in everything from Chaos Magic to Painting and Tantra to Scientology – with Burroughs revealing how much animosity he still felt toward the movement's founder, L. Ron Hubbard. With regard to Burroughs and Tantra, Phil remarked:

I'm not so sure if he had specific interest in Tantra itself, but he definitely was interested in that whole kind of strain of ascetic practices . . . He was mainly interested in practices like pole-sitting – or become like anchorites and go out into the desert, or roll from one temple to another.[349]

One of the consequences of the meeting was that when Hine came to rewrite his second book, *Prime Chaos: Adventures in Chaos Magic*, he was able to get permission to use a detail of a painting by Burroughs, *The Creation of the Homunculus*, for the cover-art – although he explains that there was some initial resistance from the publishers, New Falcon, who didn't seem quite sure who Burroughs *was*, or perhaps his relevance to a book on Chaos Magic! Phil was also present at the gathering of the IOT in Austria at which *William S. Burroughs Addresses The Magickal Pact of the Illuminates of Thanateros* was played, and remarks:

. . . there were at least 4 or 5 people going "what the fuck's this about?" But again it's like because he's not an occultist they didn't quite see the relevance . . .[350]

Occultism aside, Hine remarks that his "lasting impression of Burroughs is his old world courtesy and his care to his guests" – explaining how during his visit with the elderly writer:

> . . . at some point me and Bob and – some other guy who was there, I can't remember his name – I think he was one of the guys that ran the October Gallery? [Author's note: most likely José Férez Kuri, former Director of The October Gallery and latterly independent Curator, who was in effect the main Art Dealer for WSB's paintings] – and William were all having this really heavy duty magical conversation, mostly between ourselves – and Maria felt a bit left out, I think. She went over and looked at one of the paintings. He got out of his chair, and he was very like doddery and frail by that point, and he took her on a complete tour of his house – showed her all the paintings: y'know, his paintings, Brion Gysin's paintings – and just talked to her about it, 'cos she's an artist – and I just thought, wow, y'know that's just . . . It showed for me his utter humanity and his care for other people.[351]

After Burroughs had died, Douglas Grant would write:

> Through a mutual interest in Hassan Ibn Sabbah, contact was made with William S. Burroughs. William expressed interest in the IOT and was subsequently initiated into the IOT, by myself and another Frater and Soror. William did not receive an honorary degree, he was put through an evening of ritual that included a Retro Spell Casting Rite, an Invocation of Chaos, and a Santeria Rite, as well as the Neophyte Ritual inducting William into the IOT as a full member . . . Though it is not included in the list of items buried with William, James Grauerholz assured me that William was buried with his IOT Initiate ring.[352]

For his part, in an interview conducted some years after William's death, James Grauerholz affirmed: *William was very serious about his studies in, and initiation into the IOT . . . Our longtime friend, Douglas Grant, was a prime mover; William met and liked Peter Carroll and Phil Hine, I am pretty sure.*[353]

As a footnote to this, I would just like to add that Eric K. Lerner – who, as well as having been partner to Cabell McLean for the last 18 years of his life, is also an initiated Santero: that is, a Priest of Santeria – informs me that, having seen papers relating to Burroughs' initiation into the IOT, "the Santeria part was put together by somebody who really knew what they were doing . . ."[354]

The Medicine Man
& The Ugly Spirit

> Listen, baby, I've been coping with this for so many years. I
> know this invasion gets in. As soon as you get close to
> something important, that's when you feel this invasion, and
> that's the way you know there's something there . . .[355]

But there was also still the loss, the pain, and – perhaps more than ever? –
The Ugly Spirit. During the writing of *With William Burroughs*, Victor Bockris
relates how Burroughs would attend a séance to try and make contact with
the spirit of Ian Sommerville, as well as another lost *amigo*. As well as the
séance (which proved inconclusive), through the auspices of his good friend,
the poet John Giorno – who was also a Tibetan Buddhist practitioner – he
would have an audience with His Holiness the Dudjom Rinpoche, who
specialized in "locating people who have died and informing the interested
party as to their well-being"[356] – but it was bad news all round: the monk
had looked at the photos of Ian which Burroughs had provided and
determined that Ian did not realise that he had died, and had been reborn as
an animal. Dudjom had then burned the photos in a purification ritual,
which further upset Burroughs as he didn't have copies.

In many ways, Burroughs' engagement with the many-and-varied aspects
of the Magical Universe – and just how it shaped his thinking, and then, of
course, by extension his work – became increasingly self-evident after his
return to the United States, and in no small part after his "return to narrative"
as it came to be known. The same book of interviews compiled and
conducted by Victor Bockris includes a section *On Dreams*, in which is stressed
just how important a source dreams have been to Burroughs as a writer:

> I keep a regular dream diary. Then, if they're particularly

interesting or important I'll expand them into dream-scenes that might be usable in a fictional context . . . Sometimes I get long sequential narrative dreams just like a movie, and some of these have gone almost verbatim into my work.[357]

A particularly striking section is one entitled *On Psychic Sex*, which is initiated by Bockris confiding in Burroughs that he has been experiencing what he can only describe as *strange dreams* and "extremely intense . . . sexual, hallucinations."[358] He is quite frank in describing how:

> Bill first expressed surprise . . . at my ignorance about such a visitation, explaining that this was clearly "a visit by the demon lover, my dear!"[359] *Bockris admits his ignorance of the subject – asking "What is a succubus?" – prompting Burroughs to explain:*

> My dear, according to the dictionary, a succubus is "a female demon supposed to descend upon and have sexual intercourse with a man while he sleeps." In the male form it is called an incubus . . .[360]

Warming to his theme, Burroughs expands on the whole area of psychic phenomena, such as out-of-the-body-experiences, stating his belief that "We urgently need explorers who are willing to investigate these uncharted possibilities"[361] and recommending Robert Monroe's book *Journeys Out of the Body*, which apparently includes a chapter on what is described as "Sex in the Second State" i.e. out-of-the-body, or "astral" encounters. Burroughs suggests that "This phenomenon has been going on since the beginning of time"[362] and quotes from Lewis Spence's *Encyclopedia of Occultism* concerning the pre-Old Testament myth that:

> "Adam was having sexual intercourse with Lillith, Adam's first wife and the Princess who presided over these demons known as succubi, for 130 years before the creation of Eve."[363]

Burroughs proceeds, once again, to recommend *Psychic Self Defence* by Dion Fortune, but cautions that "although she was an adept explorer into the occult" her attitudes to sex "were still bound by the period she lived in, so she was always outraged by the lewd sexual approach of these creatures."[364] He goes on to liken this to the received opinions and preconceptions he sees as having compromised the so-called "objectivity" of so many scientists, a favourite personal example for Burroughs being:

> . . . I suggested to a psychiatrist for example that witchcraft may have foundations in fact. "NO! The witch is an hysteric and the victim is a paranoid!" he screamed. "As a scientist, I must believe this." Scientists turn out to be as emotional about their dogma as medieval ecclesiastics . . .[365]

An example of how Burroughs was often able to bridge or apparently combine what might, at least at first glance, appear to be the contradictory impulses of science and magic, was his keen interest in some of the unusual devices or gadgets produced. Maybe it had something to do with the fact that while one of his grandfathers had been, of course, the inventor of the famous "Burroughs Adding Machine" the other had been a "circuit-riding Methodist minister" and church builder, so on some level his heritage was a strange combination of DIY Yankee pragmatism and spiritual non-conformity.

A number of curious gadgets had caught Burroughs' interest down the years because of their alleged psycho-spiritual benefits, or other such therapeutic properties. One of the first and best known was Wilhelm Reich's famed Orgone Accumulator: at its simplest, a box of alternating organic and metallic layers, said to somehow concentrate the life energy that Reich claimed he had discovered and named "orgone" and thereby confer energising and health-enhancing benefits on a test-subject. As his friend from Tangier, John Hopkins, recorded in his diary after visiting Burroughs once he had settled back in New York:

> Bill proudly showed me his fur-lined Wilhelm Reich orgone box where he spends several hours each day hoping to revive his creative powers.[366]

From the farm in Pharr, Texas to Duke Street in London, the Bunker on New York's Bowery to Learnard Avenue in Lawrence, Kansas – wherever Burroughs lived for long enough and was able, he would have an Orgone Accumulator built that was big enough to sit in.

Another such device was the E-meter central to the processing known as "Auditing" of the Scientologists. Although vociferously denied by Hubbard and his followers ever since, the E-meter – in its simplest form a pair of tin cans attached by wires to a galvanometer – is basically a device for measuring electrical resistance and skin conductance, and so, in effect, akin to a lie-detector. Although at the height of his interest in the methods of Scientology, Burroughs wondered whether the apparent subtle feedback effects of the E-meter during therapy sessions might not be "a sort of sloppy form of electrical brain stimulation"[367] that could also, perhaps, be used as "a lie-detector and a mind-reading machine"[368] in the end he declared:

> With further use of the E-meter I'm not at all sure that it isn't quite valueless.[369]

One of the last such "mind machines" to catch Burroughs' imagination was the so-called "Wishing Machine" – described by James Grauerholz as "a psycho-electronic device that can hold a small photo or object and be used to focus the wisher's intention"[370] – which he had read about in the book *On the Frontiers of Science* by G. Harry Stine (later republished as *Mind Machines You Can Build*.) Clearly Burroughs was very taken with the idea, mentioning it at length to his students in a lecture at Naropa, entitled *"The Technology and Ethics of Wishing"*[371] – although as Geff Rushton of the band Coil later commented, "To Burroughs' dismay nobody seemed interested"[372] – including it in a key episode towards the end of *The Western Lands*, and actually approaching an acquaintance, Lawrence eccentric Len McGruder, to build one for him:

> Directions for use are simple. You put a picture, nail clipping,

hair or anything connected with the subject of your wish
between two copper plates activated by a patented magnetic
device that runs on standard current. Then you make your
wish.[373]

Burroughs had always been a great believer in the power of the Will, of
wishing, and saw all these contested experiences, such as telepathy, ESP, and
astral projection, as being just as real as any of our so-called more "objective"
experiences – they were part-and-parcel of his belief *in* and experience *of*
the Magical Universe, and fundamental to life itself. Even with his common-
law wife, Joan, Burroughs had experienced a degree of telepathic exchange,
such as when they would play the "drawing game"[374] in which they would sit
at opposite ends of the room, divide a sheet of paper into nine squares, and
draw images at random in each square: a bottle, a dog, a scorpion. Afterwards,
when they compared images, there was often a surprisingly high degree of
correspondence between what they had both drawn.

As Burroughs would remark in an interview with his friend from the Lawrence
years, David Ohle:

> Anyone who doesn't believe in ESP simply hasn't kept his eyes
> open. It happens all the time. These dumb scientists. One said,
> 'I'll never believe in ESP, no matter what evidence there is.' The
> general tendency of scientific materialism is to deny such
> phenomena and the fundamentalists admit that it happens – but
> it's evil. The word of God says the occult is the enemy. The
> height of closed-mindedness.[375]

To Burroughs, this could not have been more at odds with what he saw as
being the fundamental purpose of writing – or ALL Art, of whatever kind,
for that matter:

> I postulate that the function of art and all creative thought is to
> make us aware of what we know and don't know that we
> know.[376]

He stated frequently throughout his career the firm belief that writing was about two things: Bringing It Back and Making It Happen – almost sacred acts, the ability or aptitude for which was akin to the calling of shaman or priest. It was also the gravest responsibility he could conceive of. In 1974, shortly after his return to the United States, Burroughs had been interviewed at length by the American academic and writer, John Tytell (author of *Naked Angels* and *Paradise Outlaws*, both about the Beat Generation, and now professor of English at Queens College, City University of New York), and one exchange in particular towards the end of their interview amounts to nothing less than a statement of position:

> JT: Rather than simply informing us of a vision of the future, as in *The Wild Boys*, I feel the ultimate end of your fiction is a kind of alchemy – magic based on precise and incantatory arrangement of language to create particular effects, such as the violation of Western conditioning.

> WB: I would say that that was accurate . . . Of course the beginning of writing, and perhaps of all art, was related to the magical. Cave painting, which is the beginning of writing . . . The purpose of those paintings was magical, that is to produce the effect that is depicted.[377]

Then, in 1986, Burroughs was asked about his more esoteric interests and inspirations in a radio interview with Tom Vitali:

> TV: So much of your work deals with the juncture between science and mystery, it seems. I mean there've been references to Orgone boxes, and Scientology, and Castañeda, it just goes on and on.

> *WB: Hm. Yes.*

> *TV: How did you get involved in this sort of area?*

> WB: Always was. I always was involved in that area from my early childhood. I was always interested in the occult and the mysterious . . . just a life-long preoccupation.[378]

Interviewed by Nicholas Zurbrugge after his return to the Mid-West, first in St. Louis in 1989 and then in Lawrence in 1991, Burroughs once again demonstrated a considerable consistency that carried over from his thinking about writing to his newly-preferred medium of painting:

> NZ: *Your work often seems more primitive, ritualistic or magical perhaps.*
>
> WB: It's supposed to be, yes. It's supposed to have an element of magical invocation.[379]

In the second of the interviews, Burroughs talks about the ecological and environmental concerns emerging in his later work, such as the *Red Night* trilogy and *Ghost of Chance*, and the connection to his more esoteric interests is made clear:

> I'm very interested in Indian shamanism now. Shamans can really call up the spirits, and there's one will be here in a couple of days, and I hope that he can demonstrate.[380]

For Burroughs, as ever, the worlds of art and the spirits and writing are all still related:

> Genet says some extraordinary things about writing. He says that 'The writer undertakes the responsibility for the characters he creates', which he regards as real – as real beings, which I do, too. As Klee says, 'Any serious artist is trying to create something with a life of its own, apart from the creator, and apart from the canvas' – the canvas and the words are very much the same thing.[381]

Enthusing about the New Age magazine, *Shaman's Drum* – "I read these from cover to cover"[382] – Burroughs explains how some of the spirits have appeared in his paintings, but when he is asked if his interest in "things like shamanism" is "because it's a return to something fundamental and substantial" he counters:

> Well, it's not necessarily a return, but going on – going on to some sort of basic change, biologic change, mutations.[383]

Speaking of changes, it was of course inevitable and even necessary that life would change for William Burroughs as he returned to the Mid-West of his birth, away from the pressures and temptations of New York, and began to gradually make at least a few concessions to his advancing years:

> Queer to think of him now living in Lawrence, Kansas, meticulously dressed in his undertaker suit and grey fedora, a cross between T. S. Eliot and Dashiel Hammett, poking through the cat food at the local Kroger's then out to aim his Smith & Wesson at backyard canvases in the pursuit of instant "shotgun art," winding up reading H. P. Lovecraft by night lamp while in the dry distance the Santa Fe railroad conductor blew his midnight whistle on the lonesome way from Wichita to Topeka . . .[384]

As it had been at the Bunker, so it continued in Lawrence, with an inevitable round of visitors: from old friends and colleagues, such as Gregory Corso, Allen Ginsberg, Timothy Leary, and Patti Smith, as well as film-makers, students and would-be writers, to occasional fans, who made the pilgrimage in hope of a brief audience with the Old Man of the counter-culture. The journals published posthumously as *Last Words* reveal dealings with the actor, Steve Buscemi – long an ardent admirer, who hoped one day to make a film of *Junkie* – to the Irish rock band, U2, who had screened Gus van Sant's short film of Burroughs' *A Thanksgiving Prayer* as part of the opening of their stadium-touring multimedia *Zoo TV* show. U2 would film Burroughs for the promo video for their single, *Last Night On Earth*, at the end of which he would surprise everybody with an unscripted moment revealing that the cane he had been carrying was, in fact, a sword-stick. The 83-year-old writer would turn to the camera, brandishing the blade, and paraphrase the words of Jesus Christ:

"I bring not peace but a sword."[385]

One of the more unusual visitors, and doubtless at the other end of the spiritual spectrum to U2, was Steven Johnson Leyba: a young painter and performance artist who claimed Mescalero Apache ancestry, and had also been initiated as a Reverend in Anton LaVey's infamous Church of Satan. Leyba courted controversy, combining extreme elements from BDSM and Body Art, such as scarification, genital piercing, and blood-letting, with trials of pain and endurance allegedly inspired by Native American Indian tribal initiation rites. Gathering together his fetishistic, graphic, artwork – utilising heavy acrylic and oil paint, multi-layered collage, and invariably adorned with semen, blood, and Indian-style bead-working – into elaborate self-published albums that are talismanic objects in their own right, Leyba had sought out endorsement from other such confrontational and transgressive artists as Genesis Breyer P-Orridge, H. R. Giger, Poppy Z. Brite and Clive Barker. Making the pilgrimage to Lawrence to show Burroughs his first collection, *My Stinking Ass*, Leyba was rewarded with the following:

> Johnson sees a subject as it is, sees an asshole or a cock as is without a stroke of simpering prurience, or irrelevant repugnance. There it is like a stone, a tendril, a plum. Like a cray fish hole, a mushroom. A crinkled leaf. He sees and puts what he sees on a canvas.
>
> Oh ass where is thy clutch?
>
> Oh cock where is thy sting?
>
> Oh shit where is thy victory?[386]

After settling in Lawrence, Kansas – a small University town, far from the distractions and temptations of New York, and very much a reminder of his Mid-Western background in St. Louis – Burroughs became friends with William Lyon, a Professor of Anthropology, who had been apprenticed to Sioux Medicine Man Black Elk. As Burroughs told an interviewer:

> A friend of mine called Bill Lyon – an anthropologist who specialises in shamanism – has spent twelve years with Wallace Black Elk, and he wrote a book – *Black Elk: The Sacred Ways of a Lakota*. He tells how Black Elk calls up spirits – animal spirits of

all kinds. He's done it in front of physicists.[387]

Lyon was now working with a Navajo Indian shaman, Melvin Betsellie, and had dug a sweat lodge next to the house he was renting – which just happened to be the old stone house on a hill outside of town that Burroughs had first lived in when he moved to Lawrence. A full purification ceremony was arranged in an attempt to evict The Ugly Spirit, which Burroughs explained was:

> . . . very much related to the American tycoon. To William Randolph Hearst, Vanderbilt, Rockefeller, that whole stratum of American acquisitive evil. Monopolistic, acquisitive evil. Ugly evil. The ugly American. The ugly American at his ugly worst. That's exactly what it is.[388]

Included among those who took part in the ceremony along with Burroughs, was his former lover and friend of over fifty years, the poet Allen Ginsberg, who wrote a detailed and revealing account:

> We sat with towels in the black dark smoky plastic igloo . . . a fire pit in center . . . as the big-bellied shaman went 'round the tent thanking each one there, Bill first, for inviting him to share the grandfathers' medicine and again giving him the opportunity to drive the bad spirit out of Bill's life and body. Then he prayed to the grandfathers, water, earth, rocks and green coal . . . to the creator, the grandfathers, the elements, to help Bill on his way, make his way easy when it's time for him to go back to the creator, make him strong to live a long long time, and to us all to think of Bill and send him our healing thoughts, get rid of the bad element that was in the coal, send the bad spirit back to the one who'd put it in Bill, maybe an animal, maybe someone angry. The spirit was caught, jiggled in the shrill flute & blown into the fire. Put the spirit into the rocky fire pit still glowing, steaming with cedar-fragrant smoke in our eyes.
>
> Last round of pipe and tobacco were passed 'round, sweet mild tobacco. We puffed three or four times each from the long-stemmed stone-headed heavy pipe. Thank ancestors, thank

water, stone, sky, wood, varied elements, spirits, crawling spirits, insect spirits, all asked to help us and help this old man on his way have a strong heart and clear head and a long happy life, peaceful life from now on, the bad spirit gone back to where it came from, who it came from.[389]

Afterwards, Ginsberg asked his old friend if the Shaman had been able to apprehend The Ugly Spirit, and Burroughs answered:

He described it as a spirit with a white skull face, but no eyes, and sort of . . . wings, like that.[390]

He also explained that he had himself caught glimpses of similar or related entities a number of times over the years, and when he showed the Shaman some of his paintings, Betsellie had pointed at details in the images and said:

"Well, there it is, there it is, and there it is."[391]

All-in-all, Burroughs was impressed by the "strength and heart" of the medicine man:

I like the shaman very much, the way he was crying . . . He was suffering, he was hurt by this spirit. And he says he hadn't realised the power of this entity, the full, evil power. And it was almost too much for him . . .

He said it was the toughest case he'd ever handled. And for a moment he thought he was going to just lose.[392]

Later, in conversation, the Old Writer and the Shaman agreed that to just clearly *identify* the enemy in such terms was in itself something of a victory. As Burroughs told his friend, Allen Ginsberg:

If you see it, you gain control of it. It's just a matter of, well, if you see it outside, it's no longer inside.[393]

He concluded:

That was much better than anything psychoanalysts have come

up with. Something definite there was being touched upon . . .
It's the means, the moment at which the spirit gained access.
This, you see, is the same notion – Catholic exorcism,
psychotherapy, shamanistic practices – getting to the moment
when whatever it was gained access. And also to the name of
the spirit. Just to know that it's the Ugly Spirit. That's a great
step. Because the spirit doesn't want its name to be known.[394]

Last Words

> The old writer couldn't write anymore because he had reached
> the end of words, the end of what can be done with words.
> And then?[395]

And then, after his death in August 1997, as well as the previously mentioned second volume of correspondence, *Rub Out The Words: The Letters of William S. Burroughs 1959-1974*, the most significant addition was without doubt *Last Words* – subtitled *The Final Journals of William Burroughs* – which had been compiled from jottings in notebooks and on file-cards during the last nine months of his life. Many felt that the memory of Burroughs – whether as Writer, Thinker, or Man – was not especially well-served by the range of entries, which are rambling in places, rather repetitive, and often seem petty. This is very much the private musings of an old man – cats, dentist and doctor appointments, fuming at critics, health worries, missed opportunities, and lost loved ones. There were also intermittent worries about his stockpile and supply of methadone, the synthetic opioid medication he had been prescribed for the last 17 years of his life in an effort to "manage" his drug dependency – a subject that was still cause for misgivings. In a moment of unflinching, self-lacerating honesty Burroughs writes:

> How can anyone endure this furtive, precarious life without
> junk? Shows me the full power that junk has over me, lying
> hypocrite that I am. 'Oh yes, oh yes – I'm off the junk.'
> Knowing that abrupt withdrawal from Methadone, 60
> milligrams per day, would in all likelihood be fatal.[396]

On the subject of damaging dependencies, Burroughs had long been convinced that "Language is a virus" – the basic mechanism of Control, the Ugly Spirit – that we have *all* somehow succumbed to, against our own best interests:

Man sold his soul for time, language, tools, weapons, and
dominance. And to make sure he doesn't get out of line, these
invaders keep an occupying garrison in his nondominant brain
hemisphere.[397]

Once, Burroughs had even joked about forming a pop-group called "The
Mind Parasites"[398] with poet John Giorno, in honour of the invaders, and
no doubt remembering Colin Wilson's novel of the same name on this very
theme.

There are still flashes of brilliance, humour, and the wit of the William
Burroughs of old, however, and still insights into The Magical Universe,
such as:

> Many spiritual disciplines establish as a prerequisite of
> advancement the attainment of inner silence. Rub out the word.
> Castaneda in *The Teachings of Don Juan* stresses the need to
> suspend the inner dialog – rub out the word – and gives precise
> exercises designed to attain a wordless state.[399]

There are also some final assessments of what Burroughs doubtless feels he
has been up against, all along, that we are *all* up against:

> Enemy have two notable weaknesses:
>
> 1. No sense of humor. They simply don't get it.
>
> 2. They totally lack understanding of magic, and being totally
> oriented toward control, what they don't understand is a
> menace, to be destroyed by any means – consequently they tip
> their hand.[400]

Edited and with an Introduction by James Grauerholz, who had not only
been an assistant, companion, friend and manager to Burroughs since 1974,
but was also his adopted son, and in death became his heir and literary
executor, *Last Words* came with something of a surprise ending – which has
actually become the final Burroughs meme with a viral, virtual life all of its

own . . . Just days before the attack of mounting chest pains which took him to hospital, where he later died of a massive heart-attack, Burroughs had scribbled what would become his last words in his Journal:

> *There is no final enough of wisdom, experience – any fucking thing.* No *Holy* Grail, No Final Satori, no final solution. Just conflict.
>
> Only thing that can resolve conflict is love . . .
>
> Love? What is It?
>
> Most natural painkiller what there is.
>
> LOVE.[401]

For William S. Burroughs, knowing that he has found his place in The Western Lands . . .

Matthew Levi Stevens, 2014.

Further Reading:

Although there is a vast wealth of material pertaining to The Magical Universe of William S. Burroughs that I could heartily recommend for further reading, I have decided to try and keep things a little streamlined. Burroughs could be remarkably consistent over his long life as to the authors, books, and subjects which he endorsed or expressed interest in, and the list that follows is a key selection from his personal recommendation of works pertaining to the esoteric, magic and the occult, or other paranormal interests.

An Encyclopaedia of Occultism (1920) – Lewis Spence

Black Elk: The Sacred Ways of a Lakota (1990) – Wallace Black Elk & William S. Lyon

An Experiment with Time (1927, revised 1934) – J. W. Dunne

Breakthrough: Electronic Communication with the Dead (1971) – Konstantîns Raudive

Journeys Out of the Body (1971) – Robert A. Monroe

Magic: An Occult Primer (1972) – David Conway

On the Frontiers of Science: Strange Machines You Can Build (1985) – G. Harry Stine

Psychic Discoveries Behind the Iron Curtain (1970) – Sheila Ostrander & Lynn Schroeder

Psychic Self-Defence: A Study in Occult Pathology and Criminality (1930) – Dion Fortune

Real Magic (1972) – Philip Emmons Isaac Bonewits

The Teachings of Don Juan: A Yaqui Way of Knowledge (1968) – Carlos Castañeda

Quotations, Footnotes, And Citations

1. "I am a man of the world. Going to and fro and walking up and down in it." – WSB, 'The Private Asshole', *Cities of the Red Night* (John Calder Ltd, 1981.) Doubtless a reference to *Job* 1:7 in *The Bible*, in which God's query "Whence comest thou?" to Satan is met with the reply "From going to and fro in the earth, and from walking up and down in it."

2. "Aside from James Grauerholz . . ." – Interview with Professor Oliver Harris, posted on *Reality Studio* website, January 2005.

3. "In the magical universe . . ." – WSB, Ted Morgan, *Literary Outlaw* (Pimlico, 1991.)

4. "As the single most important . . ." – Ted Morgan, *Literary Outlaw* (Pimlico, 1991.)

5. "Among so-called primitive peoples . . ." – WSB, 'On Coincidence', included in *The Adding Machine: Collected Essays* (John Calder Ltd, 1985.)

6. "In Mr Burroughs hands . . ." – review in *New York Times*, cited as back-cover copy during the 1970s (e.g. *Nova Express*, Granada paperback edition, etc.)

7. Details concerning the friendship between WSB, Anthony Burgess, and his first wife, Lynne, can be found in a number of sources, e.g. *The Real Life of Anthony Burgess*, by Andrew Biswell (Picador, 2005.)

8. "Mr Burroughs joins a small body . . ." – Anthony Burgess, cited as back-cover copy. Most likely originates from his review of *Naked Lunch*, 'On the end of every fork', which appeared in *The Guardian*, 20th November 1964.

9. "Hitman for the Apocalypse" – J. G. Ballard, review for the *Independent on Sunday* of Ted Morgan's *Literary Outlaw*, 1991. Also included in J. G. Ballard, *A User's Guide to the Millennium* (HarperCollins, 1996.)

10. ". . . William Burroughs has fashioned . . ." – J. G. Ballard, 'Myth Maker of the Twentieth Century', review of WSB's *Naked Lunch* in *New Worlds*, 1964. Also included in J. G. Ballard, *A User's Guide to the*

Millennium (HarperCollins, 1996.)

11. "Bill had an . . . I was in . . . It was bewildering." – Heathcote Williams, 'Burroughs in London', http://realitystudio.org/biography/burroughs-in-london/ February 2014. Also cross-posted to Jan Herman's blog, *Straight Up.*

12. "I first heard of the 23 enigma . . ." – Robert Anton Wilson, *Cosmic Trigger: Final Secret Of The Illuminati* (And/Or, 1977.)

13. "Can the world . . . Flight 23 . . ." – Throbbing Gristle, *The Old Man Smiled*, c.1980.

14. ". . . Burroughs realizes that the black magic . . ." – Eric Mottram, *The Algebra of Need* (Marion Boyars, 1977.)

15. "For me, William was . . ." – Kathy Acker, 'William Burroughs', dated 8/4/97 and with "Acknowledgement and thanks to 21.C magazine." Accessed by the author at http://www.geek.co.uk/burroughs/acker/html on 27/11/99.

16. "the only living . . . Burroughs' project . . . much funnier" – Angela Carter, review of WSB's *The Western Lands* in the *Guardian*, London 1988. Included in Angela Carter, *Expletives Deleted* (Chatto & Windus Ltd, 1992.)

17. "William seemed to have a . . . revere him enough!" – Patti Smith, speaking in Yony Leyser's documentary, *William S. Burroughs: A Man Within* (2010.)

18. "It is to be remembered . . ." – WSB, Essay on Brion Gysin for *Contemporary Artists,* ed. Naylor & P-Orridge (St. James Press, 1977.) As quoted in Brion Gysin & Terry Wilson, *Here To Go: Planet R101* (RE/Search, 1982.)

19. ". . . I will examine the connections . . ." – WSB, 'Technology of Writing', included in *The Adding Machine: Collected Essays* (John Calder Ltd, 1985.)

20. "Audrey was a thin pale boy . . ." – WSB, 'And Bury the Bread Deep in a Sty', *The Wild Boys* (Calder & Boyars, 1972.)

21. "To me 'genius' is . . ." – WSB, to author, The October Gallery, London 1988. Published in Matthew Levi Stevens, *A Moving Target: Encounters with William Burroughs* (Beat Scene Press, October 2012.)

22. "In the Carlos Castañeda books . . ." – WSB, January 1989, 'Nagual Art.' Included in the catalogue for his exhibition in Rome (Cleto Polcina Edizioni, 1989.)

23. "My concept of possession . . ." – WSB, Introduction, *Queer* (Viking Penguin, 1985.)

24. "In 1939, I became . . ." – WSB, Introduction, *Queer* (Viking Penguin, 1985.)

25. "I live with the constant . . ." – WSB, Introduction, *Queer* (Viking Penguin, 1985.)

26. "As a young child . . ." – WSB, 'The Name is Burroughs', collected in *The Adding Machine: Collected Essays* (John Calder Ltd, 1985.)

27. "I was born in 1914 . . ." – WSB, Prologue, *Junky* (Penguin, 1977.)

28. "Actually my earliest memories . . ." – WSB, Prologue, *Junky* (Penguin, 1977.)

29. "she adored crystal balls . . ." – WSB, *The Place of Dead Roads* (Viking, 1983.)

30. "My mother's character . . ." – WSB, quoted by Victor Bockris in 'A Passport for William Burroughs: Introduction', *With William Burroughs: A Report From The Bunker* (Vermilion, 1981.)

31. "Kim is a slimy, morbid youth . . ." – WSB, *The Place of Dead Roads* (Viking, 1983.)

32. "When I was four years old . . ." – WSB, *The Cat Inside* (Viking, 1992.)

33. "I was subject to hallucinations . . ." – WSB, Prologue, *Junky* (Penguin, 1977.)

34. "When they have . . ." – Pliny the Elder, *Natural History* (Penguin Classics, 1991.)

35. ". . . if there was one instance . . ." – Malcolm Mc Neill, email to author. As well as an informal "Burroughs scholar" and Collector, Jed Birmingham is also Contributing Editor to *Reality Studio*, the premier website devoted to all-things-Burroughs.

36. "seen anything unusual . . . Like what? . . . There I discovered . . . Anatole Broyard" – Malcolm Mc Neill, *Observed While Falling* (Fantagraphics, 2012.)

37. "The fact that the loft . . ." – Malcolm Mc Neill, email to author.

38. "the old nursemaid trick . . ." – Ted Morgan, *Literary Outlaw* (Pimlico, 1991.)

39. "Once he made sex magic . . ." – WSB, *The Place of Dead Roads* (Viking, 1983.)

40. "The memory he could never . . ." – WSB, 'Lee's Journals', *Interzone* (Viking, 1989.)

41. ". . . one might ask *why* . . ." – C. J. Bradbury Robinson, letter to author.

42. "'Physical' is not the only criterion . . ." – C. G. Jung, Prefatory Note to *Answer to Job*, from Vol. 11 of the *Collected Works* of C. G. Jung

(Princeton, 2010.)

43. "As soon as you walk . . ." – WSB, to author, in conversation at *The Final Academy*, London 1982. Account published in *Academy 23: an unofficial tribute to William S. Burroughs & 'The Final Academy'* ed. Stevens & Doeve (WhollyBooks, 2012.)

44. "'The Subliminal Kid' moved in . . ." – WSB, *Nova Express* (Grove Press, 1964.)

45. "Of course, when you think . . ." – WSB, interviewed by Conrad Knickerbocker, 1966, *The Paris Review*. Reprinted in *Writers at Work*, 3rd series (1967), and later collected in Burroughs & Gysin, *The Third Mind* (Viking, 1978.)

46. "once upon . . . *future* time" – WSB, according to account of Ted Morgan, *Literary Outlaw* (Pimlico, 1991.)

47. "When you experiment . . ." – WSB, lecture at Naropa College. Transcript published as 'It Belongs to the Cucumbers', included in *The Adding Machine: Collected Essays* (John Calder Ltd, 1985.)

48. "slippery times . . ." – Brion Gysin, interviewed by Terry Wilson, 'painting to palaver to polaroids', in *Here To Go: Planet R101* (RE/Search, 1982.)

49. "Brion Gysin is the only man . . ." – WSB, recorded by Corinna MacNeice, shown at the Here To Go Show, Dublin, 1992. Compare with a statement written by WSB just after hearing of Gysin's death in 1986: "He was the only man I have ever respected. I have admired many others, esteemed and valued others, but respected only him. He was at all times impeccable. Who was Brion Gysin? The only authentic heir to Hassan i Sabbah, the Old Man of the Mountain? Certainly that. Through his painting I caught glimpses of the Garden that the Old Man showed to his Assassins." [Included in John Geiger's biography of Gysin, *Nothing Is True Everything Is Permitted: The Life of Brion Gysin*, Disinformation 2005.]

50. "project for disastrous success" – Brion Gysin, 'Cut-ups: A Project for Disastrous Success', collected in *The Third Mind* (Viking, 1978.)

51. "No two minds . . ." – Napoleon Hill, *Think and Grow Rich* (Ralston Society, 1937.)

52. "complete and systematic derangement of the senses" – the expression is from Arthur Rimbaud, in the so-called 'Les Lettres du Voyant' of 1871, included in his *Collected Poems* (Penguin Classics, 1986.)

53. "almost *too* good . . ." – Terry Wilson, in conversation with the author, Summer 1988.

54. "He was looking . . ." – WSB, 'Introductions', *The Third Mind* (Viking, 1978.)

55. "The cut up method brings . . ." – WSB, 'The Cut-up of Brion Gysin', collected in *The Third Mind* (Viking, 1978.)

56. "In 1964 I made . . ." – WSB, lecture at Naropa College. Transcript published as 'It Belongs to the Cucumbers', included in *The Adding Machine: Collected Essays* (John Calder Ltd, 1985.)

57. "I have experienced a number . . ." – WSB, 'On Freud and the Unconscious', included in *The Adding Machine: Collected Essays* (John Calder Ltd, 1985.)

58. "Given the fundamental uncertainty . . ." – Malcolm Mc Neill, 'Here', in *Observed While Falling* (Fantagraphics, 2012.)

59. "You will recall . . ." – WSB, 'Introductions', in *The Third Mind* (Viking, 1978.)

60. "Perhaps events are pre-written . . ." – WSB, with Daniel Odier, 'Journey through space-time', included in *The Job* (John Calder Ltd, 1970.)

61. "The word of course . . ." – WSB, with Daniel Odier, 'Journey through space-time', included in *The Job* (John Calder Ltd, 1970.)

62. "creepy letter . . . what he's *really* saying!" – archival tape-recording, WSB, Brion Gysin, Gregory Corso & Sinclair Beiles. Released on *Nothing Here Now But The Recordings* (Industrial records, 1980.) Also included in the 4xCD box-set *The Best of William S. Burroughs* (Giorno Poetry Systems, 1998.)

63. "Words thank you . . ." – Brion Gysin, included in *The Third Mind* (Viking, 1978.)

64. "The permutations discovered *me* . . ." – Brion Gysin, interviewed by Terry Wilson, 'Ports of Entry', *Here To Go: Planet R101* (RE/Search, 1982.)

65. "William followed . . . ever fazed him." – Brion Gysin, interviewed by Terry Wilson, 'Ports of Entry', *Here To Go: Planet R101* (RE/Search, 1982.)

66. "On the wall hangs . . ." – Brion Gysin, interviewed by Terry Wilson, 'Ports of Entry', *Here To Go: Planet R101* (RE/Search, 1982.)

67. "It sounds to me . . ." – Stephen Spender, transcript, International Writers Conference: Edinburgh 1962.

68. "Cut ups often come . . ." – WSB, 'The Cut-up Method of Brion Gysin', included in *The Third Mind* (Viking, 1978.)

69. "The years in the Beat Hotel . . ." – Brion Gysin, interviewed by

Terry Wilson, 'The Torso of 1960', *Here To Go: Planet R101* (RE/Search, 1982)

70. "I hate you – I love you . . ." – WSB, to author, London 1988. Also reported in Phil Baker, *William S. Burroughs*, in the *Critical Lives* series (Reaktion Books, 2010.)

71. ". . . you see great galleries . . ." – Brion Gysin, interviewed by Terry Wilson, 'The Torso of 1960', *Here To Go: Planet R101* (RE/Search, 1982.)

72. "a coffin in the library" – WSB, letter to Brion Gysin, 17th Jan 1959. *The Letters of William S. Burroughs 1945 to 1959* (Viking Penguin, 1993.)

73. "The para-normal occurrences . . ." – WSB, letter to Allen Ginsberg, 2nd Jan 1959. *The Letters of William S. Burroughs 1945 to 1959* (Viking Penguin, 1993.)

74. "Once I looked in mirror . . ." – WSB, letter to Allen Ginsberg, 2nd Jan 1959. *The Letters of William S. Burroughs 1945 to 1959* (Viking Penguin, 1993.)

75. "What is happening now . . ." – WSB, letter to Allen Ginsberg, late July 1959. *The Letters of William S. Burroughs 1945 to 1959* (Viking Penguin, 1993.)

76. "Jacques Stern had psychic powers . . ." – WSB, to Ted Morgan, cited by Barry Miles in *Call Me Burroughs: A Life* (Twelve, 2014.)

77. "Stern in complete seclusion . . ." – WSB, letter to Allen Ginsberg, 18th May 1959. *The Letters of William S. Burroughs 1945 to 1959* (Viking Penguin, 1993.)

78. "Wickedest Man in the World" – WSB, letter to his mother, Laura Lee Burroughs, December 1959, in *Rub Out The Words: The Letters of William S. Burroughs 1959-1974*, ed. Bill Morgan (Penguin Classics, 2012.)

79. "There is also the question . . ." – WSB, interviewed by John Tytell, New York, 24th March 1974. Transcript published in *A Burroughs Compendium: Calling the Toads* (Ring Tarigh, 1998.)

80. "Interviewers: You're interested in the occult . . ." – WSB, 'Grandpa From Hell', *LA Weekly*, 19th July 1996. Included in *Burroughs Live: The Collected Interviews of William S. Burroughs 1960-1997* (Semiotext(e), 2001.)

81. "Burroughs thought he and Jimmy . . ." – WSB, with Stephen Davis, 'Rock Magic', *Crawdaddy* Magazine, June 1975. Also included in Stephen Davis, *LZ-'75: The Lost Chronicles of Led Zeppelin's 1975*

American Tour (Gotham Books, 2010.)

82. "MS: What William described . . ." – Graham Masterton, interviewed by the author, via email, November 2012. Also published in *Beat Scene* No.71a, Winter 2014.

83. ". . . Burroughs considered Crowley . . ." – James Grauerholz, interviewed by Steve Foland, 25th June 2010. Published as 'Taking the brooooooaaaaad view of things: A Conversation with James Grauerholz on William S. Burroughs and Magick', can be found online at: http://pop-damage.com/?p=5393

84. "William knew quite a bit . . ." – James Grauerholz, interviewed by Steve Foland, 25th June 2010. Published as 'Taking the brooooooaaaaad view of things: A Conversation with James Grauerholz on William S. Burroughs and Magick', can be found online at: http://pop-damage.com/?p=5393

85. "Old Aleister Crowley . . ." – WSB, in conversation with Tennessee Williams. First published in *The Village Voice*, 16th May 1977. Included as 'Orpheus Holds His Own' in *Burroughs Live: The Collected Interviews of William S. Burroughs 1960-1997* (Semiotext(e), 2001.)

86. "On the evening . . . as if nothing happened" – Malcolm Mc Neill, *Observed While Falling* (Fantagraphics, 2012.)

87. "Tom introduces Kim . . ." – WSB, *The Place of Dead Roads* (Viking, 1983.)

88. "barbarous names of evocation" – a term used within the Western Magical Tradition to denote the long strings of often unintelligible words that are often found in spells that have come down from Antiquity, e.g. the *Graeco-Egyptian Magical Papyri*. It is thought most likely that these words originate from corruption or misunderstanding of older, often forgotten, languages. It has been suggested that the very unintelligibility of these complex phrases is what lends them their evocative power, e.g: "It may be conceded in any case that the long strings of formidable words which roar and moan through so many conjurations have a real effect in exalting the consciousness of the magician to the proper pitch . . ." – Aleister Crowley, 'Of Silence and Secrecy: and Of the Barbarous Names of Evocation', Chapter IX, *Magick in Theory and Practice,* ed. Symonds and Grant (Guild Publishing, 1988.)

89. "Chris has set up a stone altar . . ." – WSB, *The Place of Dead Roads* (Viking, 1983.)

90. "I've got a real muse thing . . ." – WSB talking to David Ohle, 26th

January 1985. Transcript published in *My Kind of Angel*, ed. Rupert Loydell (Stride, 1998.)

91. "well constructed hoax" – Professor Owen Davies, *Grimoires: A History of Magic Books* (Oxford University Press, 2010.)

92. "It was about that time . . ." – Khem Caigan, in Daniel Harms & John Wisdom Gonce III, *Necronomicon Files: The Truth Behind Lovecraft's Legend* (Weiser, 2003.)

93. "Humwawa . . . Pazuzu . . . Kutulu . . ." – *The Necronomicon*, edited and with an introduction by "Simon" (Schlangekraft, Inc., 1979.)

94. "Io Pan! Io Pan!" – Aleister Crowley, 'Hymn to Pan' (1913.) Included in *Magick in Theory and Practice*, ed. Symonds and Grant (Guild Publishing, 1988.)

95. "It seems that M[*ichaux*] . . ." – WSB, letter to Allen Ginsberg, 30th October 1959, in *Rub Out The Words: Collected Letters of William S. Burroughs 1959-1974*, ed. Bill Morgan (Penguin Classics, 2012.)

96. "planetary perspective" – Mary McCarthy, 'Dejeuner sur l'Herbe', review of WSB's *Naked Lunch*, in *The New York Review of Books*, February 1963.

97. ". . . witness to an era . . ." – Bill Morgan, 2011, Introduction, *Rub Out The Words: Collected Letters of William S. Burroughs 1959-1974*, ed. Bill Morgan (Penguin Classics, 2012.)

98. "Burroughs and I saw each other . . ." – Brion Gysin, interviewed by Terry Wilson, 'painting to palaver to polaroids', *Here To Go: Planet R101* (RE/Search, 1982.)

99. "I have met . . ." – WSB, letter to Allen Ginsberg, 2nd December 1959, in *Rub Out The Words: Collected Letters of William S. Burroughs 1959-1974*, ed. Bill Morgan (Penguin Classics, 2012.)

100. ". . . Brion dispenses . . ." – Timothy Leary, *Jail Notes* (Grove Press, 1972.)

101. "Hash-Head Assassins" – from the title of Brion Gysin's article 'A Quick Trip to Alamut: The Celebrated Castle of the Hash-Head Assassins' commissioned by *Rolling Stone* in 1973, but rejected. Included in *Back in No Time: The Brion Gysin Reader*, ed. Jason Weiss (Wesleyan University Press, 2001.)

102. "Magic calls itself . . ." – Brion Gysin, liner notes for *Brian Jones presents The Pipes of Pan at Joujouka* (text written 1964, LP released Rolling Stones Records, 1971.)

103. ". . . I recognized very quickly . . ." – Brion Gysin, interviewed by Terry Wilson, 'Terminal Tourist', *Here To Go: Planet R101* (RE/

Search, 1982.)

104. "Their secret, guarded even . . ." – Brion Gysin, 'Cut-ups: A Project for Disastrous Success' in *The Third Mind* (Viking, 1978.)

105. "The boy . . . dances . . . Listen . . . music on earth." – WSB, 'Face to Face with the Goat God' in *Oui* vol.2 no.8, August 1973. Also quoted in the liner notes of the CD reissue of *Brian Jones presents The Pipes of Pan at Jajouka* [sic] (Point Music, 1995.)

106. "Mariners sailing close . . . down the sky." – WSB, *Apocalypse*. An illustrated catalogue of 20 silkscreen images, collaboration with graffiti artist Keith Haring, text by WSB (George Mulder Fine Arts, 1989.)

107. "The magical theory . . ." – WSB, *The Place of Dead Roads* (Viking, 1983.)

108. "The sections entitled . . ." – WSB, Acknowledgment, *The Ticket That Exploded* (Olympia, 1962.)

109. "this kid *likes* . . ." – Harold Norse, as reported by Norse during interview for Ted Morgan's *Literary Outlaw* (Pimlico, 1991.)

110. "Ian Sommerville was a mathematics . . ." – Brion Gysin, 'Collaborators', in *The Final Academy: Statements of a Kind* (The Final Academy, 1982.)

111. "The section called 'This Horrible Case' . . ." – WSB, Foreword Note, *Nova Express* (Grove, 1964.)

112. "Had a transcendental . . ." – Brion Gysin, diary entry, 21ˢᵗ December 1958. Quoted in Brion Gysin & Terry Wilson, *Here To Go: Planet R101* (RE/Search, 1982.)

113. "Oddly enough it is . . . wiser apes." – W. Grey Walter, *The Living Brain* (Duckworth, 1953; Penguin, 1961.)

114. "Blitzkrieg the citadel of enlightenment!" – WSB, New Year 1960, quoted in Brion Gysin, 'Cut-ups: A Project for Disastrous Success' (1964), which originally appeared in the *Evergreen Review* and later in *Brion Gysin Let The Mice In*. Collected in *Back In No Time: The Brion Gysin Reader*, ed. Jason Weiss (Wesleyan University Press, 2001.)

115. "I have made . . ." – Ian Sommerville, 15ᵗʰ February 1960, as quoted in Brion Gysin, 'Dream Machine' [sic], *Olympia* magazine No.2 (Olympia Press, 1962.) Included in *Flickers of the Dreamachine*, ed. Paul Cecil (Codex, 1996.)

116. "He was an extraordinary . . ." – Brion Gysin, interviewed by Terry Wilson, 'Control . . . Control?', *Here To Go: Planet R101* (RE/Search, 1982.)

117. According to Brion Gysin: "I made a 'machine' from his ensuing description and added to it an interior cylinder covered with the type of painting I have developed in the three years since my first flicker experience. The result, eyes open or closed, warranted taking out patent, and on July 18, 1961 I received brevet no. P.V.868, 281" – in 'Dream Machine' [sic], *Olympia* magazine No.2 (Olympia Press, 1962.) Included in *Flickers of the Dreamachine*, ed. Paul Cecil (Codex, 1996.)

118. "The Dreamachine . . . one knows . . . closed eyelids . . ." – Brion Gysin, interviewed by Jon Savage, date unknown. Transcript included in *RE/Search* 4/5, credited "From a forthcoming book of interviews with Brion Gysin, edited by Genesis P-Orridge. In Paris, Jon Savage asked the questions . . ." (RE/Search, 1982.)

119. "the drugless turn-on . . ." – Jon Savage, aforementioned interview with Brion Gysin, *RE/Search* 4/5 (RE/Search, 1982.)

120. 'Conjure Man' by Kid 'Congo' Powers and The Pink Monkey Birds (In The Red, 2013.) Incidentally, the promo video was shot by Aaron Brookner, nephew of Howard Brookner, director of the 1983 documentary, *Burroughs: The Movie.*

121. "I remember going . . . Only a magical . . . never gonna fly . . ." – Marianne Faithfull, in Nik Sheehan's documentary *FLicKeR* (2008.)

122. "Burroughs and I were forever saying . . ." – Brion Gysin, 'Collaborators', in *The Final Academy: Statements of a Kind* (The Final Academy, 1982.)

123. "Bill's all hung up . . ." – Allen Ginsberg, letter to Lucien Carr, 28th July 1961.

124. ". . . with the pouty . . ." – Ted Morgan, *Literary Outlaw* (Pimlico, 1991.)

125. "Miguel [Michael] Portman's beauty . . ." – WSB, letter to Brion Gysin, 7th October 1960, included in *Rub Out The Words: Collected Letters of William S. Burroughs 1959-1974*, ed. Bill Morgan (Penguin Classics, 2012.)

126. "A much more beautiful . . ." – WSB, letter to Brion Gysin, 1st October 1960, included in *Rub Out The Words: Collected Letters of William S. Burroughs 1959-1974,* ed. Bill Morgan (Penguin Classics, 2012.) The pidgin Spanish translates as something like "You called Meester [Mister.] What do you want?"

127. "Some staff difficulties . . ." – WSB, letter to Brion Gysin, 9th April 1962, included in *Rub Out The Words: Collected Letters of William S. Burroughs 1959-1974*, ed. Bill Morgan (Penguin Classics, 2012.)

128. "When I went round to Duke Street . . ." – Heathcote Williams, 'Burroughs in London', http://realitystudio.org/biography/burroughs-in-london/ February 2014. Also cross-posted to Jan Herman's blog, *Straight Up.*

129. "Mikey, it is terrible . . ." – as reported by Terry Wilson, in conversation with the author, Summer 1988, and confirmed by Felicity Mason. Compare with WSB, to Ted Morgan, as reported in Barry Miles, *Call Me Burroughs: A Life* (Twelve, 2014.)

130. "make use . . . uncorrupt, pure" – PGM VII.540-78, *The Greek Magical Papyri In Translation*, ed. Hans Dieter Betz (University of Chicago Press, 1986.)

131. "You should bring . . ." – PDM xiv.68, *The Greek Magical Papyri In Translation*, ed. Hans Dieter Betz (University of Chicago Press, 1986.)

132. "Victory to Aleister Crowley!" – Michael Portman, as reported by Terry Wilson, in conversation with author, London, Summer 1988.

133. "When he fixes me with . . ." – Ian Sommerville, as reported in Barry Miles, *El Hombre Invisible* (Virgin, 1992.)

134. "Everybody does . . . I can't tell . . . Bill's getting better" – Ian Sommerville, in conversation with Harold Norse at the Beat Hotel, Paris, 1959, as reported by Norse during interview for Ted Morgan's *Literary Outlaw* (Pimlico, 1991.)

135. "He was standing . . . lover's arrival . . . reeled in . . ." – Ira Cohen, as reported by Terry Wilson, in conversation with author, London, Summer 1988. Also confirmed by Felicity Mason in her account of the relationship between WSB and Sommerville.

136. "He was a very talented young man . . ." – WSB, as reported in Barry Miles, *The Beat Hotel* (Atlantic Books, 2001.)

137. "almost the founding document . . ." – Ronald Hutton, *Pagan Religions of the Ancient British Isles: their nature and legacy* (Blackwell, 1995.)

138. "I not only felt it . . . dying feeling" – WSB, reported in Barry Miles, *Call Me Burroughs: A Life* (Twelve, 2014.)

139. "electric-razor queen . . . rough trade" – Bill Levy, 'Electric Ian', quoted in Phil Baker's *William S. Burroughs*, the *Critical Lives* series (Reaktion Books, 2010.) Perhaps not surprisingly, to this day Levy is antagonistic and contentious with regard to Sommerville's death, maintaining that it was a suicide – although, as the accident in question was the result of another driver taking a wrong turn and driving into him, it is difficult to see how the unfortunate Sommerville could possibly have *willed* this to happen, even *if* suicide *was* his intent . . .

Jed Irwin, one of Levy's former partners in the *Insect Trust Gazette* – a magazine which took the inspiration for its name from WSB, and was happy to publish his work, and thereby profit from an association with him! – has stated *". . . Sometime after Bill* [Levy] *moved to London — and, I think, before he moved on to Amsterdam — he published two pieces in a magazine called* The Fanatic. *In one, he claimed actual magical power for words / language, a concept derived from his studies in Jewish mysticism; he said "words can kill". In a second piece, a review or bit of criticism, he referred with extreme negativity to some work by Burroughs acolyte / collaborator Ian Sommerville (involved I believe with the creation of the "Dream Machine"). Bill essentially wrote that Sommerville was a worthless piece of shit and did not deserve to live."* See *Jed Irwin on the Insect Trust Gazette*, online @ http://realitystudio.org/bibliographic-bunker/bunker-interviews/jed-irwin-on-the-insect-trust-gazette/

140. "Antony *[Balch]* swears . . ." – WSB, letter to Brion Gysin, 5th November 1968, included in *Rub Out The Words: Collected Letters of William S. Burroughs 1959-1974*, ed. Bill Morgan (Penguin Classics, 2012.)

141. "the two worked at the centre . . ." – Tim Cummins, Review of *Rub Out The Words: Collected Letters of William S. Burroughs*, in the *Independent*, 6th April 2012.

142. "It should never be forgotten . . ." – Aleister Crowley, *Magick Without Tears* (Llewellyn, 1973.)

143. "complete and systematic derangement . . ." – the expression is from Arthur Rimbaud, in the so-called 'Les Lettres du Voyant' of 1871, included in his *Collected Poems* (Penguin Classics, 1986.)

144. "paranoiac-critical . . . delirious phenomena" – Salvador Dali, in collaboration with David Gascoyne, *Conquest of the Irrational* (Julien Levy, 1935.)

145. "L. Ron Hubbard, the founder of Scientology . . ." – WSB, *My Education: A Book of Dreams* (Viking, 1995.)

146. "He must be one . . ." – Brion Gysin on WSB & Scientology, interviewed by Terry Wilson for *Here To Go: Planet R101* (RE/Search Publications, 1982.)

147. "a dream come true" – David S. Wills, *Scientologist! William S. Burroughs and the "Weird Cult"* (Beatdom Books, 2013.)

148. "This foreword . . . is an essay . . ." – WSB, in Graham Masterton, *Rules of Duel* (Telos Publishing Ltd, 2010.)

149. "When you read look listen . . ." – WSB, in Graham Masterton, *Rules*

of Duel (Telos Publishing Ltd, 2010.)

150. "Start with newspapers . . ." – WSB, 'The Moving Times'. Originally in Jeff Nuttall's *My Own Mag* (1969), included in *The Burroughs File* (City Lights, 1984.)

151. ". . . when I first wrote to him . . ." – Graham Masterton, email to author. This is actually not dissimilar to an experience the author had meeting WSB for the first time: I was wearing a Sony Walkman, loaned to me by Peter 'Sleazy' Christopherson, then of Psychic TV (co-organisers of *The Final Academy*), on which I was listening to David Bowie's *Low*. When WSB asked me "What's your name, kid?" I answered "Matthew, Matthew Stevens – Stevens with a 'v' . . ." as was my custom. He looked at me, as if something was meaningful – then asked, indicating the Walkman, what I was listening to? I replied "*Low*, by David Bowie" – and then he really did look at me as if something was meaningful. Later he told me about his *amigo*, Steven Lowe, who would always introduce himself as "Steven-with-a-v" for the same reason, to avoid the alternative "ph" spelling, and whose surname, of course, sounded the same as "Low." All small details, easy to dismiss as "just coincidence" or trivia I know, but what was readily apparent was that to WSB, it *meant something*: I believe *that* was why he chose to talk to me, and why he invited me to take a walk with him. He later described this to me as "an intersection", and said it was the kind of thing a writer should look out for: the apparent connections *between* and hidden meanings *in* things.

152. "a scattering . . ." – Graham Masterton, January 2010, Introduction to *Rules of Duel* (Telos Publishing Ltd, 2010.)

153. ". . . depended on the writer . . ." – Graham Masterton, Introduction to *Rules of Duel* (Telos Publishing Ltd, 2010.)

154. "The Ancient Mayans possessed . . ." – WSB, 'Journey through time-space', *The Job* (John Calder Ltd, 1969.)

155. "mistakes too monstrous for remorse / to tamper or to dally with" – this line, frequently quoted by WSB throughout his life, is a slight misremembering of "There are mistakes too monstrous for remorse / To fondle or dally with" from *Arthurian Poets (Tristram)* by American poet Edwin Arlington Robinson (1869-1935.)

156. "The method is eclectic . . ." – Angela Carter, review of WSB's *The Western Lands* in the *Guardian*, London 1988. Included in Angela Carter, *Expletives Deleted* (Chatto & Windus Ltd, 1992.)

157. "To consolidate revolutionary gains . . ." – WSB, 'The Revised Boy

Scout Manual', released first as a pair of limited edition tape-cassettes, transcription of one tape later appearing in *RE/Search* 4/5 (RE/Search Publications, 1982.)

158. "The Colonel decides . . ." – WSB, 'The Discipline of DE', included in *Exterminator!* (Viking Press, 1973.)

159. "the system began . . . 1. Terre Haute . . . and Wiener . . ." – WSB's 'Dream Calendar' details based on the account given in *William Burroughs, El Hombre Invisible* by Barry Miles (Virgin, 1992.)

160. "Dear Brion . . . Land's End" – WSB, letter to Brion Gysin, 21st January 1970, included in *Rub Out The Words: Collected Letters of William S. Burroughs 1959-1974*, ed. Bill Morgan (Penguin Classics, 2012.)

161. "The above idea came to me . . ." – WSB, letter to Brion Gysin, 21st January 1970, included in *Rub Out The Words: Collected Letters of William S. Burroughs 1959-1974*, ed. Bill Morgan (Penguin Classics, 2012.)

162. ". . . the priests could calculate . . ." – WSB, *The Job* (John Calder Ltd, 1969.)

163. "Man is a being . . ." – Alfred Korzybski (1879-1950), *Manhood of Humanity: The Science and Art of Human Engineering* (E. P. Dutton & Co, 1921.)

164. "I'm primarily concerned with survival . . ." – WSB, keynote statement, 'What The Nova Convention Is About', for the "counter-cultural conference" in celebration of WSB organised by Sylvère Lotringer with assistance from James Grauerholz and John Giorno, held 30th November – 2nd December, 1978 in New York, and featuring a line-up including Laurie Anderson, John Cage, Allen Ginsberg, John Giorno, Philip Glass, Brion Gysin, Timothy Leary, Patti Smith, Terry Southern, Anne Waldman, Frank Zappa, and of course, William S. Burroughs. A 2-LP set of the event, *The Nova Convention*, was released by Giorno Poetry Systems in 1979.

165. "We postulate that man . . ." – WSB, 'Civilian Defense', included in *The Adding Machine: Collected Essays* (John Calder Ltd, 1985.)

166. "To travel in space . . ." – WSB, *The Job* (John Calder Ltd, 1970.)

167. "The hope lies in . . ." – WSB, interviewed by Conrad Knickerbocker, *The Art of Fiction*, No. 36 (The Paris Review, 1965.)

168. "An Ishmalian and Gnostic . . ." – WSB, interviewed 1984 by Gregory Corso, published as 'Attack *Anything* Moving' (London, 1986.) Later included in *Burroughs Live: The Collected Interviews of William S.*

Burroughs 1960-1997 (Semiotext(e), 2001.)

169. "All of my work . . ." – WSB, interviewed by Conrad Knickerbocker, *The Art of Fiction*, No. 36 (The Paris Review, 1965.)

170. "Mr Bradley-Mr Martin . . ." – WSB, 'The Future of the Novel.' Statement to the International Writers Conference, Edinburgh, 1962. Transcript included later that year in issue number 11 of *The Transatlantic Review*.

171. ". . . Burroughs' writing, in the manner . . ." – Gregory Stephenson, 'The Gnostic Vision of William S. Burroughs', in his collection *The Daybreak Boys: Essays on the Literature of the Beat Generation* (SIU Press, 1990.)

172. "Yen Lee sat down and . . ." – WSB, 'We see Tibet with the binoculars of the people', *Cities of the Red Night* (John Calder Ltd, 1981.)

173. "They had to be careful about sex . . ." – WSB, 'Cheers here are the nondead', *Cities of the Red Night* (John Calder Ltd, 1981.)

174. "The human body is . . ." – WSB, 'Civilian Defence', in *The Adding Machine: Collected Essays* (John Calder Ltd, 1985.)

175. "Of course the sands of . . ." – Brion Gysin, *The Process* (Jonathan Cape Ltd, 1969.) Also cited on the back cover of *Here To Go: Planet R101* (RE/Search, 1982.)

176. "I consider that immortality . . ." – WSB, 'Statement on The Final Academy' July 1982, in *The Final Academy: Statements of a Kind* (The Final Academy, 1982.)

177. "All tape recorder tricks . . ." – WSB, Postscript to 'The Invisible Generation' in 'Abstract' magazine. Also International Times magazine, and included as appendix to *The Ticket That Exploded* (Olympia, 1962.)

178. "With their diseases . . ." – WSB, *Nova Express* (Grove Press, 1964.)

179. "Honour thy error as a hidden intention . . ." – Brian Eno & Peter Schmidt, *Obliques Strategies*, (Opal Records, 1978.)

180. "Why did you . . . Advertising!" – Genesis P-Orridge, interviewed by V. Vale, *RE/Search 4/5* (RE/Search, 1982.)

181. "At the moment I'm trying . . ." – WSB, to David Bowie. Craig Copetas, 'Beat Godfather meets Glitter Mainman', *Rolling Stone*, 28th February 1974. Also included in *Burroughs Live: The Collected Interviews of William S. Burroughs 1960-1997* (Semiotext(e), 2001.)

182. "When David Bowie came . . ." – Victor Bockris, *With William Burroughs: A Report From The Bunker* (Vermilion, 1981.)

183. "Since the word 'magic' . . ." – WSB, with Stephen Davis, 'Rock

Magic', *Crawdaddy* Magazine, June 1975. Also included in Stephen Davis, *LZ-'75: The Lost Chronicles of Led Zeppelin's 1975 American Tour* (Gotham Books, 2010.)

184. "Magick is the Science and Art . . ." – Aleister Crowley, Introduction to Part III, included in *Magick in Theory and Practice* (Guild Publishing, 1988.)

185. "Over margaritas . . ." – WSB, with Stephen Davis, 'Rock Magic', *Crawdaddy* Magazine, June 1975. Also included in Stephen Davis, *LZ-'75: The Lost Chronicles of Led Zeppelin's 1975 American Tour* (Gotham Books, 2010.)

186. "Mr Burroughs is back . . ." – Patti Smith, quoted by Victor Bockris in *With William Burroughs: A Report From The Bunker* (Vermilion, 1981.)

187. "I was very privileged . . ." – Patti Smith, interviewed by Michael Hendrick, 15th May 2012. Transcript published as 'Talking Barefoot: A Chat with Patti Smith' in *Beatdom* no.12, Winter 2012.

188. "Patti Smith is not only . . ." – WSB, endorsement for *Patti Smith Complete: Lyrics, Reflections, and Notes for the Future* (Doubleday, 1998.)

189. "He comes stumbling . . . William Burroughs was simultaneously old and young . . ." – Patti Smith, *Just Kids* (Bloomsbury, 2010.)

190. "Harry Smith another wrong number . . ." – WSB, letter to Allen Ginsberg, 26th October 1961, included in *Rub Out The Words: Collected Letters of William S. Burroughs 1959-1974*, ed. Bill Morgan (Penguin Classics, 2012.)

191. ". . . amazed to see the rival wizards . . ." – interview with Barry Miles, quoted by Sherill Tippens, *Inside the Dream Palace* (Simon & Schuster, 2013.)

192. "Riot sound effects . . ." – WSB, *Nova Express* (Grove Press, 1964.)

193. "This is machine strategy . . ." – WSB, *Nova Express* (Grove Press, 1964.)

194. "Get it out of your head . . ." – WSB, 'The Invisible Generation', published in *The International Times*, no.5.5, 1966. Later included as appendix in *The Ticket That Exploded* (revised edition, Grove Press, 1967), and *The Job* (John Calder Ltd, 1969.)

195. "He was an expert . . ." – Brion Gysin, 'Collaborators', in *The Final Academy: Statements of a Kind* (The Final Academy, 1982.)

196. "Mr Ian Sommerville . . ." – WSB, Acknowledgment, *The Ticket That Exploded* (Olympia, 1962.)

197. "you need a Philips . . ." – WSB, 'The Invisible Generation', pub-

lished in The International Times, no.5.5, 1966. Later included as appendix in *The Ticket That Exploded* (revised edition, Grove Press, 1967), and *The Job* (John Calder Ltd, 1969.)

198. "stopped at customs . . . a pale boy . . . Tony Balch" – Jeff Nuttall, *Bomb Culture* (Paladin, 1970.)

199. "Through the casual drift . . ." – Jeff Nuttall, *Bomb Culture* (Paladin, 1970.)

200. "– Innarested in – Mag . . ." – Jeff Nuttall, *Bomb Culture* (Paladin, 1970.)

201. "Two short months later . . ." – Jeff Nuttall, *Bomb Culture* (Paladin, 1970.)

202. "I hope you have been able . . ." – WSB, letter to Bruce Holbrook, 4th October 1965, included in *Rub Out The Words: Collected Letters of William S. Burroughs 1959-1974*, ed. Bill Morgan (Penguin Classics, 2012.)

203. "He put his hands . . ." – 'A Letter from Carl Weissner: Mannheim, West Germany, 1974', included in Victor Bockris, *With William Burroughs: A Report From The Bunker* (Vermilion, 1981.)

204. "Look, man, what you do . . ." – WSB, as reported in Barry Miles, *Call Me Burroughs: A Life* (Twelve, 2014.)

205. ". . . I am doing a job on Scientology . . ." – WSB, letter to Brion Gysin, 7th September 1967, included in *Rub Out The Words: Collected Letters of William S. Burroughs 1959-1974*, ed. Bill Morgan (Penguin Classics, 2012.)

206. "William Burroughs stalked the night . . ." – Mick Farren, *Give the Anarchist a Cigarette* (Random House, 2010.)

207. ". . . I found Burroughs' phone number . . ." – Terry Wilson, in conversation with the author, Summer 1988. Transcript published as *Soul-to-Soul* (WhollyBooks, 2012.) Excerpts also appear in *Beat Scene* No.71a, Winter 2014.

208. "Phony magicians . . ." – Terry Wilson, *Perilous Passage* (Synergetic, 2012.)

209. "You think that . . ." – John Buchan, *The Power-House* (Blackwood, 1916.)

210. "the company of predatory 'magical' . . ." – Terry Wilson, in conversation with the author, Summer 1988.

211. "It was almost closing time . . ." – Terry Wilson, 'The Man From Nowhere', *Perilous Passage* (Synergetic, 2012.)

212. "I will speak now for magical truth . . ." – WSB, 'On Coincidence',

included in *The Adding Machine: Collected Essays* (John Calder Ltd, 1985.)

213. "Now anyone who has lived . . ." – WSB, 'Mind War', *The Adding Machine: Collected Essays* (John Calder Ltd, 1985.)

214. ". . . while getting the restaurant ready . . ." – 'Terminal Tourist', Brion Gysin, interviewed by Terry Wilson, *Here To Go: Planet R101* (RE/Search, 1982.)

215. "I live with the constant threat . . ." – WSB, 'Introduction', *Queer* (Viking Penguin, 1985.)

216. "Sorcery!" – WSB, in conversation with the author, at the time of *The Final Academy*, London 1982.

217. "As soon as you start . . ." – WSB, quoted in Barry Miles, *El Hombre Invisible* (Virgin, 1992.)

218. "MS: You are quoted . . ." – Terry Wilson, in conversation with the author, recorded Summer 1988, published as *Soul-to-Soul* (WhollyBooks, 2012.)

219. "100% swishy . . . score a goal . . ." – Terry Wilson, in conversation with the author, London, Summer 1988. Brion Gysin's "pseudo sister," Felicity Mason, related similar anecdotes to the author during an informal "In Conversation" alongside Terry Wilson, George Dowden, and Bob Copping at the London Film-Maker's Co-Op.

220. "TW: The cut-up techniques . . ." – 'Ports of Entry', Terry Wilson and Brion Gysin, *Here To Go: Planet R101* (RE/Search, 1982.)

221. "Lock them out and bar the door . . ." – WSB, narration for *Häxan* (1922), distributed by Antony Balch as *Witchcraft Through the Ages*.

222. "I have frequently . . ." – WSB, 'Playback From Eden To Watergate', included in *The Job* (John Calder Ltd, 1970.)

223. "Here is a sample . . ." – WSB, 'Playback From Eden To Watergate', included in *The Job* (John Calder Ltd, 1970.)

224. "I collaborated with him on . . ." – Cabell McLean, 1st May 1999. Preface to *Machine*, an as-yet unpublished memoir.

225. "At 17 Audrey is handsome . . ." – 'From Gay Gun' by William S. Burroughs and Cabell McLean, *Washington Review*, Summer-Fall 1977.

226. "[William] continued going to the bar . . ." – Cabell McLean, 'Playback: My Personal Experience of Chaos Magic with William S. Burroughs, Sr.', first published in *Ashé Journal of Experimental Spirituality* Vol.2 Issue 3 (2003), and later collected in *Playback: The Magic of William S. Burroughs* (Rebel Satori Press, 2009.)

227. "You know Cabell . . ." – WSB, quoted in Cabell McLean, 'Playback:

My Personal Experience of Chaos Magic with William S. Burroughs, Sr.', first published in *Ashé Journal of Experimental Spirituality* Vol.2 Issue 3 (2003), and later collected in *Playback: The Magic of William S. Burroughs* (Rebel Satori Press, 2009.)

228. "These voices are in a number of accents . . ." – WSB, 'It Belongs to the Cucumbers', *The Adding Machine: Collected Essays* (John Calder Ltd, 1985.)

229. "They are somehow imprinted . . ." – WSB, 'It Belongs to the Cucumbers', *The Adding Machine: Collected Essays* (John Calder Ltd, 1985.)

230. "Remember that your memory . . ." – WSB, 'It Belongs to the Cucumbers', *The Adding Machine: Collected Essays* (John Calder Ltd, 1985.)

231. "Horse and hattock! . . . in the Devil's Name . . . owre the muirs and fells." – Sarah Anne Lawless, 'Horse and Hattock: The Origin of the Witch's Chant' which is available to download as a PDF from her website, http://sarahannelawless.com/wp-content/uploads/2013/04/Horse_and_Hattock.pdf. I am indebted to Emma Doeve for bringing this excellent article to my attention.

232. "Now horse, and hattock . . . hattock speedily" – Sir Walter Scott, *The Black Dwarf* (Oxford University Press, 1908.)

233. "aids to concentration." – Dion Fortune, *Psychic Self-Defence* (Red Wheel Weiser, 1971.)

234. "It's true then . . . I use any methods . . ." – WSB, 'The private asshole', *Cities of the Red Night* (Viking, 1981.)

235. "I will explain exactly how . . ." – WSB, 'The private asshole', *Cities of the Red Night* (Viking, 1981.)

236. "Burroughs, and Gysin, both told . . ." – Genesis Breyer P-Orridge, 'Magick Squares and Future Beats', *Book of Lies* ed. R. Metzger (Disinformation, 2003.)

237. "A lot of what we did . . ." – Richard H. Kirk, interviewed by Biba Kopf, 'William Burroughs: Ghost of Chance', *The Wire*, October 1997.

238. "Tell me about . . . No, I don't . . . you know . . ." – Genesis Breyer P-Orridge, 'Magick Squares and Future Beats', *Book of Lies* ed. Metzger (Disinformation, 2003.)

239. "what we see is . . ." – WSB, 'The Invisible Generation', published in *The International Times*, no.5.5, 1966. Later included as appendix in *The Ticket That Exploded* (revised edition, Grove Press, 1967), and *The Job*

(John Calder Ltd, 1969.)

240. "I was already being taught . . ." – Genesis Breyer P-Orridge, 'Magick Squares and Future Beats', *Book of Lies* ed. Richard Metzger (Disinformation, 2003.)

241. "Magic calls itself . . ." – Brion Gysin, liner notes for *Brian Jones presents The Pipes of Pan at Joujouka* (Rolling Stones Records, 1971.)

242. "Given that we were meeting . . ." – Genesis Breyer P-Orridge, 'Magick Squares and Future Beats', *Book of Lies* ed. R. Metzger (Disinformation, 2003.)

243. "William, Brion and the poet John . . ." – Genesis P-Orridge, interviewed by Chris Bohn, 'A Leak Into The Future', *New Musical Express*, 25th September 1982.

244. "The original intentions of cut ups . . ." – Coil, interviewed for *Fist* magazine (issue 5, 1992 – interviewer unknown), concerning their ground-breaking third album, *Love's Secret Domain* (Threshold House, 1991), which was highly acclaimed for its innovative and original use of both analogue and digital sampling.

245. "This book is the original handbook . . ." – Geff Rushton (writing as 'John Balance'), Introduction, *The Electronic Revolution* (Maldoror Stichting, 1988.)

246. "It changed my life!" – Peter Christopherson, to author.

247. "My perception of Burroughs' work . . ." – Peter Christopherson, quoted in David Keenan, *England's Hidden Reverse* (SAF Publishing, 2002.)

248. "too much like . . ." – Peter Christopherson, to author.

249. "Nothing to do . . ." – Peter Christopherson, to author. Also confirmed in Biba Kopf, 'William Burroughs: Ghost of Chance', *The Wire*, October 1997.

250. "I remember getting very, *very* drunk . . ." – Peter Christopherson, interviewed by Biba Kopf for 'William Burroughs: Ghost of Chance', *The Wire*, October 1997.

251. ". . . I suggested that it would be . . ." – Peter Christopherson, interviewed by Biba Kopf for 'William Burroughs: Ghost of Chance', *The Wire*, October 1997.

252. "I thought of doing the LP . . ." – Genesis P-Orridge, uncredited interview, *Burroughs/Gysin/P.Orridge – Interviews & Readings* (Cold Spring Tape, 1989.)

253. "He just agreed to us . . ." – Genesis P-Orridge, interviewed by V. Vale, *RE/Search* 4/5 (RE/Search, 1982.)

254. ". . . they had used some Burroughs samples . . ." – Geff Rushton (aka 'John Balance'), to Tony Dickie, for *Compulsion* magazine no.1, Winter 1992.

255. "William, that's a *lot* . . . cats to feed." – Peter Christopherson, to author.

256. ". . . I'm fed up of hearing him . . ." – Geff Rushton (aka 'John Balance'), to Tony Dickie, for *Compulsion* magazine no.1, Winter 1992.

257. "We got him to speak . . ." – Geff Rushton (aka 'John Balance'), to author.

258. "We did hot knives . . ." – Geff Rushton (aka 'John Balance'), to Jas Morgan and Diana Trimble, for *Mondo 2000* magazine, 1992.

259. "If you got him on Thursday . . ." – Geff Rushton (aka 'John Balance'), to David Keenan, in *England's Hidden Reverse* (SAF Publishing, 2002.)

260. "As the poet says . . ." – WSB, 'Voices in Your Head', Introduction to John Giorno, *You Got To Burn To Shine* (High Risk Books/ Serpent's Tail, 1994.)

261. "Ketamine may disrupt . . ." – Todd Girard, in J. A. Cheyne, T. A. Girard and L. K. Wilkins, *Ketamine as a primary predictor of out-of-body experiences associated with multiple substance use* (Department of Psychology, Ryerson University, Toronto, ON, Canada.) Also quoted in 'Science News', *Wired* magazine, February 2011.

262. "He was charming . . ." – Peter Christopherson, quoted in David Keenan, *England's Hidden Reverse* (SAF Publishing, 2002.)

263. "From the diary . . ." – WSB, *The Job* (John Calder Ltd, 1969.)

264. "a bit old-fashioned . . . some good information" – WSB, to author, at the time of *The Final Academy*, London 1982. Compare with other interviews at the time, e.g. V. Vale, 'Under Psychic Attack' (San Francisco, 1982), included in *Burroughs Live: The Collected Interviews of William S. Burroughs 1960-1997* (Semiotext(e), 2001.)

265. "Mind parasites, malignant beings . . ." – WSB, review of Colin Wilson's *The Mind Parasites* in *Rat*, 19th June 1969. Also appears as *Burroughs Academy Bulletin 20*, 'The Voracious Aliens', in *Mayfair* Vol.4 No.8, August 1969.

266. ". . . somebody rang me . . ." – Colin Wilson "interviewed at Tetherdown" 11th September 2007, according to http://colinwilsononline.com/interview/

267. "that *dreadful* man!" – Colin Wilson, reported to author by David Conway.

268. "I was taught this . . . still the basic fear." – WSB, to author, at the time of *The Final Academy*, London 1982.

269. "You are no more invaded . . ." – WSB, interviewed by Victor Bockris for *Interview* magazine Vol.XXII No.4 April 1991, added to Revised Edition of *With William Burroughs* (St. Martin's Griffin, 1996)

270. "Whenever you . . . Whenever anyone . . . My saga will shine . . ." – WSB, *The Place of Dead Roads* (Viking, 1983.)

271. "The old writer couldn't write . . ." – WSB, *The Western Lands* (Viking Penguin, 1987)

272. ". . . *Western Lands* is just the end . . ." – WSB, to author, at The October Gallery, London 1988. Transcript published in Matthew Levi Stevens, *A Moving Target: Encounters with William Burroughs* (Beat Scene Press, October 2012.)

273. "Evidence indicates that cats . . ." – WSB, *The Cat Inside* (Viking, 1992.)

274. "I have said that cats . . ." – WSB, *The Cat Inside* (Viking, 1992.)

275. "He once said to me . . ." – C. J. Bradbury Robinson, letter to author.

276. ". . . any writer who hasn't jacked off . . ." – WSB, interview with Bockris-Wylie, 1974. Included in Victor Bockris, *With William Burroughs: A Report From The Bunker* (Vermilion, 1981.)

277. "dreams are a fertile source . . ." – WSB, 'The Technology of Writing', *The Adding Machine: Collected Essays* (John Calder Ltd, 1985.)

278. "And so dreams tell stories . . ." – WSB, *My Education: A Book of Dreams* (Viking, 1995.)

279. "The Land of the Dead . . ." – WSB, *My Education: A Book of Dreams* (Viking, 1995.)

280. "It was a hectic, portentous time . . . Remember when . . . Who will ever know?" – WSB, *The Western Lands* (Viking Penguin, 1987.)

281. "Burroughs often wrote . . ." – James Grauerholz, speaking 'On Burroughs and Dharma' for the Summer Writing Institute 24th June 1999, Naropa University. Transcript published in *Beat Scene* magazine No.71a, Winter 2014.

282. "Do I want to know?" – WSB, *Last Words: The Final Journals of William Burroughs*, ed. James Grauerholz (Grove, 2000.)

283. "We talked a great deal . . ." – Graham Masterton, to author, Summer 2012.

284. "Bill was only interested . . ." – Alex Trocchi, to author, London 1984. Also confirmed by Felicity Mason, "In Conversation" with author.

285. ". . . saw group concentration . . ." – WSB, *Last Words: The Final Journals of William Burroughs*, ed. James Grauerholz (Grove, 2000.)

286. "America is not a young land . . ." – WSB, *Naked Lunch* (Olympia, 1959.)

287. "totally white . . ." – Victor Bockris, *With William Burroughs: A Report From The Bunker* (Vermilion, 1981.)

288. "More advanced and detailed incantations . . ." – WSB, *The Place of Dead Roads* (Viking, 1983.)

289. "Fear and the Monkey" – WSB, August 1978, written as a submission for Larry Fagin's *Bombay Gin* magazine. Later included in *Die Alten Filme*, ed. Carl Weissner (Maro Verlag, 1979), and subsequently collected in the section *The Old Movies* in *The Burroughs File* (City Lights, 1984.)

290. "Most of the material . . ." – Malcolm Mc Neill, *Observed While Falling* (Fantagraphics, 2012.)

291. "get high with the Pope of Dope" – James Grauerholz, interviewed in Yony Leyser's documentary, *William S. Burroughs: A Man Within* (2010.)

292. "a disease of exposure" – WSB, reported by Robert Anton Wilson (writing as 'Ronald Weston') in his article, 'William Burroughs: High Priest of Hipsterism', in Ralph Ginzburg's *fact* magazine, Volume 2, Issue 6, Nov-Dec 1965. WSB stated and re-stated a number of different versions of this opinion at different times: for instance, see his reply in *The Paris Review* interview, *The Art of Fiction* No. 36, when Conrad Knickerbocker asks him about regarding addiction as an illness – "It's as simple as the way in which anyone happens to become an alcoholic. They start drinking, that's all. They like it, and they drink, and then they become alcoholic. I was exposed to heroin in New York—that is, I was going around with people who were using it; I took it; the effects were pleasant. I went on using it and became addicted . . . The idea that addiction is somehow a psychological illness is, I think, totally ridiculous. It's as psychological as malaria. It's a matter of exposure."

293. "An old man with a cane . . ." – Grant Hart, interviewed in Yony Leyser's documentary, *William S. Burroughs: A Man Within* (2010.)

294. "On how I injected . . ." – Gerard Peter Pas, *How I came to know William Burroughs*, online at: http://www.gerardpas.com/library/memoirs/burrough.html

295. ". . . a writer has to take it . . ." – WSB, 'The Retreat Diaries' (1976),

included in *The Burroughs File* (City Lights, 1984.)

296. "As far as any system . . ." – WSB, 'The Retreat Diaries' (1976), included in *The Burroughs File* (City Lights, 1984.)

297. "by the method outlined . . ." – WSB, 'The Retreat Diaries' (1976), included in *The Burroughs File* (City Lights, 1984.)

298. "I was thinking about Bradbury Robinson . . ." – WSB, 'The Retreat Diaries' (1976), included in *The Burroughs File* (City Lights, 1984.)

299. "Telepathy, journeys out of the body . . ." – WSB, 'The Retreat Diaries' (1976), included in *The Burroughs File* (City Lights, 1984.)

300. "Cabell McLean was one . . ." – Emma Doeve, introducing 'Legend Days Begun' by Cabell McLean, during *Final Academy/2012* (an informal celebration of the 30th anniversary of *The Final Academy* events, organised by Joe Ambrose, with film, music, and spoken word by Emma Doeve, Paul A. Green, Lilian Lijn, Scanner, Matthew Levi Stevens, & Tony White) The Horse Hospital, London, October 2012.

301. James Branch Cabell (1879-1958), *Jurgen, A Comedy of Justice* (Robert M. McBride, 1919.)

302. "Where you need . . . Go see Bill." – Cabell McLean, extract from *Machine*, published as 'My Friend, The Teacher', *Academy 23: an unofficial tribute to William S. Burroughs & The Final Academy* ed. Stevens & Doeve (WhollyBooks, 2012.)

303. "Although I had seen many images . . ." – Cabell McLean, extract from *Machine*, 'My Friend, The Teacher', in *Academy 23: an unofficial tribute to William S. Burroughs & The Final Academy* ed. Stevens & Doeve (WhollyBooks, 2012.)

304. "for me he was just . . ." – Leslie Winer, email to author, February 2013.

305. "I *am* a master . . . cool queer . . ." – Marc Olmsted, 'American Mutants Spawned In The Bunker' in *Beatdom* no.14, Winter 2014.

306. ". . . I lived with Bill . . . days of my life" – Cabell McLean, 1st May 1999. Preface to *Machine*, an as-yet unpublished memoir.

307. "Cabell Lee Hardy was Burroughs companion . . ." – James Grauerholz, Notes for WSB, *Last Words: The Final Journals* (Grove, 2000.)

308. "Boulder at sunrise . . . Cabell was me . . ." – WSB, *My Education: A Book of Dreams* (Viking, 1995.)

309. "Both writers are masters . . ." – WSB, Foreword to Denton Welch, *In Youth Is Pleasure* (Exact Change, 1994.)

310. "The Mayan codices . . ." – WSB, 20th September 1975, in the Foreword to *Ah Pook Is Here* (John Calder, 1979.)

311. "When I was writing The Place of Dead Roads . . ." – WSB, Introduction, *Queer* (Viking Penguin, 1985.)

312. "At first Denton did not believe . . ." – Michael De-la-Noy, *Denton Welch: The Making of a Writer* (Viking, 1984.) Incorporates quotation from *A Voice Through A Cloud* by Denton Welch (John Lehmann, 1950.)

313. "It was not until I reread Denton . . ." – WSB, Foreword to Denton Welch, *In Youth Is Pleasure* (Exact Change, 1994.)

314. "I'm greatly indebted to Burroughs' writing . . ." – Phil Hine, 'Bitter Venoms: The Magical Worlds of William Burroughs', *Mektoub* 2(7), also in *A Taste of Things to Come* (Revelations 23 Press, 1991.)

315. "angst-ridden teenage outsider" – Phil Hine, to author, Summer 2012.

316. ". . . mid-to-late-80s . . ." – Phil Hine, to author, Summer 2012. Included in *Academy 23: an unofficial celebration of William S. Burroughs & 'The Final Academy'* (WhollyBooks, October 2012.)

317. "a bit wary of the sexuality angle" – Phil Hine, to author, Summer 2012. Included in *Academy 23: an unofficial celebration of William S. Burroughs & 'The Final Academy'* (WhollyBooks, October 2012.)

318. "Well I think it's pretty clear . . ." – Phil Hine, to author, Summer 2012. Included in *Academy 23: an unofficial celebration of William S. Burroughs & 'The Final Academy'* (WhollyBooks, October 2012.)

319. ". . . we asked him to recite . . ." – Geff Rushton ('John Balance'), to David Keenan, interviewed for *England's Hidden Reverse* (SAF Publishing, 2002.)

320. "My perception of Burroughs' work . . ." – Peter Christopherson, interviewed by Biba Kopf for *The Wire*, 1997. Referenced by David Keenan, *England's Hidden Reverse* (SAF Publishing, 2002.)

321. "I believe that a re-reading . . ." – Genesis Breyer P-Orridge, 'Magick Squares and Future Beats', in *Book of Lies* ed. Richard Metzger (Disinformation, 2003.)

322. "I strongly advise any . . ." – Genesis Breyer P-Orridge, 'Magick Squares and Future Beats', in *Book of Lies* ed. R. Metzger (Disinformation, 2003.)

323. "Bill had gone upstairs . . ." – as reported in Barry Miles, *Call Me Burroughs: A Life* (Twelve, 2014.)

324. "If we are going to investigate . . ." – WSB, to Victor Bockris, 'On

Psychic Sex', in *With William Burroughs: A Report From The Bunker* (Vermilion, 1981.)

325. "One of the most useful . . ." – Zeena and Nikolas Schreck, *Demons of the Flesh* (Creation, 2002.)

326. "homosexual sex magic . . . credible" – Zeena and Nikolas Schreck, *Demons of the Flesh* (Creation, 2002.)

327. "Back at the loft we decided to try . . ." – WSB, 'Are you in salt', *Cities of the Red Night* (Calder, 1981.)

328. "a flower at each cardinal point . . . works of discord . . ." – David Conway, *Magic: An Occult Primer* (Jonathan Cape Ltd, 1972.)

329. "For kliphothic intentions the name of Seth . . ." – David Conway, *Magic: An Occult Primer* (Jonathan Cape Ltd, 1972.)

330. ". . . we pledged that our exchanges . . ." – David Conway, email to author.

331. "in the event . . ." – David Conway, email to author.

332. "What I can mention . . ." – David Conway, email to author.

333. "WSB was a man . . ." – David Conway, email to author.

334. "This book is . . ." – WSB, Invocation, *Cities of the Red Night* (Calder, 1981.)

335. "the worst disaster . . ." – WSB, interviewed at the time of *The Final Academy* by Mick Brown, published in *The Guardian*, 1st October, 1982.

336. "an independent Magickal . . . Illuminates of Thanateros" – details concerning the history of Templum Nigri Solis culled from 'Authors' Introduction' in *Between Spaces: Selected Rituals & Essays From The Archives Of Templum Nigri Solis* (privately published by Templum Nigri Solis, Samhain 2010.)

337. "a working manual . . . the exercises . . . immediately workable" – WSB, Introduction, *Between Spaces: Selected Rituals & Essays From The Archives Of Templum Nigri Solis* (privately published by Templum Nigri Solis, Samhain 2010.)

338. "Science should be more Magical . . ." – WSB, Introduction, *Between Spaces: Selected Rituals & Essays From The Archives Of Templum Nigri Solis* (TNS, 2010.)

339. "Now the outer and the inner . . ." – WSB, Introduction, *Between Spaces: Selected Rituals & Essays From The Archives Of Templum Nigri Solis* (TNS, 2010.)

340. "Nothing is more dangerous . . . Keep moving, Pilgrim." – WSB, Introduction, *Between Spaces: Selected Rituals & Essays From The Archives*

Of Templum Nigri Solis (TNS, 2010.)

341. ". . . Douglas went shooting . . ." – email from "Alex S", IOT USA member.

342. "What did Hassan i Sabbah . . ." – WSB, *The Western Lands* (Viking, 1987.)

343. "Burroughs utilized Polaroid technology . . ." – Douglas Grant, 'Magick and Photography', *Ashé Journal of Experimental Spirituality* Vol.2, Issue 3 (2003), also in *Playback: The Magic of William S. Burroughs* (Rebel Satori Press, 2009.)

344. ". . . oh yes, as a child . . ." – WSB, speaking in the video interview *William S. Burroughs Addresses The Magickal Pact of the Illuminates of Thanateros*. Transcript published in the American *Kaos Magic Journal* No.1, Summer 1994.

345. "Well, I've heard people . . ." – WSB, speaking in the video interview *William S. Burroughs Addresses The Magickal Pact of the Illuminates of Thanateros*. Transcript published in the American *Kaos Magic Journal* No.1, Summer 1994.

346. "It seems to me . . ." – WSB, speaking in the video interview *William S. Burroughs Addresses The Magickal Pact of the Illuminates of Thanateros*. Transcript published in the American *Kaos Magic Journal* No.1, Summer 1994.

347. "William S. Burroughs' 1969 novel . . ." – Phil Hine, 'Zimbu Xototl Time' (2000), published in *Ashé Journal of Experimental Spirituality* Vol.2 Issue 3 (2003), and later collected in *Playback: The Magic of William S. Burroughs* (Rebel Satori Press, 2009.)

348. "Phil Hine's book is . . ." – WSB, blurb for Phil Hine, *Condensed Chaos: An Introduction to Chaos Magic* (New Falcon, 1995.)

349. "I'm not so sure . . ." – Phil Hine, interview with author, Summer 2012.

350. ". . . there were at least . . ." – Phil Hine, interview with author, Summer 2012.

351. ". . . at some point . . ." – Phil Hine, interview with author, Summer 2012.

352. "Through a mutual interest . . ." – Douglas Grant, 'Magick and Photography', *Ashé Journal of Experimental Spirituality* Vol.2, Issue 3 (2003.) Although omitted from the later *Playback* anthology, this statement is still included in the online version of Douglas Grant's text found at: http://ashejournal.com/index.php?id=166

353. "William was very serious . . ." – James Grauerholz, interviewed 25th

June 2010 by Steve Foland. Published as 'Taking the brooooooaaaad view of things: A Conversation with James Grauerholz on William S. Burroughs and Magick', online at http://pop-damage.com/?p=5393

354. "the Santeria part . . ." – Eric K. Lerner, phone conversation with author.

355. "Listen, baby, I've been coping . . ." – WSB, to Victor Bockris, revised edition of *With William Burroughs: A Report From The Bunker* (St. Martin's Griffin, 1996.)

356. "locating people who have died . . ." – Victor Bockris, 'Looking for Ian', in *With William Burroughs: A Report From The Bunker* (Vermilion, 1981.)

357. "I keep a regular dream diary . . ." – WSB, to Victor Bockris, 'On Dreams', in *With William Burroughs: A Report From The Bunker* (Vermilion, 1981.)

358. "extremely intense . . ." – Victor Bockris, 'On Psychic Sex', in *With William Burroughs: A Report From The Bunker* (Vermilion, 1981.)

359. "Bill first expressed surprise . . ." – WSB, to Victor Bockris, 'On Psychic Sex', in *With William Burroughs: A Report From The Bunker* (Vermilion, 1981.)

360. "My dear, according . . ." – WSB, to Victor Bockris, 'On Psychic Sex', in *With William Burroughs: A Report From The Bunker* (Vermilion, 1981.)

361. "We urgently need explorers . . ." – WSB, to Victor Bockris, 'On Psychic Sex', in *With William Burroughs: A Report From The Bunker* (Vermilion, 1981.)

362. "This phenomenon . . ." – WSB, to Victor Bockris, 'On Psychic Sex', in With *William Burroughs: A Report From The Bunker* (Vermilion, 1981.)

363. "Adam was having sexual . . ." – WSB, to Victor Bockris, 'On Psychic Sex', in *With William Burroughs: A Report From The Bunker* (Vermilion, 1981.)

364. "although she was . . . were still bound . . . these creatures" – WSB, to Victor Bockris, 'On Psychic Sex', in *With William Burroughs: A Report From The Bunker* (Vermilion, 1981.)

365. ". . . I suggested to a psychiatrist . . ." – WSB, to Victor Bockris, 'On Psychic Sex', in *With William Burroughs: A Report From The Bunker* (Vermilion, 1981.)

366. "Bill proudly showed me . . ." – John Hopkins, *The Tangier Diaries 1962-1979* (Cadmus Editions, 1998.)

367. "a sort of sloppy . . ." – WSB, interviewed by Robert Palmer for *Rolling Stone*, London 1972. Included in *Burroughs Live: The Collected Interviews of William S. Burroughs 1960-1997* (Semiotext(e), 2001.)

368. "a lie-detector . . ." – WSB, interviewed by Robert Palmer for *Rolling Stone*, London 1972. Included in *Burroughs Live: The Collected Interviews of William S. Burroughs 1960-1997* (Semiotext(e), 2001.)

369. "With further use of the E-meter . . ." – WSB, interviewed by Eric Mottram, originally published in *Snack* (Aloes Books, 1975.) Included in *Burroughs Live: The Collected Interviews of William S. Burroughs 1960-1997 (Semiotext(e), 2001.)*

370. "a psycho-electronic device . . ." – Notes for WSB, *Last Words: The Final Journals of William Burroughs*, ed. James Grauerholz (Grove, 2000.)

371. "The Technology and Ethics of Wishing" – WSB, lecture given 25th June 1986 at Naropa: https://archive.org/details/ naropa_william_s_burroughs_class_on7

372. "To Burroughs' dismay . . ." – Geff Rushton, writing as 'John Balance', Introduction, *The Electronic Revolution* (Maldoror Stichting, 1988.)

373. "Directions for use . . ." – WSB, *The Western Lands* (Viking Penguin, 1987.)

374. "drawing game" – as described by Allen Ginsberg, Lucien Carr and others, for example to Ted Morgan, *Literary Outlaw* (Pimlico edition, 1991.)

375. "Anyone who doesn't believe in ESP . . ." – WSB, interviewed by David Ohle, Lawrence, Kansas, 26th January, 1985. Transcript published in *My Kind of Angel*, ed. Rupert Loydell (Stride, 1998.)

376. "I postulate that the function of art . . ." – WSB, 'Sects and Death'(1979), The Church of the SubGenius anthology, *Three-Fisted Tales of "Bob"*, ed. Reverend Ivan Stang (Fireside, 1990.)

377. "JT: Rather than simply . . ." – WSB, interviewed by John Tytell, New York, 24th March 1974. Transcript published in *A Burroughs Compendium: Calling the Toads* (Ring Tarigh, 1998.)

378. "TV: So much of your work . . ." – WSB, radio interview by Tom Vitali, 26th November 1986. Transcript published as 'A Moveable Feast' in *Burroughs Live: The Collected Interviews of William S. Burroughs 1960-1997* (Semiotext(e), 2001.)

379. "NZ: Your work often . . ." – WSB, interviewed by Nicholas Zurbrugge, St. Louis, 27th April 1989. Transcript published in *My*

Kind of Angel, ed. Rupert Loydell (Stride, 1998.)

380. "I'm very interested in Indian shamanism now . . ." – WSB, interviewed by Nicholas Zurbrugge, Lawrence, Kansas, 10th June 1991. Transcript published in *My Kind of Angel*, ed. Rupert Loydell (Stride, 1998.)

381. "Genet says . . ." – WSB, interviewed by Nicholas Zurbrugge, Lawrence, Kansas, 10th June 1991. Transcript published in *My Kind of Angel*, ed. Rupert Loydell (Stride, 1998.)

382. "I read these . . ." – WSB, interviewed by Nicholas Zurbrugge, Lawrence, Kansas, 10th June 1991. Transcript published in *My Kind of Angel*, ed. Rupert Loydell (Stride, 1998.)

383. "Well, it's not necessarily a return . . ." – WSB, interviewed by Nicholas Zurbrugge, Lawrence, Kansas, 10th June 1991. Transcript published in *My Kind of Angel*, ed. Rupert Loydell (Stride, 1998.)

384. "Queer to think of him . . ." – Douglas Brinkley, 'The Death of William S. Burroughs', in *A Burroughs Compendium: Calling the Toads* (Ring Tarigh, 1998.)

385. "I bring not peace . . ." – WSB, clearly a paraphrase of the words attributed to Christ in *Matthew* 10:34, "I came not to bring peace, but to bring a sword."

386. "Johnson sees a subject . . ." – WSB, 9th October 1992. Used as Introduction to *My Stinking Ass*, included in *Coyote Satan Amerika: The Unspeakable Art and Performances of Reverend Steven Johnson Leyba* (Last Gasp, 2001.)

387. "A friend of mine called Bill Lyon . . ." – WSB, interviewed by Nicholas Zurbrugge, Lawrence, Kansas, 10th June 1991. Transcript published in *My Kind of Angel*, ed. Rupert Loydell (Stride, 1998.)

388. ". . . very much related to the American tycoon . . ." – WSB, interviewed by Allen Ginsberg, Lawrence 1992. Published as 'The Ugly Spirit' in *Burroughs Live: The Collected Interviews of William S. Burroughs 1960-1997* (Semiotext(e), 2001.)

389. "We sat with . . ." – Allen Ginsberg, 'The Ugly Spirit', in *Burroughs Live: The Collected Interviews of William S. Burroughs 1960-1997* (Semiotext(e), 2001.)

390. "He described it as a spirit . . ." – WSB, interviewed by Allen Ginsberg, Lawrence 1992. Published as 'The Ugly Spirit' in *Burroughs Live: The Collected Interviews of William S. Burroughs 1960-1997* (Semiotext(e), 2001.)

391. "Well, there it is . . ." – WSB, interviewed by Allen Ginsberg,

Lawrence 1992. Published as 'The Ugly Spirit' in *Burroughs Live: The Collected Interviews of William S. Burroughs 1960-1997* (Semiotext(e), 2001.)

392. "I like the shaman very much . . ." – WSB, interviewed by Allen Ginsberg, Lawrence 1992. Published as 'The Ugly Spirit' in *Burroughs Live: The Collected Interviews of William S. Burroughs 1960-1997* (Semiotext(e), 2001.)

393. "If you see it . . ." – WSB, interviewed by Allen Ginsberg, Lawrence 1992. Published as 'The Ugly Spirit' in *Burroughs Live: The Collected Interviews of William S. Burroughs 1960-1997* (Semiotext(e), 2001.)

394. "That was much better . . ." – WSB, interviewed by Allen Ginsberg, Lawrence 1992. Published as 'The Ugly Spirit' in *Burroughs Live: The Collected Interviews of William S. Burroughs 1960-1997* (Semiotext(e), 2001.)

395. "The old writer . . ." – WSB, *The Western Lands* (Viking Penguin, 1987.)

396. "How can anyone . . ." – WSB, *Last Words: The Final Journals of William Burroughs*, ed. James Grauerholz (Grove, 2000.)

397. "Man sold his soul . . ." – WSB, *Ghost of Chance* (High Risk, 1995.)

398. "The Mind Parasites" – WSB, 'Voices in Your Head', Introduction to John Giorno, *You Got To Burn To Shine* (High Risk Books/Serpent's Tail, 1994.)

399. "Many spiritual disciplines . . ." – WSB, *Last Words: The Final Journals of William Burroughs*, ed. James Grauerholz (Grove, 2000.)

400. "Enemy have two . . ." – WSB, *Last Words: The Final Journals of William Burroughs*, ed. James Grauerholz (Grove, 2000.)

401. "There is no final . . ." – WSB, *Last Words: The Final Journals of William Burroughs*, ed. James Grauerholz (Grove, 2000.)

Index

CPSIA information can be obtained
at www.ICGtesting.com
Printed in the USA
BVHW042048210221
600749BV00008B/144